"Whether you're learning the craft, revising your manuscript, or looking to position it for the best chance of getting published, read Elizabeth Lyon. *Manuscript Makeover* maps out exactly how to revise and rewrite. *A Writer's Guide to Fiction* provides practical tips to bring your characters to life and to improve your plot, and *The Sell Your Novel Tool Kit* is the best book I've ever read on how to write a query letter and synopsis that will get an agent and an editor's attention. I wouldn't be published without either book."

—Robert Dugoni, author of *New York Times* bestseller
The Jury Master and *Damage Control*

"In her new book, *Manuscript Makeover*, Elizabeth Lyon makes excellent use of her years as a book editor. Any writer is sure to take away some inspiring anecdote or advice that will make their writing go where it could not before."

—Kathy Hepinstall, bestselling author of
The House of Gentle Men and *Absence of Nectar*

"Elizabeth Lyon is a writer's best friend. With masterful clarity and gentle humor she coaches us through the full range of techniques (from liberating our voice to producing a presentable product) that will improve and enhance our manuscripts and make us better at what we do. *Manuscript Makeover* is a must."

—Barbara Corrado Pope, author of *Cézanne's Quarry*

"With *Manuscript Makeover*, Elizabeth Lyon converts the complex process of revision into a step-by-step method of upgrading your plot, style, and characters. The book answers the daunting question of 'Where do I begin?' and is loaded with simple revision techniques any writer, at any level, can use to craft a better novel."

—Carolyn Rose, author of the Casey Brandt series

"From overhauling structure to deepening characters, fine-tuning imagery, mastering mechanics, and setting your style apart—*Manuscript Makeover* does it all. This is the one book on revision every writer should own."

—Mike Nettleton, coauthor of *The Hard Karma Shuffle*

continued...

A Writer's Guide to Fiction

"*A Writer's Guide to Fiction* is a terrific resource for authors; positive in tone (*very* important to aspiring writers), well organized (a critical point for both authors and the librarians who are often called upon to advise them in these matters), and concise."
    —Jayne Ann Krentz

"A must-read for anyone about to embark on fiction writing or anyone enjoying a writing career. As agents, we are recommending all our clients read it either as an inspiration or as a valuable refresher course. Lyon never talks down to the writer but simply puts up clean, clear signposts to follow the fiction rules of the road. Highly recommended."
    —Anna Cottle and Mary Alice Kier, Cine/Lit Representation,
      literary agency and media consultants

"A superb introduction to the basics. Don't start your novel without it."
    —Donald Maass, literary agent and author of
      Writing the Breakout Novel

"A detailed, confident, no-nonsense guide for the serious fiction writer...Highly recommended."
    —*Library Journal*

The Sell Your Novel Tool Kit

"If you're serious about selling your novel, Elizabeth Lyon is here to coach you with the skills, the inside information, and the inspiration you'll need."
    —Chuck Palahniuk, author of *Fight Club* and *Diary*

"Every novelist...should own this gem."
    —Kathleen Dougherty, novelist and editorial associate
      for Writer's Digest School

"Elizabeth Lyon has written a masterly work that belongs on any writer's bookshelf."
    —Jean Naggar, literary agent

"[Not] just another how-to puff, this is an operations plan. Read it."
    —Donald E. McQuinn, author of eight novels

"A pragmatic marketing guide written for and about real writers in the trenches. It's like having a five-star general drop into your foxhole not only to show you a map of the entire battlefield, but to give you tips on marksmanship and battlefield survival."
—M. K. Wren, author of eight Conan Flagg mysteries

"Here's the work writers must research *before* they approach me or any agent. This will be required reading for any potential client."
—Denise Marcil, literary agent

"Throw away all of your other how-to books; *The Sell Your Novel Tool Kit* is the only book you'll need to break into print. My dog-eared first edition helped me draft a query that landed an agent, which ultimately resulted in a three-book, six-figure deal."
—J. A. Konrath, author of *Whiskey Sour*

A Writer's Guide to Nonfiction
"In [Lyon's] confident, optimistic writing primer, the first in the Writer's Compass series, she shows would-be authors how to find their area of expertise and turn it into an article, essay, or even a book...Lyon crafts a detailed and practical course for the nonfiction novice. This detailed and practical guide may not guarantee writing hopefuls a book deal, but it distinguishes itself from other writing how-tos by its concrete and economical advice."
—*Publishers Weekly*

"Readers interested in the practicalities of publishing and marketing their work will find [*A Writer's Guide to Nonfiction*] useful."
—*Library Journal*

Nonfiction Book Proposals Anybody Can Write
"The perfect tool with which to create a successful book proposal."
—Mary Alice Kier and Anna Cottle, Cine/Lit Representation, literary agency and media consultants

"Elizabeth Lyon knows book proposals the way a surgeon knows anatomy."
—Gary Provost, author of twenty-two books including *100 Ways to Improve Your Writing*

Manuscript Makeover

REVISION TECHNIQUES NO FICTION WRITER
CAN AFFORD TO IGNORE

Elizabeth Lyon

A Perigee Book

A PERIGEE BOOK
Published by the Penguin Group
Penguin Group (USA) Inc.
375 Hudson Street, New York, New York 10014, USA
Penguin Group (Canada), 90 Eglinton Avenue East, Suite 700, Toronto, Ontario M4P 2Y3, Canada (a division of Pearson Penguin Canada Inc.)
Penguin Books Ltd., 80 Strand, London WC2R 0RL, England
Penguin Group Ireland, 25 St. Stephen's Green, Dublin 2, Ireland (a division of Penguin Books Ltd.)
Penguin Group (Australia), 250 Camberwell Road, Camberwell, Victoria 3124, Australia (a division of Pearson Australia Group Pty. Ltd.)
Penguin Books India Pvt. Ltd., 11 Community Centre, Panchsheel Park, New Delhi—110 017, India
Penguin Group (NZ), 67 Apollo Drive, Rosedale, North Shore 0632, New Zealand (a division of Pearson New Zealand Ltd.)
Penguin Books (South Africa) (Pty.) Ltd., 24 Sturdee Avenue, Rosebank, Johannesburg 2196, South Africa

Penguin Books Ltd., Registered Offices: 80 Strand, London WC2R 0RL, England

While the author has made every effort to provide accurate telephone numbers and Internet addresses at the time of publication, neither the publisher nor the author assumes any responsibility for errors, or for changes that occur after publication. Further, the publisher does not have any control over and does not assume any responsibility for author or third-party websites or their content.

First edition: April 2008

Library of Congress Cataloging-in-Publication Data

Lyon, Elizabeth, 1950–
    Manuscript makeover : revision techniques no fiction writer can afford to ignore / Elizabeth Lyon.—1st ed.
        p. cm.
    Includes index.
    ISBN-13: 978-0-399-53395-2
    1. Editing.   2. Fiction—Technique.   I. Title.
    PN162.L96 2008
    808.3—dc22   2007046161

PRINTED IN THE UNITED STATES OF AMERICA

10   9   8   7   6   5   4   3   2   1

Most Perigee books are available at special quantity discounts for bulk purchases for sales promotions, premiums, fund-raising, or educational use. Special books, or book excerpts, can also be created to fit specific needs. For details, write: Special Markets, Penguin Group (USA) Inc., 375 Hudson Street, New York, New York 10014.

Dedicated to my beloved and amazing family:
Ella, Don, and Jim Redditt
Louis, Chris, and Elaine Lyon

"Fiction is the single best means for arriving at the truth."
—Don DeLillo, winner of National Book Award for *White Noise*

"I learned to separate the *story* from the *writing*, probably
the most important thing that any storyteller has to learn—that
there are a thousand right ways to tell a story, and ten million
wrong ones, and you're a lot more likely to find one of the latter
than the former your first time through the tale."
—Orson Scott Card, Hugo and Nebula Award–winner for *Ender's Game*

CONTENTS

Preparing to Revise

The novel is complete, the short story finished. Maybe you're not satisfied with all of the writing. Maybe another writer or your critique group has indicated you have more work before your story is ready to market. Or maybe you've sent out a dozen manuscripts and all of them have come back with rejection letters. What's next? Revision. Or, as the title of this book says, a makeover, as sweeping as demolition or as minor as a new coat of paint.

Revision, as part of writing terminology, has multiple meanings. Defined, it means to make changes in what you have written with the intention of producing an improved version. Although used as an all-encompassing word, it includes three processes: finding or marking what needs change—in other words, *editing*—deciding what changes to make, and then making them.

Yet, here lies the conundrum: Presumably, you've written your story or novel to the best of your ability and understanding of craft. If so, you'll begin the revision process in a quandary. You may have a notion about what needs change, a whispered premonition just enough beyond the range of awareness to capture it. Like a bloodhound, you've found the scent. But where do you begin and how do you discover and make needed improvements? This book will answer these questions.

Whether your story needs a little or a lot of work, the fact is that revising fiction involves skills apart from writing. Learn and apply the techniques in this book and your present novel will be vastly improved. Apply your newfound revision skills on all future stories, and you'll begin to break in, selling one work, selling another, and in time, becoming a professional, published fiction writer.

Develop Your Own Revision Method

Because this art of ours has specific elements of craft and stylistic conventions, it also has patterns. In two decades of helping writers as a book editor and teacher, I've discovered scores of these patterns. Is there a secret shortcut for revising a novel or short story, one that the pros know and you'll discover in this book? No. But that's not a bad thing. While this book doesn't reveal the "one secret" behind successful revision, it will help you develop a system for finding and correcting errors—a method that works for you.

Dean Koontz has his own method. In the revealing afterword to *Whispers*, the last book he drafted on a typewriter, and his first big success, he wrote: "When I finished *Whispers*, [my wife] informed me that she had tracked our office supplies, and that for every page in the final manuscript, I had used thirty-two pages of typing paper, which meant that I had done thirty-one discarded drafts for every page, typing eight hundred pages of text again and again to polish it. Although I was aware of my obsessive-compulsive rewriting, I hadn't realized quite how many revisions I usually undertook." What Koontz describes would bring looks of horror to other published authors, yet he reveals one writer's perfectionism to arrive at a polished work he's happy with.

Later, his publisher told him to "slash the manuscript in half," that he was "'a midlist suspense writer' who had overreached." Yet, Koontz found only five pages to cut of the eight hundred pages of manuscript and declined to cut more. The novel rose to number five on the *New York Times* paperback bestsellers list, was published in over thirty-three languages, and remained in print for over two decades.

On the opposite end of the spectrum, two novelists—a married couple, Dean Wesley Smith and Kristine Kathryn Rusch—who have over 100 published novels of all types between them, revise differently. They tell aspiring short story writers and novelists to research, write a first draft quickly, and revise no more than three times before marketing. Expect rejection, but keep marketing. While waiting for your probable rejection, start a new work. Through practice, sheer volume of words, and encountering different situations in each new piece, you'll build your repertoire and skill. Eventually, they say, you'll write well enough to break in. At first you'll be published sporadically and then most of the time. What a different opinion about revision from Dean Koontz's!

When asked what a writer should do when he or she encounters a problem or a shortcoming about an element of craft, Smith and Rusch have a practical answer: Go find out. Study, ask someone who knows the answer, gain that missing knowledge, and put it into practice. Shift that newfound understanding from left brain to right brain. Put it into action so that it gets integrated into your skills, and keep writing.

I heard about another style of revision at one conference where I sat in on a workshop about revision taught by novelist Jonis Agee, author of five literary novels (of which three were selected as Notable Books of the Year by the *New York Times*). She told the audience that she typically writes and discards her first draft and most of her second draft. *She throws them away!* You should have heard the collective gasp in the room. She explained that the third draft captures the heart and soul of her characters and her author voice. She deems her third drafts as worthy of final polishing and publication.

These examples represent but three philosophies of revision, but as many methods exist as there are writers.

Techniques Common to All Methods of Revision

Two basic approaches to revision are featured in this book: revising from the "inside-out" and revising from the "outside-in." The first refers to using your self-knowledge to plumb the depths of your life experiences to improve your writing. The second is more technical. It reveals the "tricks of the trade"—known techniques for writing well and revising well. At "ground level," five working techniques are common to all methods:

- Add
- Delete
- Rearrange
- Enhance
- Transform

How to Use This Book

Reading about revision is different than applying it. If you know a specific area of craft you want to concentrate on, such as giving your characters more personality or creating greater suspense, find those sections of this book. No one learns everything about revising fiction, then closes the book and implements it. Plan to return to this book again and again, to improve every novel or short story, and to bolster improving your weakest areas of writing. Each chapter begins with a heading called "Options," designed to direct you how to get the most value for your time, and where to find topics.

I recommend that everyone read chapters one and two to understand the two basic approaches: inside-out revision and outside-in revision.

Even if you select particular chapters, every element of craft is related to every other element of craft. Therefore, I do believe you'll gain the most understanding by reading this guidebook from cover to cover. However, when you are ready to revise, choose one task—such as varying your sentence beginnings or clarifying scene goals—and make those changes; then choose another task or two. Eventually, you will be able to do multiple revision tasks during each pass through your book.

As you read, you'll think, "I'll have to remember that." Write it down! Make a list. You'll start customizing the techniques in this book to meet your individual needs. I've included boxes and end-of-chapter Makeover Revision Checklists for easy reference and future review.

Here is my promise to you: The end result of reading this book will be enhanced knowledge and superior techniques that with practice will lead to polished and publishable stories.

PART ONE

Style Speaks

CHAPTER ONE

Inside-Out: The Voice of Style

Options If you like building your knowledge block by block, read on. Maybe you've been told that your writing needs to become more exciting, more distinctive. The techniques in this chapter will help you. On the other hand, you may be eager to make instant improvements on a sentence-by-sentence basis. Then skip ahead to chapter two.

Most writers who are intent upon selling their work will at some time attend a writers' conference. Imagine that you're sitting in one of the ballrooms of a large hotel on the first day of a four-day conference. The moderator has just asked the dozen literary agents and editors sitting behind a large table on stage what they most look for when they receive a novel submitted by a previously unpublished writer.

"Above all, I look for original style," an agent answers, adding, "distinctive voice, and then story." She passes the microphone to the editor sitting next to her.

"I agree. Geraldine has identified what we all look for—fresh, original style. Individuality of the author's voice."

You're mulling over the answers when the man next to you shoots his hand in the air. When acknowledged, he stands and asks, "Would anyone on the panel define what is meant by 'voice' and how that differs from 'style'?"

After a moment of silence while the agents and editors shift around and glance at each other, one agent takes the microphone and clears his throat. "It's difficult to put in words, but we know it when we see it." The nodding heads confirm what he says, and the moderator moves on to take another question.

The terms *style* and *voice* are often used interchangeably and are seldom defined. The reason is because they are inextricably twined—components of each other. Readers and aspiring fiction writers most often mention *style*, I've noticed, while agents and editors use the term *voice*. Although there may be a single hair that everyone is splitting, I've adopted a simple definition of the two words: Style is based on "wordsmithing," choosing and tweaking words to create the desired effect and to fit a character and genre. Voice is the author's natural use of language to create authentic and original characters and unique storytelling. More simply stated, style is an outcome of voice, more so than vice versa.

One individual might write, "The house fell into disarray." Someone different writes, "Pride of ownership had long-ago vanished, replaced by heaps of reeking garbage and half-empty rusting food cans littering the weed-infested yard." Yet another person writes, "The place was trashed out, like the crummy yard of the busted crack dealer down my block." For writing about the same content, these writers chose different images, diction (manner of speaking), and therefore express different styles. Each voice is unique to the writer.

Literary agents and editors complain that most manuscripts they read have writers' voices as distinctive and delicious as fast food; in other words, not distinctive at all. Writing can be so original that nearly anyone familiar with an author recognizes who wrote it: James Lee Burke, Stephen King, Ray Bradbury, Alice Walker, Janet Evanovich, J. K. Rowling.

How, then, do you cultivate your natural voice and learn how to adapt it for characters and story?

The following six processes will help you undo the negative aspects of society and upbringing and free the imprisoned artist within.

- Cultivate deep listening.
- Silence critics; banish censors.

- Practice riff-writing.
- Revise from your truth.
- Harvest your emotions.
- Catch fireflies.

Cultivate Deep Listening

The ear rarely deceives. You can see—read—your story and not catch many errors. However, if you listen to your story, you'll hear clunks, hisses, and coughs. Yet, there is listening and there is *listening*. As you know, it is possible to hear without really listening, either to oneself or to others. Developing the perspective of inside-out revision means tuning inward, trusting your own senses and intuition as you read your story silently or aloud.

Deep listening means giving your undivided attention; in this case, to your own writing. It means that you begin with the intention of listening fully, pushing away mind clutter and preparing to focus. Then take a full, cleansing breath, as a yogi might before meditation or a religious person prior to prayer.

As you carefully and slowly read what you have written, listen to the words as you hear them in your mind. Also read aloud—*and alone*—making sure you don't perform your writing. Theatrics, including inflections, modulations, and dialects can too easily disguise problems or glamorize the ordinary. Read in a straightforward manner and more slowly than normal, which facilitates deep listening.

Listen for obvious dissonances, clunky rhythms, unintended repetitions, monotone voices, and jarring transitions. Tune in to your own responses. Are you bored with long pages of your brilliant narration? Do you laugh at places you intended to be humorous, or do they now sound lame? Stop and revise or merely note the problem and continue reading and listening. Catching the obvious "glitches" will help center you for yet deeper listening, the aspect of inside-out revision that involves feeling what your character might be feeling, in body and emotions.

Keep your correction pen handy as this reading will be stop-and-go. Listen for awkward writing, incorrect word choice, and on the same or a subsequent reading, become your characters facing the conflicts, needs, and goals of your plot. Where in your body do you, or would you, experience your characters' anger, elation, worry, fear, and so forth? Add your human and realistic responses where you have omitted them when writing. Later, after you have read more chapters in this book, you can listen for particular problems in craft and style, using deep listening while reading silently or aloud. Don't take on too many pages at one time because you can easily lose your edge, dull out to the task, and begin to read for pleasure or somnolence. You'll also tend to lose your perspective of the whole story and flow, which is why several readings are worthwhile.

Because your stories are your offspring, it can be easy to get caught up in the dream of your creation, lulled by the words you are so familiar with that they all sound right. Fiction writing can be like daydreaming with a keyboard or notepad. Revision works best when you have the acuity that follows a great night's sleep or the edge that comes after drinking a double espresso.

Another form of reading aloud involves making a tape recording. The tape recorder method allows you to catch problems as you record your voice, and catch more as you listen to the recording, now freed from thinking about performing the task.

A real test for deep listening occurs when you share your work with others. Ask someone else to read your story aloud (this could be tape-recorded as well). Tell your reader to speak in a casual way, not to give you a dramatic performance. Take and release a deep breath. Listen closely; listen deeply. You'll be stunned by what you hear. You'll need to block out any concerns about what the other person thinks about you or your writing and listen to and note your mistakes, weak areas, and strengths—which you may hear with new ears. Pay attention to the words your reader stumbles over, where he or she slows down or speeds up. If you are following along on a printout of your story, as you listen, circle problem areas on your manuscript or use a plus mark or minus mark to correspond with "well done" or "needs improvement."

Many writers obtain this kind of feedback within the context of a critique group, also called a writers' workshop. Janet Fitch, author of a bestselling debut literary novel, *White Oleander*, had reported having a terrible time writing a follow-up novel. She wrote an historical novel of 300 pages, twice, then threw it away when her editors agreed with her that it would be better to put it aside. She turned to hosting a writers' workshop and, out of that mutual editing and feedback process, she wrote—and saw the publication of—her second novel, *Paint It Black*.

Training in critique and editing does help writers revise more effectively, but all writers—and listeners—have blind spots. Obviously, avoid groups (or individuals) that seem ego-driven or pull punches with soft-pedaled feedback. To end up with a publishable revision, you need constructive criticism.

Deep listening will serve you well for double-checking all of your revisions. It also refers to listening to your own heart, mind, soul, and body to use your own reactions to infuse your writing with vitality and originality.

Silence Critics; Banish Censors

As you turn inward and listen closely, you may hear internalized voices of critics. "Why don't you give it up—you write trash." Much has been written about the writer's "inner critics." They are not to be confused with your inner editor, the voice that says things like, "Oops, misspelled Mississippi" or "I'm using too many passive verbs—better dedicate one of my revisions to strengthening them." By "inner critic," I'm referring to a form of self-talk that interferes with both the writing and revision process.

The reason you want to silence these critical voices is that their advice is worth absolutely nothing. They judge you like a criminal rather than offer constructive criticism; they set up roadblocks to creative and original writing. Psychologists, coaches, and writers have faced and overcome this problem in various ways.

Your problem may also be not so much inner critics as real-life ones. What other people say may sink deep into your mind. Remember, there is a difference between a critic and someone offering a critique. The critic will level judgments against your writing, your chances of succeeding, or you personally. How do you handle these people? If a response of silence and leaving the person's company doesn't help you, then tell the individual that her remarks are "unhelpful" (a nonjudgmental word) and leave. If you're like me, you will still have to deal with what was said in your internal world because these remarks have a way of feeding insecurities that nourish the voracious inner critics. While a full treatise on overcoming inner obstacles is beyond the scope of this book, a few suggestions may help you with this nearly universal problem.

Recognition of the existence of an inner critic, whether you have one or a marauding horde, is a necessary first step. They go by many recognizable names: What If, If Only, Borrowing Trouble, It's No Good, Give It Up, Why Try, and the three blind mice: Doubt, Distraction, and Perfectionism. Sometimes that is all a writer needs to do—turn the blinding light of recognition onto a critic and let it shrink up and die like the Wicked Witch of the West.

For many writers, recognition of the critical voices alone is not enough. It's as if they are too powerful. They simply won't shut up. A number of "guerrilla" techniques may help you:

- Say affirmations—positive statements such as "I will write, revise, and publish."
- Repeat the word *no*, silently, until the naysaying natterers cease and desist.
- Visualize success—your chat with Oprah, endorsing fat royalty checks, or winning a contest.

Use deep listening as you write and revise but keep one ear bent toward these two intruders—inner and outer critics. It's especially important not to think, while you are writing or revising, of your mother or father or beloved grandmother or minister and what they would say. With time and practice, you'll quiet the choir and dull their impact. In their place, you'll be able to rely upon the inner editor to give you sound advice for revision—*if* you don't have the interference of one other problem: inner censors.

In the writer's internal universe, inner censors are parallel bad guys to inner critics. They are more insidious because they often live in the subconscious, although their development is a necessary stage of the socializing process of children through adulthood. Nobody brings his imaginary friend to the first day of college, for instance. (Notice I did not mention high school; I don't know about you, but I needed my imaginary friend to get through those years.)

Inner censors interfere with effective revision in a number of ways. For instance, most fiction writers act like protective parents toward their characters, especially the hero and his or her friends. Writers are too nice. You not only don't have to treat your characters nicely, but in revision you should look for ways to make the obstacles bigger, the complications seemingly endless, and their suffering worse. Avoid the temptation to rescue your characters. Instead of showing your hero running out of the rain into the shelter of a nearby building, make it a downpour with wind and hail and no way to quickly escape. Instead of another character being miffed at your hero, let him yell and cry and threaten—or shove, push, beat, or wound. A canon of good writing is *never write away from a good fight*. The inner censor would send you to reform school. But as a creative writer, you need full literary license to create suspense, which springs from conflict. Your one obligation is to be authentic to your characters and the story.

Another manifestation of the inner censor is drawing a blank. Perhaps you've been told that your story needs more development of setting, description, emotions, or characterization in general. Yet, when you reread your writing with the intent to revise, you can't get past the big stifling nada—nothing comes to mind. Your tabula rasa blank screen stares back. For whatever reasons, your imagination is restricted, you must kick the inner censors where it hurts, and liberate your creativity. You have to figure out how to not draw a blank when you do indeed draw one.

Most early drafts of novels are "tight"—they are shells of what they need to be, outlines or condensed versions of the full story. The most powerful technique I've discovered for silencing inner critics, banishing the inner censors, and developing any part of your story is a technique I call "riff-writing."

Practice Riff-Writing

We've all seen and heard a riff, in person or on TV. Whenever a musician, often playing jazz or rock, departs from the practiced notes of the band or sheet music and takes off on a spontaneous solo, he or she is playing a riff. Applied to our art, I call this "riff-writing."

It is similar to what has been called free writing or writing to a prompt—a picture or word or memory—or free association on paper. These methods fill your pages with writing, they help loosen you up and stick it to the censors, and they generate ideas for manuscripts. Riff-writing differs from these methods by being expressly applied to *revising a portion of your writing*. In this way, it is not "free" writing; it's very directed. You already have your "art," your novel or short story. Riff-writing helps you expand your imagination around a particular problem or need—to lengthen a section, to add images, or to develop more characterization, for instance. You then take the riffs and fold them into your story.

Here are the steps to practice riff-writing:

- Select a sentence or paragraph from your story that seems tight, brief, or could have more behind it.
- Choose a jumping-off place, such as a character's feeling, an object, a memory, an attitude, the setting, or any other element of craft or part of speech that arrests your attention and needs revising.
- Start your riff-writing, opening up that jumping-off point and

developing it. Follow it like a winding creek and allow yourself to express whatever great, good, nonsensical, lewd, or dumb phrases come to mind. You have no limits or boundaries. Overwrite; don't stop when you have the first impulse to. Keep writing; keep writing.

• Later, when you edit and revise, after the riff-writing has had a chance to "cool off," you'll have more distance from which to delete what doesn't fit your story, and you may have even more ideas for refining the added material.

As a not-great flute player, I used to improvise with a professional guitarist. I once lamented to a friend, a jazz pianist, how I wasn't competent enough to avoid hitting lots of wrong notes. They made me cringe or want to melt right through the floor. He enlightened me when he answered, "There are no wrong notes. You work them and they become a part of the riff."

Consider this before-and-after example of what I call riffing. I've selected an excerpt from *Prodigal Summer* by Barbara Kingsolver. I altered it to make it similar to what an underdeveloped first draft might look like. It's tight; it's "pre-riff." Then, I've followed my version with her original, fully developed writing.

Before riff (my condensing of Kingsolver's writing):
   "Called home. He's with the Savior now."
   "He looks real natural."
   She hadn't looked at the body and couldn't contemplate it. She opened her eyes for fear she would fall into the darkness. A tiny old woman was there, kneeling in front of her, startling Lusa by putting both hands very firmly on her knees.

After riff (Kingsolver's full writing):
   "Called home. He's with the Savior now."
   "He looks real natural."
   She hadn't looked at the body and couldn't contemplate it. She could not really think it was in there, not his body, the great perfect

table of his stomach on which she could lay down her head like a sleepy schoolchild; that energy of his that she had learned to crave and move to like an old tune inside her that she'd never known how to sing before Cole. His hands on her bare back, his mouth that drew her in like a nectar guide on a flower—these things of Cole's she would never have again in her life. She opened her eyes for fear she would fall into the darkness. A tiny old woman was there, kneeling in front of her, startling Lusa by putting both hands very firmly on her knees.

I hope you agree how inadequate the "before" is and how satisfying the "after," even though Barbara Kingsolver may or may not have had to revise to produce this wonderful writing. The most important thing is to *overdo* riff-writing as an aspect of revision. Later, you can revise and polish your riffs. In twenty years as an independent editor, I have rarely seen a manuscript overwritten, containing too many riffs. The Kingsolver example shows what the agents and editors mean when they say, "I know it when I see it," referring to original voice and a fully developed story. That's what you're aiming for.

Revise from Your Truth

Some literary agents have said they have a kind of sixth sense about detecting inauthentic prose. One telltale sign: Your reader is unmoved or bored. The writing might be technically well-executed, but it comes across as without heart or passion; emotion is absent or rings falsely, even when dramatic events are happening to the characters.

You can try on a style like you can try on clothing that is not *you*. You can also cultivate a voice that is hollow and superficial. You can become a good wordsmith—a master puppeteer—and the result may fool some of the people some of the time, including agents and editors. You may get published; most of us have read published prose that puts puppet characters through the motions of a puppet plot.

But I encourage you to summon the courage and develop the skill (through practice and riffing and other techniques) to write with a strong and open connection with your truth—from your heart, mind, and spirit.

Writers and editors have long struggled with an apparent contradiction. We have been discussing the author's voice, yet characters, often dramatically different from their creators, live out pretend stories. The characters might be magicians, monsters, mobsters, cheerleaders, Border collies, caterpillars, or any other sentient, or nonsentient, beings. How does author voice compare with character voice, not only in dialogue but in narration?

Your heroes are usually on a quest to resolve big problems that are recognizable if not common to the human condition. Multidimensional characters reflect the panoply of universal human needs and emotions: desires, yearnings, compulsions, fears, secrets, drives, and other inclinations and qualities that all of us possess.

A superficial or false-sounding voice can stem from a separation between the author and the point-of-view characters, especially the protagonist—the hero or heroine. Often, as fiction writers craft their first drafts, they see their stories visually, as movies on the screen of their minds, and do a lot of intellectual problem solving. Writers are understandably preoccupied by the demands of laying down characterization, viewpoint, dialogue, setting, narration, theme, and many other elements of craft covered in future chapters. You might say that first drafts are often author-driven, not character-driven. There is one exception to this statement: stories written entirely in an omniscient—all-seeing, or author—viewpoint. In this case, the writer's use of language comes through as dominant for all characters, in narration and in active scenes and dialogue. The success—and authenticity—of voice in this kind of writing depends greatly on the originality of style and the uniqueness of the story.

Although your characters may be vastly different from you, they too experience basic human emotions and their myriad variations. Even a Spock-like or robotic character with an absence of emotion matches the human who feels numb. You may have a character like that—or you may be a character like that. But ninety-nine percent of the time, your characters should approximate emoting human beings.

Chances are you have written your first drafts intellectually, which is as if an electrical short has cut you off from emotions. Your task in revision is to reconnect with your deepest feelings and yearnings and those specific ones your characters should experience. In life, the difficulties and suffering of others elicit empathy. Empathize with your characters and their difficulties, and you'll reconnect with the full range of your emotions. Once you have done that, you can imbue your story people with full authentic responses.

Harvest Your Emotions

Because most first drafts of a story or novel omit many emotional responses and visceral reactions, I developed a method to join emotion and prose. I call it "harvesting the emotions." This method is designed to breathe life into your characters, to make them emotionally authentic to the human experience, which in turn improves your voice. Here are the steps:

1. Choose a time and setting where you can be alone and without distractions for an extended period of time, depending upon how much material you will tackle. Have a printed-out copy of your manuscript and a pen at the ready.
2. Begin reading your selection ever so slowly. You first goal is to "become" your character, to vicariously experience his or her (or its) inner reality and the external story or plot. This is also what you hope your reader will do.
3. As you read places where a character should have an emotional reaction—tune into yourself. Use deep listening to your reactions to the situation faced by your character. The late writing teacher and prolific novelist Jack Bickham discussed the technique of stimulus and response. Action and reaction. In most situations in life, we react to a "stimulus" within our bodies first, then translate that into an identified feeling and thought.

Writers can figure out either one first, the emotion and then where it expresses itself in the body, or the body response and what emotion corresponds to it. Begin with your own body or feeling. If you have trouble feeling or imagining a response, then recall any experience you've had that is parallel to your character's experience.

Let's say your character gets slugged in the gut. How would you react? What emotion would you feel and where in your body would you feel it? A surge of adrenaline that powers white-hot rage to spew out in screaming invectives? That's one reaction, for sure. What next action would you take? What would be authentic to your character?

4. Harvest your emotions and those visceral, physical responses that reflect feelings—variations of mad, sad, and glad. Tap your vast accumulation of life experiences. Make notes of your emotions and responses. Add ones appropriate to your character into the manuscript.

5. Repeat this same five-step process, but now read aloud.

Your reader will share the experience and stay fully engaged. Your reader will care what happens to your characters. As you read your writing to yourself, cultivating deep listening, and harvest your emotions and visceral responses, you will most definitely catch previously invisible omissions and mistakes, especially related to character development.

Catch Fireflies

The late futurist and inventor Buckminster Fuller is purported to have said that we have about fifteen seconds to capture an idea before it vanishes. They are fireflies, difficult to catch if you don't act quickly. Carry a notepad; write them down. As you work on your revision, words, images, and solutions will strike you at odd times. When you imagine something, or when a phrase or line of dialogue runs through your mind, write it down.

Dreams and daydreams are rich with images and ideas, if you hold on to them. Taking walks and showers, washing dishes, and riding in cars all facilitate connection with your muse. Perhaps you are waiting in your dentist's office—grim but necessary—and you catch yourself fixating on a plastic model of a set of human teeth. You stare at the perfect white incisors; they remind you of squares of Chiclet gum. Or, if the model is meant to scare you into flossing, perhaps it shows damaged and decayed teeth. If you're Dean Koontz, you might grab your notepad and write this line that appeared in his novel *Seize the Night*: "His teeth were as small as kernels of white corn, and his smile was a cold dish, which he served in generous portions as he swung the club he was holding."

Like fireflies in the summer night, these flashes of the muse at work are fleeting. With encouragement, they come more often. I'm certain that many poets are accomplished firefly catchers. Establish a regular practice of reading poetry. Doing so will help awaken your inner poet. You'll build a sturdy conduit into your so-called subconscious mind, beneath or behind the wall of censorship, allowing formerly buried treasures to rise into consciousness and replace some of your pedestrian prose with poetic lyricism. Like this excerpt from *Riding with the Queen* by Jennie Shortridge:

> The sun rises red-hot in the rearview mirror like an Atomic Fireball, one of those jawbreakers that always sound like a good idea until you're halfway through it and sweating from the cinnamon burn and can't find a good place to spit it out.

Shortridge may have started with a captured firefly and then revised the first draft of it into this evocative sentence. You, too, have within you words and imagery every bit as delightful or profound as any poet or novelist, living or dead. An important aspect of revision is adding *what is not there*, and the fireflies you catch and use will light up your style.

As you reread your novel or short story, use deep listening. Ignore interfering inner critical voices as well as internalized censorship of your creativity. Select some crimped or tight sections for riff-writing. Open up the characters' responses. Add what would be your own visceral reactions to the events in your characters' lives. Harvest your emotions from inside you to outside—on the page. Make plot complications and obstacles greater. Intensify conflict. Empathize with and become your character, and follow the energy that surges through your fingertips into more development, more emotion, more style, *your style*, your emerging voice.

Release your imagination.

In the next chapter, we'll switch perspectives, from the inside-out to the outside-in. You'll learn how to enhance your style by manipulating aspects of the language, called wordsmithing, from changing sentence structures to utilizing power positions.

MAKEOVER REVISION CHECKLIST

Inside-Out: The Voice of Style

☑ Cultivate deep listening.
- Read silently and listen.
- Read aloud and listen.
- Tape-record and listen.
- Let others read aloud and listen.
- Take notes or make revisions as you go.

☑ Silence critics; banish censors.
- Silence inner and outer critics.
- Recognize criticism versus inner editing.
- Ignore judgmental inner criticisms.
- Say affirmations, silently repeat the word "no," or visualize success.
- Banish inner censors.
- Circumvent them by increasing conflicts, obstacles, and suffering for your characters.

☑ Practice riff-writing.
- Select a sentence or paragraph.
- Choose a jumping-off point (object, emotion, memory, and so on).
- Write everything that comes to mind.
- Keep writing; keep writing.
- Later, edit and revise.

☑ Revise from your truth.
- Recognize the source of the disconnection between yourself and your characters.
- Distinguish author-driven from character-driven writing.
- Reconnect through deep listening and by empathizing with your characters and story.

☑ Harvest your emotions.
- Choose a quiet place when you have plenty of uninterrupted time.
- Read slowly; slip into your character's persona.
- Capture your emotions and your physical reactions as you identify with your character's experience.

- Make notes of your responses.
- Revise to add these authentic emotions and reactions.

☑ Catch fireflies.
- Carry a notepad.
- Capture fleeting images and ideas, daydreams and dreams.
- Read poetry for inspiration.
- Cultivate an open channel with your muse.

CHAPTER TWO

Outside-In: Simple Revisions for Style

Options This chapter features simple but powerful ways to enhance style—by manipulating sentence structure and knowing how to increase the impact of your writing. Before you call anything you write "finished," review this chapter.

I love the expression "You be stylin'," brought to mainstream culture by African-Americans. It refers to a put-together look—in clothes, shoes, hairdo, makeup, jewelry, body movement, and attitude. A "stylin'" twenty-year-old woman might dress in a way that is sexy yet dignified. Put the same everything on an eighty-year-old and you create cognitive dissonance: She not be stylin'. What seems natural on one person is a disaster on another person.

In the previous chapter, we discussed inside-out revision techniques that foster discovery and refinement of your writer's *voice*, the individuality in your writing. In this chapter, we'll discuss outside-in techniques that foster *style*. I use "outside-in" to refer to "wordsmithing," a collection of uncomplicated revision techniques that don't require you to plumb the depths of yourself. These techniques rely upon easy-to-implement steps that result in improved style. They include:

- Model favorite authors.
- Revise for sentence variety.
- Revise for impact.

Model Favorite Authors

It's said that all writers are thieves. It's also said that imitation is the best form of flattery. Both sayings are true. You already model the writing style of others, whether you're aware of it or not. Intentional imitation of favorite authors is a technique that can expand your creativity and repertoire. Plan to model *many* writers, not just one. To use the following techniques specifically to help with a revision, find passages in published works that involve similar situations or problems as those in your novel—for example, describing an office, expressing an emotion, or increasing the pace.

Comparable to the results of riff-writing, the following two methods of modeling—copying excerpts from favorite authors and imitating writing of favorite authors—should expand your repertoire.

COPY EXCERPTS BY FAVORITE AUTHORS

Type slowly, word for word, thinking about the author's word choices and sentence construction, feeling the patterns and rhythms in your fingers, and imprinting them in your body-mind. Don't type like a robot, copying mindlessly. Connect with the author's writing in a deep-listening way. Copying excerpts is a technique that will help you break restrictions and allow you to experience, through muscle memory and new patterns of thinking, many different styles. When you return to your own manuscript, it can be as if you have gained coaches looking over your shoulder, making suggestions.

IMITATE WRITING OF FAVORITE AUTHOR

This technique can help you improve upon a particular aspect of your story, whether it is character description, setting, movement, or any other element of craft. Pick short excerpts written by favorite authors and imitate the focus, emotion, syntax (the ordering and relationship of the words), and imagery (descriptive comparisons), but apply what you learn to your own manuscript.

During your revision, keep focused on the particular need you have for your story. If you need to add more setting details but you're not sure how, read how other authors handle that element of craft. Model several authors' development of setting. Consider starting a file for outstanding examples of it. As you read novels and short stories and come across passages that have the "wow" factor, or seem unusual or remarkable, type or photocopy them and add to a file on that aspect of craft.

During revision, you'll find a lot of "things"—nouns, that are flat, without color or distinctiveness. The example below shows how to make your writing parallel; that is, similar to the writing you are modeling. This imitation shows how to create a feeling using a simile for a piece of furniture. Here is one partial sentence, the original, from *The Bonesetter's Daughter* by Amy Tan, and then my modeling of that line. The two sentences are parallel in type, function, order, and use of an image.

Original: The claw-footed iron tub was as soothing as a sarcophagus....

Modeling: The moth-eaten, springy couch was as welcoming as a bed of nails.

Not all of your modeling will be successful. It doesn't matter. You're experimenting, expanding your skill. A mistake in both writing and in revision is to settle for the first way you write something. Imitation helps you by introducing more than one option. You get unstuck.

This next, longer excerpt comes from a short story, "Everything's Eventual," by Stephen King. My imitation of it follows. Can a writer take some liberties with his or her modeling? That's the idea—to effect the chosen author's expression in your own writing.

Original: I've got a house, okay? My very own house. That's fringe benefit number one. I call Ma sometimes, ask how her bad leg is, shoot the shit, but I've never invited her over here, although Harkerville is only seventy or so miles away and I know she's practically busting gut with curiosity. I don't even have to go see her unless I want to. Mostly I don't want to. If you knew my mother, you wouldn't want to, either. Sit there in the living room with her while she talks about all her relatives and whines about her puffy leg. Also I never noticed how much the house smelled of catshit until I got out of it. I'm never going to have a pet. Pets bite the big one.

Modeling: I've got my first apartment, you know? My very own hobbit hole. That's awesome benefit number one. I call Momma sometimes, ask her what she's cooking for Daddy, girl talk, but I've never invited her over here, although west Phoenix is only about thirty or so miles from ASU and I know she's biting her tongue out of curiosity. I don't see her very often now, unless I want to. Mostly I do want to. If you knew my mother, you would want to, too. Sit there in her kitchen while she confides secrets about Nana and Great-Nana, and initiates me into what she calls the Mystery School of Wise Wonderful Women by lowering her voice as if we're, like, some terrorist cell plotting to use the weapons of cardamom or ginger or saffron, the secret ingredients in family recipes. Also I never noticed how much the house smelled of spice until I left it. I'm going to have a humongous kitchen someday. With a big butcher block and a rack of a hundred spices and herbs.

In modeling Stephen King's passage, I felt like I was riff-writing. I felt relaxed, no hurry, no rushing from a brief cameo of a character to a next action. I felt the enjoyment of developing a character and a first-person voice for my character, and then building a relationship with her mother that would be parallel—but contrasting—to King's. Because of his character's antipathy to his ma, his character experiences conflict. Because my character admires her momma and is shown going through a rite of passage, I have omitted conflict. It can be profitable to examine what you have missed—and why—as much as to notice what you have learned and done well.

Although some of your efforts will be wimpy compared to the original, other imitations might prove stronger than the original. Like all revision techniques, you're striving to reach beyond your own limits to expand your creativity. The imitation technique is very much like a student artist adopting a teacher's brush stroke for achieving a special effect. Every time you model successful writing, you strengthen your own "muscles." You upgrade your knowledge and skill in subsequent revisions—and in all future writing.

Revise for Sentence Variety

Outside-in revision for style can also come from methodical word-smithing; that is, from making seemingly mundane changes that result in significant improvement of your writing.

What's your habitual type of sentence or length? It's easy to fall into a rut and use one or two types most of the time, which can bore the reader and contribute to the indictment of a "flat style." Some writers use short sentences ninety-nine percent of the time, while other writers overuse breathlessly long sentences. Do you rarely write a question? Never let a character make a command? Sentence construction varies by type, function, parts of speech, and other considerations.

TYPE

The five types of sentences are simple, compound, complex, compound-complex, and complicated.

Simple: subject, verb, object. This also refers to an independent clause or a complete sentence. Examples: "Sylvia opened the envelope." Here's a longer simple sentence, with added adjectives and adverbs, modifiers of subjects and verbs: "Anxious, Sylvia tore open the envelope and yanked out her first publishing contract."

Too many simple sentences can sound choppy and amateurish; the rhythm is reminiscent of the kinds of sentences used to teach children how to read: "Dick ran down the hill. Jane followed him. Spot barked at the ball." However, during a dramatic scene, short sentences pick up the pace like a quickened heartbeat. That's why mysteries, thrillers, and suspense novels often have more simple sentences than historical novels or literary novels. But for some writers, simple sentences may reflect their original style—and work well. Consider the following excerpt from a winner of the Booker Prize, Michael Ondaatje, for *The English Patient*:

> She lights a match in the dark hall and moves it onto the wick of the candle. Light lifts itself onto her shoulders. She is on her knees. She puts her hands on her thighs and breathes in the smell of the sulphur. She imagines she also breathes in light.

The paragraph above begins a section that is about 325 words. Of the twenty sentences, fourteen begin with "she," although about half are simple sentences by type.

Compound: more than one independent clause (a complete sentence), connected by a conjunction (and, or, nor, but, for, yet, so). Example: "Sylvia's fingers trembled and she jumped up and down." A longer compound sentence: "Sylvia hopped into her Toyota and sped to her husband's law office, but he had left for the courthouse."

Overuse of the compound type can turn into a stream of run-on sentences. The writing style can seem tedious. Another drawback is that novices often raise a question in the first clause and answer it in the second, thus missing a chance to hold the reader in suspense.

No suspense: "She ran to the bus stop, and she caught the Nonstop 12 just before the doors closed." This compound sentence ends on an emotional low, the reader's thirst for answers quenched, no reason to return to the well. A question planted in a reader's mind creates curiosity. It often implies conflict to come. The reader must read on, which creates movement and suspense, the rocket fuel of successful fiction. Revision: "She ran to the bus stop." A question lingers: "Did she make the bus in time?"

Continuing: "She caught the Nonstop 12 just in time." The second sentence answers the aforementioned question. Depending upon the plot of this story, the second sentence could answer the first and raise yet another question, and so forth. For instance, the end of the second sentence could read: "...just in time, but where was her pass?" Did she lose it? Then what will she do?

Complex: one simple sentence (an independent clause) and at least one dependent clause (an incomplete sentence), in either order. There can be other add-on clauses. Examples: "After leaving the law office for the courthouse, Sylvia called her husband on her cell phone. She hoped he would get a break, despite Judge Mudd's habit of presiding nonstop through the afternoon."

Compound-complex: more than one independent clause and at least one dependent clause. In the following example, the first independent clause is supplied by the first four words, and the second by the last five words. Example: "She dashed through security, up the stairs, and down a long corridor, reading the room numbers above the doors and finally locating room 428, at precisely the same time as the judge ordered a recess."

Overuse of complex or compound-complex sentences can wear out your poor readers or put them in a trance. These sentences force them to work to retain and understand all of the thoughts. At the end of the sentence, readers must be able to remember and connect everything. If you pile up complex and compound-complex sentences, it's like assigning your reader to hard labor on a chain gang.

Complicated: This fifth type can cause havoc for all but the most accomplished of writers. Complicated sentences may include many or all of the prior four types within it. When the sentence is tortured,

I call the result *convoluted*. When written well, the complicated sentence, often very long, can be the hallmark of that writer's style. Think Faulkner; think James Joyce. Remember Michael Ondaatje's proclivity for the simple sentence that begins with the same part of speech—the pronoun *she*? He ends his one-page section with a long and completely satisfying one-sentence, one-paragraph, grammatically complicated sentence:

> She leaps up and in midair turns so she lands facing the other way, then skips forward even wilder now down the black hall, still landing on squares she knows are there, her tennis shoes banging and slamming onto the dark floor—so the sound echoes out into the far reaches of the deserted Italian villa, out towards the moon and the scar of the ravine that half circles the building.

This sentence-paragraph is intentionally long and has great impact. Its length parallels how the character abandons herself to movement, to her need to *move*. Because the sentence continues beyond her, its length and flow emphasizes her aloneness and the power of her private actions to reach beyond her to the greater universe.

In revision, examine your story or novel specifically to determine if you overuse one sentence type—or omit any. Generally, vary your sentence types, not only for variety's sake, but to fit the events of your story and development of character, for mood, dramatic effect, and emotional power. If you believe that one of the five types, in repetition, best serves your story and style, follow this rule: Rules are meant to be broken. When can you break them? When the result works. However, develop "fluency" with all types, another step on your quest to write well, revise well, and sell.

FUNCTION

A sentence can function in one of four ways: make a statement (declarative), give a command (imperative), ask a question (interrogative), or make an exclamation (exclamatory). Omitting or failing to vary your functions is like failing to include a wrench, screwdriver, hammer, and vise grip in a mechanic's basic tool kit. After all, in manuscript makeovers you need the right tool for the right job. Like overuse of the sentence types, overuse—or under use—of one of these four functions may weaken style.

In writing, as I suspect in life, we use more statements than we do questions, and more questions than commands. Least of all—for most people (except teens)—we exclaim. Sometimes, writers favor one or two functions to the exclusion of the others, limiting their expression. Most storytelling relies upon making statements. Show (action) and tell (narration) both use statements in abundance.

If you pepper the reader with questions, the writing may seem melodramatic. For instance: "Why had she left the scene of the crime? Why hadn't she called 911? What did she have to hide? Could the answer be found in the package they found near the body?"

Be very careful when you use the rhetorical question, a question asked without expectation of an answer, or with the answer already known. If you use it mindlessly, the effect may come across as coercive, or melodramatic, like this: "How would you like to receive a million tax-free dollars?" I'll take mine in one-dollar bills, thank you very much. Yet, in dialogue a rhetorical question may perfectly capture a sarcastic tone and add to characterization. "You think I was born yesterday? Huh?"

It's unlikely that you'll overuse commands. This function obviously fits characters in roles that require dishing them out. "Put your hands over your head!" The command also fits dramatic moments: "Don't open that door!"

It's important to show strong emotion and surprise, yet these "exclamations" can lose impact with overuse of the exclamation mark. In my experience of editing novels, I see about one in fifty manuscripts riddled with exclamation marks. Riddled = Ridiculous! The use of this punctuation mark cannot substitute for building tension or emotion. I once listened to a panel of agents and cringed when an obviously clueless writer asked, "How many exclamation points should I use per novel?" This, I thought, is going to be interesting. Deadpan, an agent said, "One exclamation mark per novel. Next question."

Like all the tools of our trade, exclamations punctuated with the exclamation mark are appropriate for certain situations: "Help, I can't swim!" But when you delete the marks, don't throw out the baby, too; keep the surprise or strong emotion. A good example of this is by Hugo and Nebula Award–winner Octavia E. Butler, from *Dawn*, the first in a science fiction trilogy. The "he" referred to in the passage is an intelligent alien—with tentacles—who mates with humans. Creepy.

> Was he the reason for the clothing, then? He seemed to be wearing a similar outfit. Something to take off when the two of them got to know each other better? Good god.

This exclamation at the end reflects the strong emotion of realization after she thinks through the implications of her situation. The exclamation, "Good god" is clear without the heavy emphasis of an exclamation mark. Later, when anticipation becomes reality, Butler uses exclamation marks.

Using all four types of sentences and using all four functions will improve your style score. The next revision technique introduces an easy but effective way to strengthen sentence beginnings.

SENTENCE BEGINNINGS

Human beings are creatures of habit. We writers develop habits that easily become ruts that limit our expressiveness, like artists who only use a few colors on their palettes or musicians who play only in the major keys—and never in the minor. Limitations of artistic expression make narrower opportunities for a distinctive style—unless, of course, the limitations are intentionally *for style*.

All beginnings are so important that I'll return to them in several sections of this book. On the wordsmithing level of outside-in revision, variety in sentence beginnings is as simple as remembering the parts of speech. Maybe you'll discover pockets in your novel where too many pronouns, or too many uses of a character name, begin sentences or paragraphs. Or you pile up too many gerund beginnings (verbs ending in "ing") in a row. Every writer should know how and be able to start a sentence in every way that is grammatically possible.

For simplicity's sake, I've used examples from one author, Margaret Atwood, from her novel *The Blind Assassin* to demonstrate the full spectrum of sentence beginnings:

Noun (person, place, animal, thing, or idea): "Sabrina didn't notice me." "Water runs silently onto the floor of the tent."

Pronoun (substitutes for a noun or pronoun): "I didn't know whether to be angry or alarmed." "It was a print of the photograph of the three of us." "There was also a lot of fancy dress."

Adjective (modifies a noun or pronoun): "Dark circles under eyes, downward lines etched from nose to mouth corners." (fragment)

Article (a type of adjective—a, an, the): "The heat receded; the cold advanced."

Verb (action or state of being): "Bless your soul, did you walk all the way over here?" "Don't fidget with your gloves or your hair."

Gerund (a verb turned into a noun by adding "ing"): "Cutting up the picture like that was a very strange thing to have done."

Adverb (primarily modifies a verb, and answers how, when, where, how much): "Sometimes he sets his ear against the wall to listen."

Conjunction (links phrases and clauses): "But I could not really make sense out of what I was seeing."

Preposition (links nouns, pronouns, and verbs to other parts of the sentence): "In the middle distance trains mourn and shunt, their whistles trailing into the distance."

Interjection (an exclamation expressing emotion or surprise): "Fool, I could have taught you everything!"

Determine whether you have fallen into any repetitious and limiting ruts. Mark and revise your sentence beginnings.

Revise for Impact

Becoming aware of and intentional about your patterns with sentence lengths and types, functions, and beginnings form the basics of outside-in manuscript makeovers. You'll also be amazed how you can increase the impact of your prose through the following four revision techniques:

- one-word sentences
- word or sound repetitions
- sentence fragments
- power positions

ONE-WORD SENTENCES

When most of us took English classes in high school or college, we were instructed that a sentence must have three parts: a subject, a verb, and an object. A doer, an action, and a result of the action. One word doth not a sentence make. Except in creative writing, where anything goes. Anything.

One-word sentences are a stop sign. They make the reader slam on the brakes with sudden awareness of stopping. The sleepwalking reader wakes up. One-word sentences have power. Writers must use that power well and not squander it on a meaningless word. Really.

See what I mean? The word *really* is unworthy of the emphasis. As you read, pay attention to what words authors choose, in what context, and for what impact. The next example, *The Lone Ranger and Tonto Fistfight in Heaven* by Sherman Alexie, shows his masterful use of the one-word sentence, and his strong style. Notice the impact of the one word in this excerpt and the effect of its repetition:

> Just the week before, Victor had stood in the shadows of his father's doorway and watched as the man opened his wallet and shook his head. Empty. Victor watched his father put the empty wallet back in his pocket for a moment, then pull it out and open it again. Still empty. Victor watched his father repeat this ceremony again and again, as if the repetition itself could guarantee change. But it was always empty.

In this example, Alexie has gone beyond the use of the one-word sentence, "empty," and developed it in a way that characterizes the father, reflects the life of some Indians, and symbolizes an emotional reality for Victor, the narrator. The impact of this passage is powerful.

Alexie's excerpt shows what is possible within the context of his story. Choose your one-word sentences wisely. Reread your story draft thinking about what words, in sections throughout the book, you might want to single out for greater impact.

WORD OR SOUND REPETITIONS

In the prior example, Sherman Alexie made use of two repetitions: the word "empty" and "Victor watched his father." To see the true impact of a word or phrase, the repetition needs to be seen in context. From *Amy and Isabelle* by Elizabeth Strout, notice the impact of multiple word and sentence repetitions:

> Across town Barbara Rawley, the deacon's wife, sat down on her bed. The rain tapped steadily against the windowpane. From the

family room below came the sounds of the television, and her son, Flip, hooting as he watched the baseball game.

What she couldn't get over was how the breast was gone. How simple it was. Just gone.

She heard her husband speak to Flip, the footrest of his recliner squeaking into place. All that mattered was this: the happiness of her family.

But still. Her breast was gone. She couldn't seem to get over this, to believe it. She opened her bathrobe slowly, and stared. She stared and stared. The breast was gone.

In its place was a long, red, raised line. The breast itself was simply gone.

Although word repetition emphasizes meaning and emotion above other effects, sound repetition primarily adds to the artistry—literally the style. Repeated sounds are called "alliterations." Sometimes they are obvious: "She sells seashells by the seashore." Sometimes they are less "on the nose," less obvious: In Strout's excerpt above, many words, in addition to the intentionally repeated word "breast," begin with *B*: Barbara, bed, baseball, breast, but, breast, believe, bathrobe, breast, breast. One paragraph has no *B* words; however, footrest carries the sound of breast. The letters *F* and *H* and their sounds also recur throughout this one passage.

Did Elizabeth Strout craft this alliteration intentionally? I can't tell. The two-word alliterations in "the long, red, raised line" are more likely to have been intentional because they are obvious. Even so, like the accomplished artists they become, established authors often write and revise without having to think about each and every technique.

The alliterations in children's literature may be obvious. While too many alliterations too close together can shout amateur, an occasional density can be quite pleasing. In the middle-reader's novel *Before the Lark* by Irene Bennett Brown, I sense she enjoyed writing the following:

The fence about her potato patch had been mashed down as if it were a spider web. White bubbling backs of sheep filled the green of her garden.

Now that you have the hard work of getting a full draft done, play with sounds, rhythmic repetitions, and add alliterations to your work.

SENTENCE FRAGMENTS

Some fiction writers avoid using sentence fragments, often because their grade-school English teacher lowered a composition score by a full grade for each fragment. As you can see in the prior excerpts, sentence fragments are a fiction writer's friend. They contribute to style, they contribute to changes in pace and sentence variety, and they mimic a natural voice. Exclusive use of complete sentences can seem stilted. Artificial.

POWER POSITIONS

For reasons inexplicable to me, most writing instruction omits mention of power positions, which include "firsts" and "lasts":

- first and last words
- first and last sentences
- first and last paragraphs (in sections or chapters)
- first and last pages (in chapters, short stories, and novels)
- first and last chapters (in novels)

Dedicating one round of revision to utilizing power positions will reward you with greater dramatic impact. Don't feel as if you must always take advantage of a first and last power position. As always in writing, nothing is *always*! Look for opportunities and consider whether you want the emphasis. Use your intuition and your instincts as guidance. This round of revision will be slow, but don't rush it. You are likely to see many other changes while you are working on the power positions. (Mark, revise, or take notes so you don't forget.)

When a word, phrase, or sentence is in a first position, it serves as a hook to draw the reader in. The impact of the last position should cinch the meaning of the sentence or paragraph, and create suspense and curiosity leading to the next hook.

Again, from Irene Bennett Brown's award-winning novel for nine- to twelve-year-olds, *Before the Lark*, she often uses fragments to enhance the power position of beginning paragraphs. In this next example, she also uses the power position of the last question, which is a demand with high emotional stakes: What happened to Jocey's father. Notice how this use of a last power position raises suspense. To learn the answer, the reader must continue to the next sentence.

> Sneaking? Ruin? What was he talking about? Jocey pulled the boulder away, at last, and wiped the sweat from her forehead. Keeping a muddied hand on her hatbrim, to hide her face, she turned toward him. "What about my father? What are you talking about? I want to know."

In *White Mountain*, Dinah McCall, a prolific romantic suspense and romance writer, takes special care to open her chapters with powerful hooks. Here is one such first sentence, from chapter six, followed by the last short paragraph in this section:

> *First line:* "It took all Jack had to let Isabella go."

> *Last paragraph of section:* "He started to go into the dining room, and then changed his mind and headed for the stairs instead. He needed to wash up and change his shirt. He wasn't about to eat a meal with Bobby Joe Cage's blood on his sleeves."

Notice how the emotion of the paragraph is located in the first sentence and the last sentence. Notice how the second sentence leaves a question hanging about why he changed his mind and decided to go upstairs. Notice, too, how the one word with the most impact is "blood."

Although the role of short story or novel beginnings (and endings) will be taken up again when addressing characterization and plot, novel beginnings are always in a power position. The openings of some stories are legendary. In the following famous first lines of novels, notice how dramatic they are. Notice, too, how the last word (or words) of most of these openings is emphasized.

- "Call me Ishmael." *Moby Dick* by Herman Melville
- "It was a pleasure to burn." *Fahrenheit 451* by Ray Bradbury
- "Marley was dead: to begin with." *A Christmas Carol* by Charles Dickens
- "Far out in the uncharted backwaters of the unfashionable end of the Western Spiral arm of the Galaxy lies a small unregarded yellow sun." *The Hitchhiker's Guide to the Galaxy* by Douglas Adams
- "As Gregor Samsa awoke one morning from uneasy dreams he found himself transformed in his bed into a gigantic insect." *The Metamorphosis* by Franz Kafka

Pay attention to the opening lines of novels and short stories. Jot down sentences that you find particularly well crafted. Review these notes and apply the techniques covered in this book to help you create a first line as powerful, if not as legendary, as these famous openings.

The work of outside-in revision ends on the day you mail your manuscript. Later, in part four on marketing, we'll return to more outside-in revision related to copyediting and format. Although outside-in revision techniques are simple, they are sometimes admittedly tedious. Yet the end result is keeping your reader stimulated and engaged, and often emotionally moved. The next chapter features revision techniques that are also from the outside-in, yet entirely different from manipulation of sentence and word location. The next style booster is all about creating and revising for imagery.

MAKEOVER REVISION CHECKLIST

Outside-In: Simple Revisions for Style

☑ Model favorite authors.
  - Copy excerpts word for word, slowly.
  - Pick short excerpts and model the focus, emotion, syntax, and imagery, but in your own words and for your story.

Revise for sentence variety.
  - Vary your types of sentences: simple, compound, complex, compound-complex, and complicated.
  - Vary and appropriately use the four sentence functions: statements, commands, questions, and exclamations.
  - Limit use of exclamations.
  - Use all parts of speech for sentence beginnings.
  - Vary or intentionally repeat the same part of speech for style.

☑ Revise for impact.
  - Use one-word sentences.
  - Use word or sound repetitions, including alliterations.
  - Use sentence fragments.
  - Use power positions: first and last words, first and last sentences, first and last paragraphs, first and last pages, first and last chapters.

CHAPTER THREE

Outside-In: Advanced Revisions for Style

Options If you're concerned that your writing might be lackluster or if you've been told that it would benefit from imagery, read on. Even if you feel confident of your descriptive language, review the Makeover Revision Checklist at the end of this chapter to strengthen your use of similes and metaphors.

A clear picture is worth a thousand words; a blurry one is worth nothing. Writing fiction is the fine art of creating pictures, of taking the reader into a visual and sensory world peopled by characters with conflicts.

The pictures we create with words can be literal—factual descriptions, as in "A two-hundred-foot Douglas fir stood in the center of the small valley." Imagery, however, is symbolic, nonfactual. Authors use imagery to create alternate, or symbolic, meaning of something literal. For example: "A giant sentinel, ever green and ever watchful, stood guard over the small valley." Symbolically, the fir tree becomes a guard whose job it is to watch for trouble.

During revision, experienced fiction writers work to add imagery. Why? Because an effective image evokes emotion, atmosphere, or mood. It adds to characterization and style. Imagery can also be a way to slow pace. Almost simultaneously, but not quite, the reader connects the literal and the figurative: giant "tall, old evergreen tree" *with* "ever watchful sentinel." Some details of the initial "snapshot" have been lost: two-hundred-foot and Douglas fir. If these facts are important, a writer can easily add them through character observation or reaction, following the image: "A giant sentinel, ever green and ever watchful, stood guard over the small valley. Mabel shaded her eyes to see the top of the old Douglas fir. So that's how tall two hundred feet is, she thought. As she took a deep cleansing breath, all the tightness and stress she'd held inside melted away, and she felt an immediate bond with her protector."

If your image is successful, then the time lag between reading it and matching it up to the story is almost imperceptible. Not only that, the story deepens by what meaning the image evokes. The meaning read into images by a reader may be quite different from what the author intended. In this wonderful way, the reader enters the story artistically, adding his or her life experiences and free associations. It is said that there are three stories in any novel: the one intended by the author, the one written on the page, and the one readers interpret from their lives.

Here is what I read into the Mabel paragraph: Her last line of internalization, "she felt an immediate bond with her protector," alludes to insecurity. Why insecure? The image evoked a sentry or guard, and they offer protection. Why would she need protection? By the word choices *sentinel* and *protection*, you learn something about the character. *Sentinel* is a higher diction word than *guard*, so she probably is a college graduate, or well-read. Is there any military context in her backstory that would indicate her choice of a protector? Maybe the story will reveal that her big brother died in Afghanistan, and she yearns for the security and protection he provided, so much so that she unconsciously attributes those qualities to the tall tree.

I find an additional meaning to the image "ever green, ever watchful." To me, these words imply permanency. The fact that this tree is a "giant sentinel" is on the order of an archetype, a god-tree guaranteeing everlasting protection and security. The mood generated by this image is comfort and safety, and perhaps awe. That's my interpretation of the symbolism, and you may come up with a different one.

You can see why imagery is often a task left for revision. You may need to remove imagery that came to mind while writing, because it really doesn't work well or it symbolizes something you don't want. Or you may see that style or characterization or pace will improve if you add similes and metaphors.

If your readers are confused by your image, the spell is broken. They pop out of the imaginary world, detach their emotions from identification with your characters, and go through their left-brain files trying to decipher what in the heck you mean. Yet, as hard as you try for clarity, you're always going to have some readers "who don't get it." Don't worry about it. As a teenager, I read Robert Frost's poem "Mending Wall" for the first time and thought it was amazing. Sharing it with my dad created a long, frustrating communication. "The wall's symbolic, Dad. It's about relationships," I insisted. He said, "I don't know what you're driving at. A wall's a wall. If it's got a hole in it, you'd better repair it. That's what makes a good fence." My dad doesn't do symbolism.

Two types of imagery will enhance your revised draft: similes and metaphors. They are comparisons of a literal "picture" in terms of something else. That something else is usually visual, but similes or metaphors also offer substitutions that relate to sound, smell, taste, and touch, as well as emotions, ideas, and beliefs.

Create Similes

Similes compare one thing to another through similarity. The simile is typically preceded by the words "like" or "as." They abound in our everyday language, often in the form of clichés: "like two peas in a pod," "hot as hell," and "light as a feather." In fiction, clichés used in dialogue add to characterization. However, in narration—that is, telling—your style will be stronger if you create original similes.

Like all imagery, similes can compare anything to anything. However, most imagery relies upon the dominant visual sense.

Visual: "His brain was like a brightly lit factory, full of flying wheels and precision." *Edith Wharton*
"Something in her face spilled over me like light through a swinging door." *Sue Grafton*
"I watched her wide, full mouth sweep through her sentences like a figure touring a dark house, flipping on spots and banks of perfectly drawn light." *Chang-Rae Lee*
"Buildings as badly painted as old whores." *Larry McMurtry*

In the writing stage, writers often overemphasize the visual sense to the exclusion of others. Revision is the time to add similes that describe sound, smell, taste, touch/temperature, and touch/sensation, as well as sight.

Sound: "Silently as a dream." *William Cowper*
"A small silence came between us, as precise as a picture hanging on a wall." *Jean Stafford*

Smell: "The air smelled like damp flannel." *Jonathan Kellerman*
"A kitchen odor hung about like a bad mood." *Tom MacIntyre*

Taste: "My mouth tasted like an old penny." *Robert B. Parker*
"Tasted like it had been fried in tar." *Larry McMurtry*

Touch/Temperature: "Colder than a banker's heart." *William Diehl*
"It was like being inside a radiator." *David Brier*

Touch/Sensation: "Shame came over me like a blanket of steam." *Mary Gordon*
"A big pulse of sickness beat in him as if it throbbed through the whole earth." *D. H. Lawrence*

Every aspect of your created world can become fodder for imagery, not only the physical world and the five senses of your characters but also abstractions such as emotions, ideas, ideals, and opinions.

As you reread your stories, be especially aware of adjectives and adverbs, which could be replaced with imagery. You may be using modifiers to prop up general or nonspecific nouns or weak verbs. For instance, "a beautiful woman" or "a ruggedly handsome man" suffers with clichéd, vague adjectives. You'll earn a big fat *F* in style if you use clichés like these. Replace them with similes that capture the essence of characters or describe their physique and appearance. A different use of simile is to describe what a character isn't: "He was nothing like a butterfly, but he gave a sense of floating, hands and arms flittering, when he walked."

Weak verbs and their crutches, the adverb, need some form of triage, especially clichés like "stopped cold." Sometimes the verb and adverb are not clichés as much as simply lackluster, such as "looked angry" (or sad, or curious, or any other adverb). "Walked quickly," for instance, has what I consider the wimpy verb "walked" coupled with an adverb-crutch, "quickly." One solution replaces these two words with one strong verb that conveys the same or even a more precise meaning; in this example, a verb such as "hurried, rushed, dashed, darted, or strode." A second solution replaces "walked quickly" with a simile. "Carolyn dashed across the street like the Roadrunner being chased by the Coyote." Or, "Carolyn's walk conveyed a woman on a time clock, every second measured and either paid for or lost."

In revision, you may have to search the catacombs of your mind for apt similes. Double-check to assure they work and are appropriate. A really bad simile is like getting the Norovirus flu on a honeymoon cruise: memorable—for the wrong reasons.

Reread and think about all of your similes, because some are likely to end up like an almost-made-it *American Idol* singer. Here's an almost-made-it from a story set in the Old West: "The cowpokes leaned back in creaky wooden chairs and uncoiled their legs, like lariats." Certainly, cowpokes and lariats go together and with the times, but are legs as long as lariats? The following simile was in a story set in India, in a village, and was describing a small boy: "...his head straining forward like a baby elephant." Even though the setting has elephants that work with and for the people of the village, the head of a baby elephant is much larger than the head of a small boy. Neither simile makes the cut.

Create Metaphors

The other type of imagery is the metaphor. The comparison here is a complete substitution, not a side-by-side comparison. Once again, our language is rich with metaphors drawn from all areas of human experience, so much so that many have become familiar clichés. Here is my play with cooking and food metaphors:

> He was salt of the earth, the spice of my life, but depending on his changing moods, he could fry my ass, toast my buns, or roast me with one-liners. On the other hand, he always said my sour grapes was just the pot calling the kettle black, and I would tell him, "Better close your trap, honey pie, because you're about to step out of the frying pan and into the fire."

It's not as difficult to use metaphoric words as it is to find the right metaphoric word, phrase, or paragraph that fits your era, setting, character, plot, or theme. A metaphor that does not fit will sound false in a reader's ear. There are several types of metaphors, two that you should add to your repertoire and three that you should (mostly) delete or replace. Add: simple and extended. Delete or replace: mixed, inappropriate, and clichéd.

SIMPLE

A metaphor can be as simple as one word or a phrase. One word: "Boy did we *roast* him at his sixtieth birthday party." "I've worked on our taxes so long, I'm *fried*." Phrase: "He had to get his *butt in gear* if he was going to make the bus stop on time." "Hey, dude, don't get your *feathers ruffled*."

Notice the effectiveness of this one sentence (well, two) from *The Jury Master*, a first novel that made the *New York Times* bestseller list. Written by Robert Dugoni, the imagery throughout this thriller is a joy to read. With it he also makes superb use of the last power position, ending a chapter with impact, as follows:

> "Yes," he said, hearing the low whistle of the guillotine blade sliding down the rack and hitting the wood stump with a dull thud. "I felt guilt."

If you were a literary agent and the above line was all you had to go on before deciding to request or reject seeing more of Dugoni's novel, what would you say? I would say, "Send me more." Imagery is such a powerful aspect of style, it can literally make the difference between a request and a rejection.

EXTENDED

Metaphors that are more than a word, phrase, or short sentence might tax your brain; they do for most of the writers I know. Dean Koontz is an extended metaphor master. The following example comes from his novel *Seize the Night*:

> The trick, however, is to remember that hope is a perilous thing, that it's not a steel and concrete bridge across the void between this moment and a brighter future. Hope is no stronger than tremulous beads of dew strung on a filament of spiderweb, and it alone can't long support the terrible weight of an anguished mind and a tortured heart....

Koontz's extended metaphor provides sophisticated development of an idea. Here is a second example from the same novel, a metaphor that is less abstract but no less developed:

> Bobby Holloway says my imagination is a three-hundred-ring circus. Currently I was in ring two hundred and ninety-nine, with elephants

dancing and clowns cartwheeling and tigers leaping through rings of fire. The time had come to step back, leave the main tent, go buy some popcorn and a Coke, bliss out, cool down.

Because the goal of creating an extended metaphor can seem intimidating, take your person, place, animal, object, thing, or idea (noun)—and do riff-writing. Open it up; explore it, even if everything you write is non-metaphoric. In an outside-in technique, look up your word in a thesaurus, simile dictionary, and quotation reference, and expand your "language" about it. You'll get the hang of it.

Next, think about your character from many angles, and consider the geographic location, era, immediate environment or setting of the scene, and the emotional realities of the character. This will help you know where to insert your extended metaphor. Then work it. Eventually, the words will come. They will. You've gathered your tools, thought about the context, and used riff-writing. Like playing the five notes calling the aliens in the movie *Close Encounters of the Third Kind*, or E.T. phoning home, your spaceship will land. The extended metaphor is difficult for most writers, and that is why imagery is an advanced revision technique.

MIXED METAPHORS

As you reread your manuscript with an eye to imagery, you may find you have written short metaphors too close to one another such that the images clash. These are called "mixed metaphors." They may be as slight as one word or involve many lines. For example, a simple mixed metaphor: "At last the sun set on this chapter of his life." Where the simple metaphor leaves off and the extended metaphor begins is one of those gray areas of terminology. The next example begins as an extended metaphor but one paragraph later changes into an extended mixed metaphor. The excerpt is from *Icy Sparks* by Gwyn Hyman Rubio, and features a protagonist with Tourette's syndrome.

I could feel little invisible rubber bands fastened to my eyelids, pulled tight through my brain, and attached to the back of my head. Every few seconds, a crank behind my skull turned slowly. With each turn, the rubber bands yanked harder, and the space inside my head grew smaller.

This extended metaphor works well for me. It is clear, and I quickly make the shift from the image of taut rubber bands and a crank to powerful, visceral feelings of incredibly uncomfortable sensations. I believe the author has relayed to the reader what is called "dystonic tics," an affliction some people suffer with Tourette's syndrome.

A few paragraphs later, Rubio's paragraph is chock-full of mixed metaphors. Remember the number one rule: All rules can be broken, but only if the result works. See what you think of the following excerpt:

...hoping that the itchiness and tightness would go away, but instead I felt my eyelids, rolling up further like shades snapping open, and my eyeballs, rolling back like two turtles ducking inside their shells, and the space inside my head, shrinking smaller and smaller until only a few thoughts could fit inside; and, terrified of the contraction, of each thought's strangulation, I threw back my head and cried, "Baby Jesus! Baby Jesus!"; and, not knowing what to do or how to stop it, I gave in completely to the urge. Out popped my eyes, like ice cubes leaping from a tray.

Do the mixed metaphors work? In close proximity to each other, Rubio's imagery includes window shades, turtles, strangulation, and ice cubes. I do think Gwyn Hyman Rubio is a powerful stylist with great passion in her writing and deep empathy for her character. Perhaps she is not breaking the rules if she intended these mixed metaphors to capture the strange speech called "coprolalia" (defined as inappropriate or involuntary utterances) of someone with Tourette's. If so, the author is indeed masterful. These passages, and many others, are imbued with emotion. I doubt that readers are neutral in their reactions. Rubio has an original voice. And style trumps most rules.

However, if you're a beginner or haven't yet sold a first novel, my advice: Don't mix your metaphors.

INAPPROPRIATE

The inappropriate metaphor is a form of the mixed metaphor, and occurs when some of the images simply don't fit in the context of the story, in the character's lexicon, or in the historical era.

Context: "He shoved her down the garbage disposal of the elevator chute." Okay, I made this up and it is very strange indeed, but obviously "garbage disposal" and "elevator chute" are inappropriately matched. They are mixed, yes, but also inappropriate. I once had a member of one of my critique groups who had us all howling when his detective pursuing a serial killer had "the strength of Popeye the Sailor slugging down spinach." Say what?!

Character's lexicon: If you're writing about an old-time farmer, who doesn't have a computer, it would be inappropriate to his manner of speaking to say, "My hard drive's full. I can't take in any more data." But if you've created a character whose diction includes metaphoric language, he might say, "My silo's full. You catch my meaning?"

Historical era: Anachronism refers to a word or words that exist out of proper time for the context. They can refer to a word from the past used in the present or a word from the present used in the past. If you saw the movie *Back to the Future*, there is a scene where actor Michael J. Fox plays a character who goes back to the 1950s and orders a Pepsi Free. Oops! Not invented yet. In this case, the humor is intended and shows a character who is outside his own time or not yet adjusted. If your novel was set in the Middle Ages and you wrote about how your Crusader's horse charged full steam ahead, the metaphor is mixed—and inappropriate. The steam engine wasn't yet invented. Writers of historical fiction have the onus of research, not only to avoid inappropriate metaphors and similes but also to create imagery and use words that could only exist in that era and place. One of my clients delighted my ear when her novel, set in the late nineteenth century had this line of dialogue: "He seems such a feckless young man." Feckless! So many words have passed out of our language just as so many enter it. Do your research!

CLICHÉD

Because metaphors are so much a part of our everyday language, it's easy to slip them into your work without realizing you are doing so. Put a sticky note on your mental file cabinet to catch clichéd metaphors. Like a Trojan horse sneaking into your computer, these insidious clichés slip past neural sensors. I don't know how they get into my own work, but they are easy to spot in the manuscripts of others. Some of the clichés I've seen in manuscripts include the following: *rakish grin, mad dash, ounce of levity, chest heaved, birds singing cheerfully, grin split his face, stopped dead in his tracks, mixed emotions,* and dozens more. In dialogue, however, any cliché can be an acceptable, and even endearing, reflection of a character.

So why bother to work so hard on imagery? Indulge my use of a simile: Writing your story or novel using literal language is like a musician playing alone. With imagery, you gain an orchestra.

Imagery adds so much to a writer's style that with all practicality and crassness, I advise you to make sure to add analogies, similes, or metaphors to any pages requested by an agent or editor. Without question, make sure your revision includes imagery on page one.

Imagery adds layers of color, texture, and mood, and mirrors a worldview; it deepens characterization. Imagery communicates through symbolism—like the giant sentinel evergreen that could symbolize security and protection, or like the father's empty wallet and the son's experience of internal emptiness in Sherman Alexie's novel. Because imagery has deep roots, it supports multidimensional, authentic characterization.

Even if style is one of your strengths, or you revise to make it stronger, it can't stand on its own. Character-driven story is the lock, and original style is the key. You need both to gain entry into the circle of published writers.

Imagery deepens the impact of your story, no matter what genre you write, although the type of imagery and symbolism and its frequency must also meet what is appropriate to your chosen genre, the subject of the next chapter.

MAKEOVER REVISION CHECKLIST

Outside-In: Advanced Revisions

☑ Create similes.

Definition: comparisons of similarity in some way of one thing to another.

Revising similes:

- Use similes for sights, sounds, smells, tastes, touch/temperature, touch/sensation, ideas, actions, and emotions.
- Use similes to replace vague adjectives and weak nouns, and vague adverbs and weak verbs.
- Rework similes that don't have enough overlapping similarity.

☑ Create metaphors.

Definition: a complete substitution for one thing with another.

Revising metaphors:

- Add simple metaphors—one word, phrase, or short sentence.
- Add extended metaphors—a long sentence or sentences, paragraph, or even longer.
- Replace or delete mixed metaphors.
- Replace or delete inappropriate metaphors.
- Replace or delete clichéd metaphors.
- Develop metaphors for setting, era, aspects of the environment, and elements of characterization.

PART TWO

Craft Works

CHAPTER FOUR

Revise for Genre

Options If you want to know how agents and editors categorize works based on story, complexity, and style, read on. If you feel certain about your book's genre and subgenre, and the requirements of them, skip to chapters five and six on whole book structure.

Throughout this book, you'll see advice to read the kind of books that you are writing. Fiction is defined by "genres," a word that refers to categorizing works according to similar style, content, and form. Agents want to be able to match what you're writing with the genres a particular editor considers. All publishers need to be confident that readers who enjoy a particular genre of book can find it. Understandably, publishers want maximum sales from any title—and so do you! In a way, the matter of categorization comes down to the very old and nonelectronic task of shelving. When a reader goes to the romance section, she or he expects to find novels of that genre. Independent of considerations of the writing, there will be a problem if a novel is a romantic mystery wrapped in a horror plot set in the fantasy realm of Chatoobetu in 14A BS (Before Sirah). Oh, and it has a time-travel ghost story set in the Old West. I'm exaggerating, of course, but mixed genres can be a problem.

Is it important to revise your novel to fit a genre? The answer is yes and no. Yes, you want to be cognizant of the basic genres, if your intent is to sell your fiction. No, if you simply want to write for pleasure and have no restrictions on creativity. Sales and name recognition buy the privilege to write outside easy categorization.

For instance, Diana Gabaldon's bestselling *Outlander* series is considered a combination of historical romance, time travel, and adventure. Dean Koontz, who refused to be stuck with the horror label, writes some books that are a combination of suspense, science fiction, romance, and horror. Stephen King's novels range from creepy nightmarish horror like *Pet Sematary* to contemporary literary works such as *Hearts in Atlantis*.

I advise every aspiring novelist who has not yet published to select *one* genre that is dominant. For instance, romance with a subplot of mystery (romantic suspense) or mystery with a subplot of romance. The reason is not only to avoid the cross-category shelving problem but also to learn how to write in the style that each genre demands. In other words, a major aspect of outside-in style involves understanding and imitating the style common to your genre of choice.

I believe that writers also find genres that correspond with their own reading preferences and that fit comfortably with their values and needs. In revision, you definitely want to think about the clarity of genre in your novel. Here is a list of considerations to help determine the genre of your novel:

- Ask several readers how they would categorize your novel.
- Visit a bookstore and determine where your novel would be shelved.
- Describe your novel to booksellers and ask how they would categorize it and where they would shelve it.
- Read novels that seem similar in type or style to yours, then determine the genre.
- Visit websites of publishers for guidelines.
- Once you determine a probable genre or subgenre, do an Internet search and read more information to confirm your guess.
- Model the length and tone of your story to fit the genre or subgenre you decide on. Revise.

For purposes of this book's focus on revision, I will necessarily refer to genres by name. What follows are definitions of the larger divisions of fiction. Although full descriptions of the requirements of genres and subgenres are beyond the scope of this book, you'll find a detailed list of genres and subgenres in this chapter's Makeover Revision Checklist.

Definitions of Genres

Earlier I defined genres as categories that group works according to similar style, content, and form. When someone asks you, "What are you writing, what genre?" they want to know what category your work fits into; for instance, police procedural. However, there is a second use of the word genre. The question here is usually this: "Is your work genre, mainstream, or literary?" Or is it other?

Genre Fiction

What classifies a novel as genre, also called "category fiction," is meeting a list of prescriptive requirements, what some people refer to as "cookbook" specifications; just follow the recipe and you're guaranteed of the same outcome. (If only any writing were that easy.) Romance fiction has the most specifications, posted by some publishers at their websites. The writer may be asked to create a protagonist, usually a female, within a specific age range and select from a list of vocations. On their websites, romance publishers sometimes present writer's guidelines that describe what kind of plot problems they do and do not want to see, and how much sex, if any, and how detailed, they allow. They may also specify types of words, such as profanities, that are allowed (and not allowed), what clichés to avoid, and what total numbers of words is acceptable.

In the past, genre fiction seemed limited to romance, mystery, suspense, science fiction, fantasy, westerns, and horror. Some people added thrillers to the list. Others added the relatively new genre chicklit, that I think of as "women's fiction lite" (featuring women ages twenty to thirty) and lady lit (featuring women over thirty, often over forty). Each of these types of category fiction has rules placed on the writer to "fit" what the reader expects. The author's style can be original but it must also conform to the style and guidelines of the genre.

When an author pushes against the specs of genre, but has a history of published genre novels, the writer is called a "breakout" author. The author has established name recognition, a loyal following, and now writes a novel that, aptly labeled, has broken out of the genre limitations. It has moved categories, usually into mainstream. For instance, after Earlene Fowler had written about a dozen "Benni Harper" category mysteries (cozy mysteries), she enjoyed the publication of her first breakout novel, *The Saddlemaker's Wife*, a family saga.

Mainstream Fiction

If authors don't follow enough rules, and take too many liberties with the guidelines, then they are probably not writing genre novels. Their stories may center on romance, mystery, suspense, science fiction, fantasy, horror, western, or thriller, which is why categorization gets confusing. Instead, they might be labeled "mainstream romance" or "mainstream mystery" or "mainstream horror." Because the western category, set in the American West in the years 1860 to 1900, has been all but buried at Boot Hill, the replacement terminology in mainstream novels is now "novel of the West," which can include contemporary stories, or "frontier novel," or "western fiction" to encompass it all.

Other categories of fiction that join the mainstream list: women's fiction and historical novels. Chicklit and lady lit are sometimes thought of as mainstream, not genre. I tend to think of thrillers as mainstream because their stories may range over multiple geographic locations, and they often have a larger cast of characters or viewpoints than genre novels. Their plot complexity is greater than most category novels. Yet, the general lack of character depth and/or scant imagery of most thrillers place them closer to genre writing than to mainstream.

In contrast to genre conventions, mainstream writing may have more character viewpoints, the plot can be more complicated, and there may be a greater number of subplots. The writing style may seem more sophisticated and feature more use of similes, metaphors, and symbolism. The ending is not preordained: the boy may not get the girl, or vice versa; the bad guy might not be found or brought to justice; the point of the story may be internal transformation rather than outer success.

Literary

The final of the three big categories of fiction is literary fiction. No different from genre and mainstream, a literary novel can be a romance, mystery, or thriller, for instance. It can be historical, futuristic, or fantasy. The "genre" doesn't determine the classification of "literary" any more than it does mainstream or category (or genre) fiction.

The distinction of literary fiction from the other two categories is most of all in the writing itself: distinctive author voice and outstanding execution of the elements of fiction writing, although one area may be more striking than another, such as the setting and realism of *The Kite Runner* by Khaled Hosseini, or the voice and stark tone of *White Oleander* by Janet Fitch. Characterization is deeper and there may be layers of intended symbolism such as Jane Smiley's use of King Lear for her Pulitzer-winning *A Thousand Acres*.

There are types of novels, or "subgenres," that are usually by definition literary: magical realism, epistolary, the picaresque, noir. Magical realism includes some element of the fantastic, the magical, as if it were a part of everyday reality as in *Like Water for Chocolate* by Laura Esquivel. Epistolary novels tell a story through exchanged letters as in *The Color Purple* by Alice Walker. The picaresque describes a journey, where the protagonist meets unique and interesting characters as in *Don Quixote* by Miguel de Cervantes. Noir means dark and describes the mood, "edgy" writing (perhaps what some people would find vulgar, shocking, or obscene) and the subject matter of novels such as *Fight Club* by Chuck Palahniuk.

The problem with the division of all fiction into three categories is that the divisions are arbitrary and many works fall "in the cracks" between genre and mainstream or mainstream and literary. Do your best to determine how your novel will be categorized and whether it fits the parameters of its genre.

Other

Some types of novels fit the category of "other" for various reasons. Children's literature for ages one through eighteen has its own divisions and conventions of style and language per the age of the reader. Nearly all of the basic types of novels, from mystery to supernatural thriller, exist within children's literature.

Religious fiction is a huge category of fiction with its own literary agents, publishers, booksellers, and fans. The novels are also divided into genre, mainstream, and literary, but the specific religious market—Christian, New Age, Jewish—adds an overlay of style and sometimes content to the genre.

When Generation X individuals (born between roughly 1965 and 1975) reached adulthood, a new type of novel emerged: the Gen X novel. Often "noir" (emotionally dark or bleak), the stories are closer to literary in their writing style than to the other two categories. Yet, they exist apart from easy categorization. Examples are *In the Cherry Tree* by Dan Pope and *Alternative Atlanta* by Marshall Boswell. Not surprisingly, coming-of-age and sexuality themes with thirty-year-old protagonists are common in Gen X.

A newcomer springing from authors of two generations, Gen X and the Millennial Generation (1977–1998), is the graphic novel, a comic-book-like presentation of stories that are written and illustrated, often with stunning artwork, for adult and young adult readers. A few examples include the Legendary Couple series such as the 160-page *Legendary Couple* #7 by Louis Cha and Tony Wong; or the 224-page Liberty Meadow series, Volume 1: *Eden—Landscape Edition*.

If you attend writers' conferences, you are likely to hear the terms "high concept" and "blockbuster." This industry jargon spells dollars. The terms can apply to any genre of novel, but the plot usually features globe-trotting, stakes of earth-shattering proportions, and a central idea that stretches the edges of possibility. Michael Crichton's *Jurassic Park* and Dan Brown's *The Da Vinci Code* both fit the definition to a *T.*

Last of all, the primary genres of novels (romance, thriller, science fiction, and so on) have subcategories, often by the dozen. Your decisions about revision should include studying novels similar to yours and reading about your genre and subcategory in particular. Review the Makeover Revision Checklist at the end of this chapter.

The point of making simple outside-in revisions is to take the style and genre in which you wrote your story or novel, probably in a largely unconscious way, and to revise it intentionally. The result will be a novel that reflects everything you selected related to genre (and subgenre), but will also improve your emerging style. As with every element of fiction craft, improvement in one area makes other areas shine as well.

MAKEOVER REVISION CHECKLIST
Find Your Genre and Subgenre

MYSTERY involves investigation of a crime that has taken place and often the prevention of future crimes. It focuses on thinking, clues, and red herrings. Mysteries leave the reader intellectually satisfied.
Subgenres: amateur detective, caper, camp, chicklit, cozy, hard-boiled/cop/PI, gritty/noir, historical, humorous/comic, lady lit, legal, medical, police procedural, puzzle/locked room, whodunit/howdunit/whydunit

SUSPENSE involves prevention of crimes not yet committed but threatened, although there may have been similar crimes in the past. In suspense, the criminal is known or soon known, and one or more characters are pursued and almost constantly in danger. The reader may know more than the protagonist. Suspense satisfies a reader's vicarious and visceral emotions.
Subgenres: action-adventure, adventure, espionage, military, paramilitary, thrillers (espionage/spy, forensic, international, legal, medical, political, psychological, romantic, techno), woman-in-jeopardy (aka "fem in jep")

ROMANCE AND WOMEN'S FICTION focus on the relationship between two people. In category romance, the relationship is one of sexual and emotional attraction, and there is a happy ending. Women's fiction focuses on relationships of interest to women, and may or may not involve sex and romantic love.
Subgenres: African-American, Americana, chicklit, comedic, contemporary, erotica, ethnic, futuristic, historical (set between 1066 and 1899, including Gothic, medieval, and Regency—set in England, between 1811 and 1820), inspirational (Christian, spiritual), lady lit, mainstream, multicultural, paranormal, period (set between 1900 through 1940), saga, suspense, sweet, time travel, traditional, vampire

SCIENCE FICTION is speculative fiction. It uses and extrapolates from known science and technology to create possible realities, times past or future, and worlds and sentient beings known and unknown, artificial and biological. In general, science fiction leaves the reader wondering about possibilities and exploring new ideas.

Subgenres: alternate history, alternate intelligence, alternate world, cyber-punk, doppelgänger, end of the world, first contact, futuristic, generation starship, genetic manipulation, graphic, hard science, humor, immortality, invasion of Earth, lost colony, lost civilization, nature in revolt, new wave, parallel world, paranormal, post-disaster, post-holocaust, post-nuclear holocaust, robot, space opera, time travel, UFO, utopian/dystopian

FANTASY is speculative fiction. It involves the magical, supernatural, or sorcery, and may also involve fictional use of science, technology, and sociology. Fantasy stirs the reader's imagination and invites the reader to believe in magic.
Subgenres: epic, fairy tale, Gothic, magic realism, myth and legend, traditional, dark fantasy, fable, folktale, ghost, haunted house, light fantasy, magical realism, modern fantasy, mystical, reincarnation, sword and sorcery, urban fantasy, witchcraft

HORROR is speculative fiction, sometimes grouped as a subgenre of fantasy. Horror may use elements of science fiction or fantasy, and imparts the feeling of terror, horror, and dread.
Subgenres: ancient evil unleashed, apocalyptic, carnival-circus, child-in-peril, erotic, Gothic, family, humor, possession, reanimated dead, small town, techno, vampire, werewolf, witchcraft

WESTERN AND NOVEL OF THE WEST are set in the American West. The traditional western takes place in the frontier during the mid to late nineteenth century. It focuses on the fight to establish law and order in the West. Novels of the West may take place in the frontier times or in contemporary times. These mainstream or literary novels often have greater focus on the life of the diverse people, their cultures, struggles, families, and communities than on law and order. Westerns recreate a former time in American history and give readers satisfaction in the assertion of morality and protection of settlers. Novels of the West also recreate the former and present-day West, but satisfy readers' interest in the unique cultures and lifestyles, as well as people—indigenous, immigrant, and established.
Subgenres: chase, Indian wars, frontier, women of the West, trail drive, wagon train

HISTORICAL takes place in times past. One definition of what constitutes historical is any time period prior to any living person's memory.

Others have set the time marker as including World War II and prior. Most recently, historical has included the era of the Civil Rights Movement. There are subgenres of historical and different locations and defined historical periods.

Subgenres: Americana, epic, multigenerational, family saga

AMERICAN

Pre-Colonial America

Early European settlements

Spanish exploration and settlements

French colonization 1655–1803

English Colonial America 1493–1776

Formation of the U.S. 1776–1789

Antebellum American South, prior to Civil War

Civil War era, 1849–1865

Post-American Civil War, 1865–1870s

American West CA, OR, WA, AK—1850–1900

Depression Era, late 1920s–1930s

World War I, 1914–1918

Roaring Twenties

World War II, 1939–1945

Civil Rights movement, 1964–1970

OTHER LOCATIONS AND TIMES

Ancient Egypt, 4th century to 1st century BCE*

Ancient Greece, mostly 5th century BCE

Ancient Rome, founding to fall, 5th century BCE

Canadian West, 19th-century frontier life

Edwardian, reign of Edward VII, 1901–1910

Elizabethan, reign of Elizabeth I, 1558–1603

French Revolution 1789–1799

Georgian, reigns of first three "Georges" in England, 18th century

Medieval 5th–15th century

Napoleonic Wars 1799–1815

Post-French Revolution

Pre-History, before the Middle Ages

Renaissance, 14th–17th centuries, in Europe

Russian Revolution, around 1917

17th century clashes between Royalists and followers of Oliver Cromwell

Victorian, during reign of Queen Victoria, 1837–1901

War of 1812

* BCE means Before the Common Era and replaces BC, Before Christ

OTHER GENRES describes novels that fit one of the three umbrella genres—genre/category, mainstream, or literary—and yet they are genres or subgenres of many of the types above. Thus you can have a science fiction coming-of-age story, a contemporary epistolary novel, or a gay/lesbian historical novel set in the Canadian West.

Subgenres: comedic, coming of age, episodic, epistolary, exotic, experimental, farce, gay/lesbian, graphic, innocent, noir, off-beat, parody, picaresque, realistic, religious or spiritual (Biblical, Christian, New Age, mystical, occult, Wiccan, or any other religion), satire, stream of consciousness, urban

CHAPTER FIVE

Whole Book: Five-Stage Structure

Options Understanding and reflecting dramatic structure is fundamental to fiction writing. Whether you are new to writing or uncertain about the five stages of dramatic structure, read on. If you are certain about structure, review the chapter's sidebars or Makeover Revision Checklist for what can go wrong and how to fix it. If you know that your novel has been written using an atypical or less common structure, read the last, big section of chapter six first, then return to this one.

Many writers seize inspiration and run with it, until the flow of imagination stops. I'm not against writing for the sheer joy of it. Without a plan or prior thought, you'll sometimes end up with a rough draft worth revising. With full-length works, however, writers who take the joy ride, with little planning, are more likely to run out of gas and end up in the middle of nowhere. Lost. Most novelists, in my experience, do a mixture of planning and creating. The art of creative writing demands both: maps or blueprints as well as riff-writing. Revision is the same: planning, implementing knowledge of skill and techniques, and seizing new ideas.

Plot is a blueprint for the way the hero or heroine must act within the architecture of the novel. If you try to develop a plot based on a weak architectural blueprint, you'll end up with a weak story. No matter what category of novel or short story you have written, the principles of gravity and basic architecture are the same for a Gothic mansion and a beach bungalow.

The term *structure* is an all-encompassing word for an organized relationship of parts to a larger whole, which means that everything in your writing has structure: the whole book, chapters, sections, scenes, paragraphs, and sentences. The idea behind the phrase *character-driven* is that any and all units of structure are in service to characterization. Who wants to live in a castle or a cottage? Different people. Castles without mortar or with too much weight on top may topple. Cottages without strong beams to support roofs and walls may crumble. When your characters walk in and out of the story houses you've built, you don't want a roof collapsing on them. Structure and characterization must support one another.

Most novels, perhaps as much as ninety percent, are built using a universal "architectural" blueprint called *dramatic structure*. Its simplest form has three sequences or stages: problem, climax, resolution. More commonly, dramatic structure includes five stages, and if you have all five, you may be looking at repair, not demolition. If your story (short story or novel) does not have a five-stage dramatic structure, either the work has a major defect or you have used a less common whole-book pattern that I discuss in chapter six. Even so, most of the following stages apply to all novels and short stories. Your analysis of what needs revision, when it comes to structure, should begin here. The five stages of structure are:

1. A character has a problem.
2. Complications arise and conflict intensifies.
3. Crises culminate in a climax.
4. The problem is resolved.
5. The hero or heroine learns something about self or life.

One of the most notable aspects of this structure is that it defines an arc. After the beginning, there is a crescendo of drama that leads to higher points of drama and suspense. The character finally overcomes all complications and foes (if the story is not a tragedy), and the arc reaches its highest point, a climax, followed by a rapid dropping off of drama. Like so many things that appear simple, each stage has hidden complexity and therefore potential problems that need examination in revision.

Stage 1: A Character Has a Problem

The reader must learn early on of a major problem. One character, your protagonist (hero or heroine), turns the problem into a goal or quest for resolution. This whole book goal is referred to as the *story goal*, to distinguish it from *scene goals*. The reader, meanwhile, turns that story goal into a question: "Will he or she reach the goal and resolve the problem?" Devising a strong story goal or problem seems deceptively simple.

Fiction is selective; life is not. On any given day, we face multiple problems: taking the garbage out, paying bills, helping a child, discussing work with a supervisor, and so forth. Occasionally, our everyday reality includes crises: a car accident, death of a relative, emergency surgery, and so on. The selectivity of fiction enhances drama by focusing reader attention on one important problem that takes an entire novel to resolve, and on a series of lesser problems related to the larger one.

TOO LITTLE AT STAKE; GOAL INCONSEQUENTIAL

For the investment of time and emotional or spiritual energy, readers want something and someone worth caring about. Stakes refer to the

---

Here are the most common traps writers fall into when crafting story problems:

- Too little at stake; goal inconsequential
- Too much at stake, goal melodramatic, unrealistic
- Too many problems, goal unclear or nonexistent
- Problem and protagonist unmatched
- Problem and situation too familiar or clichéd

---

gravity of the problem, what can be lost or gained, what's hanging in the balance. High crimes—murder, kidnap, or rape—have high stakes. Misdemeanors—driving uninsured, forging checks for a low dollar amount, or vandalism—have lower stakes. Inner emotional needs can have high stakes—healing of loss, divorce, or abuse; or low stakes—ridding the self of petty jealousy or dealing with flashes of anger.

Let's say a woman breaks a long, manicured fingernail or a man cuts himself while shaving. These are certainly problems, but unless you are intentionally writing humor, your reader will get annoyed by being offered so little to care about. A character who is preoccupied by such trivialities will also be unlikable—too whiny, narcissistic, unworthy to qualify as a protagonist.

So-called inconsequential problems can be fixed by hooking them to story problems that do have high stakes for the character. Then petty problems do matter and the reader cares. Let's say your protagonist breaks her nail directly before a commercial where she will model a hand lotion, and as a result doesn't get paid. That lost income might be the difference between a month's rent or becoming homeless. If that shaving cut happens to a bleeder, a hemophiliac, then it is a serious problem. Now the reader cares about the outcome.

As you reread your novel, make notes about your character's problems from page to page. If the high-stakes story problem, the one that defines the whole novel, doesn't show up until many pages or chapters later in the story, will the reader care long enough about a resolution to wait until something *really important* happens?

You will see instant improvement of any story you write if you raise the stakes, outer and inner, faced by your characters. If your draft includes a sick child, why not make the illness life-threatening? Or change the sickness to an allergy to peanuts, MSG, or bee stings, and put the child's life in jeopardy. If a burglar has stolen jewels, could he poison the dog, too? Maybe he also has a cache of poisoned human corpses. No misdemeanor there.

If you have a "quiet" novel, one that is more about psychological needs and relationships than about adventure and danger, the inner problems and goals will define the novel. Self-respect, redemption,

---

To catch the problem of ho-hum stakes, ask yourself at every page turn:
  "What's at stake?"
  "How might I make the stakes higher?"
  "Why should the reader care?"

---

and loyalty are needs with high stakes, just as humiliation, betrayal, and grave mistakes are problems with high stakes. If the needs and problems come across as carrying low stakes and the goal is inconsequential, you have underdeveloped characters. Review Part Three: Characterization Endures.

TOO MUCH AT STAKE; GOAL MELODRAMATIC, UNREALISTIC

Can a story have too much hanging in the balance? Plot the destruction of all humankind or the blinking out of the entire universe, or write about a run-amok flesh-eating bacteria that spreads across the Western world, and you may have created a lie too big for the reader to swallow. Similarly, your story can seem unrealistic or melodramatic if you don't create a hero with powers equal to the antagonist.

The story goals, stakes, and powers of the characters must make sense within the context of the fictive world, and often within the reader's world. There are exceptions. Unrealistic or illogical stakes, or adversaries who are anything but a fair match show up (successfully) in comedy (*The Hitchhiker's Guide to the Galaxy*), horror—where sometimes the antagonist wins or does serious damage (*Carrie*)—magical realism (*The Milagro Bean Field War*). Sometimes, even published novelists suffer criticism for creating an all-powerful malefic and unrealistic villain, as did Scott Smith in his horror thriller *The Ruins*, for "killer vines." The genres of fantasy, horror, and science fiction are among the most challenging for problems of believability.

One answer is to reduce the stakes: The fungus that spread from Australia to the island of Vancouver (true) kills dolphins and is being tested to see if it might kill people. The entire universe isn't threatened with extinction, just our moon (minor havoc on planet Earth). The flesh-eating bacterium is presently contained on the island of Hawaii, but quarantines all of the world leaders meeting there for a summit. I find these far more interesting stories. While they correspond to possibilities within the real world, they sidestep melodrama.

A second answer is to strengthen the world you have built to provide logical answers for why your antagonist could cause the end of all humankind—within the time line of your story. Once you have closed your logical loopholes, your reader is "in"—suspending disbelief and thrilled at the outcome of stupendous stakes.

TOO MANY PROBLEMS; GOAL UNCLEAR OR NONEXISTENT

In dramatic structure, the character with the story problem figures out a goal that will resolve it. Let's take a cut-and-dried example: murder. The detective's goal is to find out whodunit and catch the killer. The reader's question is: Will the murderer be found and brought to justice? Once you establish these clear, structural basics, you have the framing that will support your whole book.

Over a decade ago, I received many more novels with unclear or absent story goals than I do now (possibly because of an increased availability of instruction). Most of the time, a story without one overarching goal is called *episodic*. These novels may have a plethora of problems facing the characters. One or several problems with goals may define a chapter, only to be solved, with new ones replacing them in the next chapter. The story moves from incident to incident, or episode to episode. There is no clear understanding where the protagonist is ultimately headed or why. As a reader and editor, these kinds of goalless novels make me feel as if I am hacking with a machete through thorny brush, hoping to reach a clearing, only to face another wall of thorny brush. Episodic novels fail to reveal one primary problem, and therefore cannot foretell what success will define the novel's end. This lack of clarity has a price: There is no chance for a reader to be held in suspense wondering if the protagonist will succeed.

This kind of writing forces the reader into an act of faith, trusting that the author will eventually lead them out of the thorny thicket. But scene by scene, chapter by chapter, the reader must invest in lesser goals related to lesser problems, and reinvest repeatedly as the book rambles on. Short of killing the protagonist, a question lingers at the end of the novel: Why stop here?

Non-goal-oriented novels have a tiny piece of the structure pie. Slightly more often you'll find a mixed structure—episodic and dramatic—such as in the historical novel, multigenerational or family saga, the autobiographical or biographical novel, the kind of fantasy novel that covers large spans of time and multiple protagonists, or any novel that spans decades in the life of the protagonist or carries over to multiple books. Most of the time, these mixed novels become stronger when revised into the five-stage dramatic arc. If you are writing in one of these genres, make sure you read the discussion about episodic structure and what can go wrong in the next chapter under Less Common Whole Book Structures, on page 95.

Reread your novel, especially its beginning, and determine whether readers will spot a story problem significant enough to become a high-stakes whole book goal, one that when reached, signals the end of your novel.

Ask and answer these questions:
- Does your writing communicate one unifying theme—a message or yearning?
- Do your interim scenes or episodes contribute to the protagonist reaching the goal and resolving the story problem?
- Are these scenes or episodes self-contained and related to shorter-term goals?
- Are your longer-term goals, or the last goals in your book, only revealed in the middle or even last sections of your novel?

If your answer to these last two questions is yes, revise to ensure dramatic, not episodic, structure.

PROBLEM AND PROTAGONIST UNMATCHED

Most of us empathize with the problems of our family members and friends, but we seldom abandon the routines and necessities of running our own lives to assume the problems of others. When a stranger donates a kidney or risks her life to save another person, the public wants to know more about this individual. These spontaneous or inexplicable acts do happen in real life, but rarely in fiction. In your novel, you must show how and why the character is compelled to take such risks.

Mismatched story problems and protagonists often show up in unpublished mysteries or thrillers. Let's suppose Samson, your protagonist, learns that his next-door neighbor, Bharti, has been kidnapped. He joins other friends and neighbors in the search with involvement of law enforcement. This is realistic; many caring individuals will pitch in—for a while—on a search for a missing child or an elder who has wandered off. But Bharti has vanished. Samson abandons his job as a construction supervisor and, becoming an amateur sleuth, decides to search for her, no matter the risks. Why? In normal life, we let trained law enforcement people put themselves in harm's way to solve crimes. Citizens don't walk away from their jobs and risk their lives fighting dangerous criminals. Even if the investigation is lousy, and the case grows cold, why would Samson take on the role of amateur sleuth? This is a mismatch between the story problem and the protagonist. His actions are illogical.

If this is a problem in your novel, or short story, you can fix it fairly easily: Increase the connections between victim and protagonist, or choose a different protagonist! Obviously, you will have fewer revisions if you can use the first remedy rather than the second. In the example above, what if Bharti is nine months pregnant with Samson's baby? And what if Bharti's blood type is Rh-negative? This means that her blood antibodies could attack her baby's red blood cells, endangering the baby. Now the reader not only accepts, but expects that Samson will do everything within his power to find

Bharti, and he will risk everything, even his life, if and when the detectives stop searching for her. If the detectives have given up, then Samson has enough reason to become the sleuth seeking Bharti.

Who has the most to lose? Most of the time, your answer will guide you to select the character who should be your protagonist. If your hero is a professional in the field—a private eye or detective—then solving a crime is that person's job. Kinsey Millhone in Sue Grafton's mystery novels is a private investigator. It's her job that supplies the motivation for her to solve crimes in book after book. We accept the match between problem and protagonist.

If you cannot revise your story to give the reader a believable reason why your hero would risk loss of a job, home, family, money, or possibly his life, then guess what? You have one novel to recycle and a new novel to map out using the correct protagonist.

PROBLEM AND SITUATION TOO FAMILIAR OR CLICHÉD

In a candid moment at a workshop based on his book *Writing the Breakout Novel*, literary agent Donald Maass said, "I don't want to see any more dead baby stories." A short time later, when invited to share in-class writing, a woman read her query letter for a literary novel that centered on a baby's death. She wrote it well enough that Don later told her he would like to see the first three chapters. Style and originality create exceptions.

Editors and agents are in the best positions to spot the overly familiar story problems or clichéd situations. However, if you read novels of the type you write, and join organizations with newsletters and meetings, check websites and blogs, or attend conferences and talk with authors and others, you'll quickly become savvy about which ideas are too familiar and clichéd.

After 9/11, agents and editors suffered an avalanche of query letters for novels that involved the Twin Towers and Pentagon tragedies. They have also had to plow through query after query about Middle East terrorists and Islamic extremists; by book's end, horrible things happen to them, in this world or in the afterlife. These problems or situations are overly familiar because they relate to events covered by the news; they require distance and time before original stories based on these life events will sell.

Every genre of fiction has known clichéd plots and stereotypical characters. A simple Internet search will help you reach lists against which you can check the story you may have already written. Some websites that provide some lists are the following:

www.thrillingdetective.com/fiction/guidelines.html
www.strangehorizons.com/guidelines/fiction-common-
    horror.shtml
www.theromancereader.com/forum25.html

If you think your plot is clichéd, before you press the panic button, know that some "stock" plots are done repeatedly, like a theme and variations. If your writing is original enough and you supply some twists, you may be doing just fine. Can you revise away from the cliché? As acclaimed novelist Josef Skvorecky said about the most overused plot devices: "There are no overused devices. There are only bad and good writers."

Stage 2: Complications Arise and Conflicts Intensify

Most of your novel's action falls under two words: complications and conflict, or should. Complications include the actions of your antagonist(s) to thwart the efforts of your protagonist to reach the story goal. Complications fuel conflict. They include obstacles, such as the weather and temperature—134°F in Death Valley for forty-three days in 1917 (true); environmental factors—the terrain, flora, and fauna, including 1,300 species of scorpions (true). They include human-made obstacles—from simple objects to complex killing machines, and everything in between—even the one hundred common toxic chemicals in the average home. And they include social

---

Use the following list of problems related to complications and conflict to find areas you need to revise:
- Complications all but absent or too minor
- Too many complications—confusing, suspense is undercut
- Complication contrived, illogical, or inappropriate
- Conflicts fail to intensify

---

forces—demonstrations, vigils, millions of pilgrims gathered in Mecca. Everything of and on Earth, created by or about humans, can serve conflict. See what fun you can have with complications?

Remember: Complications fuel conflict. Conflict fuels suspense. Suspense keeps readers turning pages.

COMPLICATIONS ALL BUT ABSENT OR TOO MINOR

This problem may look as if it refers to the stakes, but the overall story goal can have huge stakes and the complications are all but absent or too easy to overcome. Writers often neglect one required source of complication: the protagonist. Virtuous, flawless, heroic characters are boring; they are untrue to real-life human beings. All characters should have weaknesses as well as strengths, and some universal need that compels them to unconscious or ill-thought-out acts. Without inner conflict, a character is creepy, like someone you might know for whom everything is always fine, fine, *fine*. If you're writing from a robot's point of view, or some other "programmed entity," then the absence of inner conflict or imperfection must be compensated for by what havoc they are capable of inflicting.

Far more writers are too nice to their characters than too mean, which can manifest in a thin character or a snoozer plot or both. Characters absent of inner conflict are two-dimensional. Multidimensional characters fight inner demons as much as outer foes. They have contradictions that can cause inner conflict. For example, a character who has mixed values: He believes in honesty, but will lie to cover his college-bound son's cheating.

Contradictions of values add tremendously to sustained, rather than temporary, conflict, with greater opportunities for complications. Your novel's suspense may also benefit from an intense moral conflict between your character(s) and the antagonist or other characters who stand staunchly on the opposite side of an issue. Of course, your story and theme must support the particular moral conflict you choose.

During revision, deepen your characters; every novel I've ever edited needs character development. One way to deepen characterization and create complications is to take every opportunity to pit characters against inner conflicts as well as outer obstacles. Be mean. You might even want to write, with a permanent black marker, or better yet have tattooed on the back of your hand, the word CONFLICT.

A related mistake is the omission of important scenes or giving them too little development. You can imagine the buildup to a first night of lovemaking. Your heroine and hero are hot; you turn the page and it's the next morning. Your heroine is in her robe and the hero is serving her coffee. They smile knowingly. The author has omitted the first sex scene! While this is an obvious example, nice writers often jump over scenes of intense emotion and great importance. Reread your novel and think about what you *haven't* written that is important as well as what you have written that is extraneous.

To combat a "snoozer" plot, look at those extraneous scenes and see if they can be "compressed," that is, folded into other ones. It's far better to expand scenes where the stakes are great, the complications many, and the conflict high than it is to hold on to scenes that don't do enough work. Examine every page of your novel and ask yourself if the situation merits opening up. If so, develop it with riff-writing. If you can, compress one scene into another that has greater dramatic value, or delete a low-stakes scene (or chapter) altogether.

The story and plot should be saturated with complications. *Every page must have conflict.* You may think that is unrealistic. But as you revise, look for multiple sources of conflict: nature/the environment; the immediate setting; social and political obstacles; and psychological conflict—within the hero. Drawing from the same list of forces, add obstacles and conflict generated by the antagonist. Have you heard the phrase, "when an irresistible force meets an immovable object"? I always think of arm wrestling, how impossible it is to look away from the opponents, how the suspense increases when one arm starts to bend backward; yet, the winner can't be determined until the hand is completely flat on the table. Your job, in revision, is to make sure you have a wrestling match, in the hero's heart and mind, and/or in the outer world, on every page.

That does not mean that the level of suspense will be identical, or through the roof, on every page. In the quiet scenes, when the outer world is calm and your character may even be alone, make sure you show inner turmoil. When the outer world is challenging your characters, develop the suspense and keep the inner turmoil going, too.

When complications and conflict are absent, telling seems to proliferate. Many writers get caught up in telling the reader a history of the region or the background of relationships, or some other chunk of briefing. For a page, a section, or a chapter or two, the author has forgotten that the primary job is to stay anchored in a character's viewpoint as he or she presses toward the story goal and toward resolving inner conflict. Narration—description, background, and information—needs to be subservient to and in service to a character in conflict, not in place of it.

TOO MANY COMPLICATIONS—CONFUSING, SUSPENSE IS UNDERCUT

The novelist's job is to create suspense. The novelist's job is to control suspense. You decide when to increase it or decrease it. As complications increase, the suspense should create a rising arc, a crescendo of conflict. Some complications form crises that break one way or the other, releasing some of the reader's suspense. But other conflicts push the suspense even higher, eventually releasing the reader from its hold precisely at the right time—at the climax of the story. If you have too few complications, conflict is not frequent enough, and the suspense for the reader jumps, lags, and sags. It's what editors refer to as "uneven."

On the other end of the spectrum, instead of keeping readers at the edge of their seats—at the right moments—you can actually have too many complications and end up with the opposite result: little suspense and a lot of confusion. In a mystery, the writer can flood the reader with too many clues, too many suspects, too many red herrings (false clues). In a romance or women's fiction, you can introduce a heroine and hero with opposite beliefs (Republican vs. Democrat, for instance), and a mother arrives for a visit, a brother dies, a supervisor piles on overtime, the hero forgets his condom, a best friend interrupts lovemaking, and the plumbing goes out—in the first three chapters. Too many complications. Only if you are writing a romantic comedy are you on the right track; then the overabundance of complications enhances humor.

Some novelists make the mistake of taking on a cast of characters that is too unwieldy for their skill. Remember that moving your protagonist, and the rest of the cast, forward in time and through the conflicts and crises of the dramatic arc is your foremost job. Too many viewpoint characters, which for many novices is more than three, can mean that story lines cut one or another off. Then superficiality of character development lessens reader interest. As you reread your novel, get rid of peripheral characters and delegate their onstage roles to more central characters. Use as few characters as will accomplish the needs of your story and genre, and increase their relatedness. In other words, a friend can also be a coworker who is married to your heroine's sister. *Employ as few developed viewpoint characters as possible.* Viewpoint characters are those for whom you provide thoughts, feelings, and physical reactions, developing their interior and external worlds.

Complex and too complicated are two different things. Complex is interesting; it shows writer finesse and control. Complicated is a chore. The reader faces too much work to figure out what the writer meant to do. Puzzles are complex; knots are complicated. A complex novel is *Any Bitter Thing* by Monica Wood, which takes place in the present and past and uses a first-person and third-person narrator (see discussion of viewpoint in chapter nine). One of the best and most complex science fiction novels is *Dune* by Frank Herbert. The author was awarded the Nebula and the Hugo for this novel. Its complexity stems from its epic nature, including several dozen characters; multiple galaxies and peoples, including three warring noble "Houses"; a secret female society that through thousands of generations of genetic engineering has produced individuals with twisted states of advanced intelligence; corporations, including drug-trafficking on an interstellar scale; and sweeping themes involving ecology, religion, political and corporate power and greed, mass manipulation of those lacking power, and destiny and fate.

In revision, make sure that your novel has *one* strong "through-line." This line, the protagonist's quest, is the structural backbone represented by the primary plot. Never bury that primary plot with too many subplots. You'll lose suspense and your reader.

Be careful, too, not to combine many genres, which can create a monstrously complicated story. I met a first-time novelist recently and listened as she described her story. "It's a whodunit," she began, "but really, it's a deep psychological portrayal of my protagonist and alternates between the present and her past, and it also has portions of it that develop the historical period—early 1800s—and it may have a little touch of the paranormal. But really, the heroine's need to find out what happened when she was molested in her childhood defines the story." Too complicated.

Be careful, too, not to mix or shift between two genres. In doing so you can unintentionally undercut suspense in a primary story line as the reader attempts to stay oriented and keep up with details. A common subgenre is romantic suspense. But is it a romance with suspense or a suspense novel with a romantic subplot? Choose one genre to dominate and define one, complete, five-stage dramatic arc. If necessary, review chapter four for clarification of genres and subgenres.

COMPLICATION CONTRIVED, ILLOGICAL, OR INAPPROPRIATE

One of my editing clients was working on a mystery, a police procedural, and his writing style was compelling. His detective-protagonist was trying to resolve the guilt he felt over abandoning a brother whose lifestyle he found intolerable. As a result, his brother left—forever. Now the detective is working a murder involving an antagonist (no, not his brother) from the same lifestyle he found so abhorrent. That's a great setup, because the psychological conflict and the plot conflict intersect.

However, the novel's complications and obstacles take place in a train station's storage room, with hidden computer terminals and keypads, the only way the secret organization that targets murder victims can communicate. Why don't the members meet elsewhere, like in someone's home or office? Because the novel is set in this century, why are they using dated technology? Why not text messaging? If your readers must stop because the author's choices seem to defy logic, you've lost them.

Other contrived complications are any coincidences that place the antagonist and protagonist at the same time and same place, without a setup for this to logically happen. Fancy meeting you in this remote village in San Salvador! Inexplicable coincidences like this happen in real life. I once held a housewarming party where one of my guests brought her friend, a visiting Tibetan monk. Another of my guests brought her brother, who had just traveled throughout Tibet and had visited the monk's village. The brother shared news from some of the monk's relatives. This real event would never wash in fiction, not without setup. Every event must convince the reader of its plausibility.

Inappropriate complications arise from the use of anachronisms. If a story set in 1990 includes use of a Taser stun gun that implants a tracking microchip into its victims that also immobilizes and disorients them, it's an anachronism; this technology wasn't in use, if yet invented, in 1990. If your administrative assistant in 2007 is using carbon copies instead of the photocopy machine, the reader will wonder why. Carbon paper might still exist, but why would anyone use it? Do your fact-checking in revision so that you don't get egg on your face later.

Be careful about "calling down the gods and goddesses" to produce conflict. A good flash flood or forest fire can raise stakes and create terrific suspense. But if these acts of nature extricate your hero at the precise moment he or she is about to be killed or give advantage to the villain, you have saved the day with the unacceptable contrivance called deus ex machina, meaning "god from a machine." During plays performed in ancient Greece, a crane lowered gods and goddesses onto the stage to save hapless mortals. In the rules of today's fiction, with the exception of some religious fiction, this is a no-no. The protagonist must solve the problems without intervention from above—or below. *Reread your story event by event, looking for causality and logic, making sure that your characters act on their own to overcome their problems.*

Most mistakes that are deemed contrived, illogical, or inappropriate stem from inadequate setup. Setup is also referred to as *foreshadowing*. If a cougar is going to leap out on a trail and threaten the life of a girl lost on a camping trip, either show a sighting of a cougar earlier or be more subtle: The girl's brother points into the trees and yells "Bear!" The father smiles and gives a little talk about how a bear hasn't been seen in X number of years, but occasionally a cougar will saunter into a neighborhood near the national park.

CONFLICTS FAIL TO INTENSIFY

Let's say that you have enough complications, conflict of some kind on every page. Your protagonist acts without outside rescue to overcome obstacles. You're doing everything right, and yet, your critique group or an agent rejection may say something like, "Well written but I didn't feel enthusiastic enough." Or, "It's good but not great." These comments could reflect inadequate rising slope. This is especially true in the middle of the book. You have probably heard the phrase "sagging middles." When conflicts seem to repeat at the same level of intensity, the reader will, at some point, get tired rather than more deeply worried about the outcome. In revision, go back through your scenes and look for those crises that need higher highs. Make sure you read chapter twelve on scenes, including big scenes.

What will also help is to let your character express escalating emotions that develop in tandem with the difficulties: frustration, irritation, anger, rage, concern, anxiety, trepidation, fear, terror. And, your ace in the hole is to create rising tension by making character weaknesses show more prominently and interfere with the characters' goals.

Stage 3: Crises Culminate in a Climax

Complications—obstacles, antagonists, and psychological conflicts—should intensify and reach points of high drama, high suspense. Crises. If you have scenes with conflict but they never rise to crises, you will have a flat line more than an arc. Flat lines are dead stories. The problem is not only one of conflict but also of characterization.

You can remedy both problems by applying a three-word command: "Make it worse." As your plot "thickens," make the obstacles greater, the opposing forces stronger, and character flaws more evident. A classic example of making things worse is *Gone With the Wind* by Margaret Mitchell. After Scarlett marries Charles to hurt Ashley, who had rebuffed Scarlett and married Melanie, Scarlett gets pregnant, Charles joins the army, and he dies of pneumonia. Scarlett, now a widow and a mother, leaves Tara and moves to Atlanta and begins her petulant relationship with Rhett. As the war progresses, food grows scarce, and the Yankees advance toward Atlanta. Ashlely is captured and imprisoned by the Yankees, and although Scarlett desperately wants to get back to Tara, she must keep her promise to Ashley and stay with pregnant Melanie. When the Yankees set Atlanta on fire, Scarlett convinces Rhett to help the three of them—Melanie, her newborn, and Scarlett—return to Tara. To make things worse, Rhett joins the Confederates, abandoning the women at the city's outskirts. Scarlett drives their cart all day and night, encountering dangerous drifters and soldiers, finally reaching Tara. Yet worse conditions meet her: Her mother is dead, her father crazy, and the marauding soldiers have stripped Tara of food and cotton. And all of this is only half of Scarlett's problems and heartbreak. In most of *Gone With the Wind*, things go from bad to worse. When in doubt about what to do in your story, make something worse!

Make a list of the following types of events in your novel:
- The plans of your protagonist go all to hell.
- The long-anticipated "big event," joyous or horrible, finally happens.
- The protagonist's life is imminently threatened; or in quiet novels, emotional or social survival is in jeopardy.
- All hope appears lost.

These types of events will mark high points of drama; some of them should be crises that tax all of your protagonist's resources. In revision, foreshadow these events. When your characters know about an event ahead of time, such as a battle, rendezvous, or celebration, build stronger emotional reactions. Some events are, by everyone's definition, big events: engagements, weddings, divorces, deaths, funerals. Special holidays and religious rituals are anticipated, known events. If the event is unknown and cannot be anticipated, then develop your characters' determined efforts to follow their plans to reach the story goal and resolve the problem. That way, the derailment will be a larger blow, the emotions more devastating. It's up to you not to give short shrift to these intense scenes.

The crisis of a novel (or short story) is the culminating event of the story, the one where you should have the highest point of drama, the greatest suspense in the outcome, and the full emotional release of the readers. This is the moment of payoff for the investment your readers made at your story's beginning. Yet, we have all probably read novels where the climax is unsatisfying, our parting emotion disappointment. How can you make sure that your novel doesn't fail in this way?

At the climax, the end of the plot, everything must come together.

Don't:

- Leave subplots hanging, their problems unresolved.
- Keep tensions low in the crises that build up to the climax.
- Give a predictable climax, too pat or clichéd.
- Cheat the reader by introducing some significant event or information at the very end.
- Omit the climax (some writers actually do this).
- Pull punches or tamp down the requisite dramatic intensity.

Do:

- Bring any unfinished subplot to its climax directly before or during the main plot climax.
- Increase the stakes in the final crises, building suspense to a peak.
- Stretch your creativity and avoid a climax that has been overdone.
- Add the missing big scene of your climax!
- Fully develop this final scene, revealing reactions, thoughts, full sensory experience, euphoria or relief or revelation or other specific emotions appropriate to the end of the story. Pull out the stops. Take portions of your present climax and riff-write to open them up to their full potential.

The climax is the point at which you hand the controls back to the reader. If you omit any of the requisites on the "do" list or include any of the mistakes on the "don't" list, you'll leave your reader with a sense of betrayal. As you revise the climax, be authentic to your characters, the story, and your artistic vision. This is your finale.

Stage 4: The Problem Is Resolved

After you have checked that stages 1 through 3 are correctly developed, the last two stages will present only a few potential trouble spots. If you have finished a draft of book one of a trilogy, you will need to tie up critical portions of the novel, including the story problem, yet communicate to the reader that there are major and important stakes left unresolved. Superb examples are J.R.R. Tolkien's The Lord of the Rings trilogy, or the C. S. Lewis The Chronicles of Narnia series, or the seven-book Harry Potter series by J. K. Rowling.

The convention for most single-title American novels is to offer a clear resolution of the problem introduced at the beginning of the novel. This is not a necessary convention in European storytelling where the ending may be mysterious, vague, or intentionally open-ended. A good example is *The French Lieutenant's Woman* by John Fowles, where the reader gets to mull over two, perhaps three, dramatically different endings. To some degree, you can leave your ending open if doing so is true to your story and style. The majority of American readers, however, have grown to expect that the problem that began the novel will be put to rest.

Other than making sure that you resolve the story problem, the only mistake I've seen at this stage is a novel that veers off into an ending that not only doesn't resolve the story problem but introduces new complications, problems, and obstacles that have no chance of being explored and developed, much less concluded. This is the case with some episodic novels where the author introduces "anti-climactic" scenes.

Stage 5: The Hero or Heroine Learns Something about Self or Life

In this final stage of dramatic structure, you must move beyond the plot goal, now reached, and the story problem, now resolved. Instead, this stage concludes the psychological or character story. Some writers, like Dan Brown, who wrote *The Da Vinci Code*, or Tom Clancy, who opened the whole genre of techno-thrillers, are "plot monsters"; they excel at plotting. Development of their heroes, as well as showing their inner transformations, is a distant, second priority. These authors are exceptions to the rule, and the rule is to show character growth. Ask yourself, "What has my hero or heroine learned that was a blind spot and source of emotional pain in the past? Is that growth clear to my reader?" You can make this explicit and, in effect, tell the theme of the book, or you can leave it subtle and understood, as long as you are sure the reader does understand.

For instance, at the end of *Gone With the Wind*, Scarlett realizes that she does love Rhett Butler and didn't really love Ashley; instead she had been in love with the ideal of true love. Unfortunately for Scarlett, her realization comes too late; Rhett's love for her has died, perhaps along with their baby girl. But in that Scarlett is the protagonist, this realization is the resolution to her character problem. She has changed from a spoiled, conniving belle into a woman capable of loyalty, hard work, and love.

Some writers introduce a brief post-climax scene in which the protagonist faces one last test of personal growth. The way in which the hero responds indicates resolution of the psychological problem that had its origins in the past. Make sure you aren't so dazzled by the climax and the conclusion of the plot that you abandon the conclusion of your character's long internal struggle. This is where the reader gets emotional closure and the take-away message, the theme, of the novel.

Five-stage dramatic structure captures the basic and necessary structure of most novels and short stories. It is simple enough that a four-year-old will naturally tell a tale that reflects it. It is spare enough to allow an experienced novelist to use it as a springboard to write a complicated story. A fair estimate is that as much as ninety percent of our literature and movies show the "bones" of this universal structure. Yet, other forms exist. The next chapter introduces the Hero's Journey, the Heroine's Journey, less common whole book structures, and offers techniques for finding and fixing related problems.

MAKEOVER REVISION CHECKLIST
Whole Book: Five-Stage Structure

Stage 1: A character has a problem.

☑ Problem 1: Too little at stake; goal inconsequential.
Solutions:
- As you reread, make notes about character problems, page to page.
- Raise the stakes wherever you can.
- Connect lesser problems to problems with higher stakes.
- Connect outer problems to inner (psychological) problems.
- If an inner problem is the story goal, make sure it matters.

☑ Problem 2: Too much at stake; goal melodramatic, unrealistic.
Solutions:
- Give the hero powers equal to, different from, the antagonist.
- Check goals, stakes, and powers against the context of the fictive world.
- Know what is typical, or an exception, in your novel's genre.
- Strengthen the created world to supply logical answers for the stakes.
- Foreshadow what would be illogical events to make them logical.

☑ Problem 3: Too many problems; goal unclear or nonexistent.
Solutions:
- Replace episodic structure with the dramatic arc and one clear story goal.
- In epics, sagas, and longer fantasy novels, select one theme, a same need that carries from one generation to another, from one book to the next.
- Reread your book and look for the greatest problem with the highest stakes and revise the whole book to turn resolution of that one into the central story goal.
- Select one universal need for your hero to create one unifying theme.
- Delete or revise scenes that do not contribute to your protagonist filling that need and reaching the plot (story) goal.
- Make sure the one story goal is implied or obvious on every page.

☑ Problem 4: Problem and protagonist unmatched.
Solutions:
- Make sure the character who "owns" the story problem is the protagonist.
- Decide who has the most to lose; usually this person should be the hero.
- Increase connections between a victim or antagonist and the protagonist.

☑ Problem 5: Problem and situation too familiar or clichéd.
Solutions:
- Connect to the writing community and learn which stories are overdone.
- Ask if your problem or situation is a rerun of something you saw on TV or in movies.
- Dig deeper for original twists on clichéd plots and universal human problems.

Stage 2: Complications arise and conflicts intensify.
☑ Problem 1: Complications all but absent or too minor.
Solutions:
- Create a conflicted character with a big flaw and a universal need whose lack drives the hero and gets in the way of the story goal.
- Be mean; make things difficult for your characters.
- Create inner demons and fears that obstruct reaching goals.
- Add contradictions in values, like a moral conflict, to add conflict.
- Add conflict, inner and outer, to every page. Saturate your story with complications.
- Never skip dramatic scenes.
- Delete extraneous, low-tension scenes, or combine with higher-stakes scenes.
- Up the obstacles and conflicts dished out by the antagonist(s).
- When the plot events are "quiet," show inner turmoil.

☑ Problem 2: Too many complications—confusing, suspense is undercut.
Solutions:
- Reduce the number of clues, suspects, and characters.

- Delete peripheral characters and delegate their roles to central characters.
- Increase relationships between characters.
- Don't confuse complex with too complicated; create one strong through-line.
- Reduce number of subplots. Make them directly related to main plot.
- Avoid mixing too many genres; make one prominent.

☑ Problem 3: Complications contrived, illogical, or inappropriate.
Solutions:
- Avoid implausible coincidence. Foreshadow the improbable to make it believable.
- Check facts for existence and appropriateness to year or era. Delete and replace anachronisms.
- Avoid deus ex machina or other last-minute "save-the-dayers."
- Reread event by event for logic and causality. Revise!

☑ Problem 4: Conflicts fail to intensify.
Solutions:
- Decide which of your crises have the biggest stakes, the most threat of loss in any way. Develop more detail of the difficulty of overcoming the opposition or antagonists, emphasizing the doubt of success in the mind of your point-of-view character.
- Add more visceral reactions to convey emotions and more interior thought about the consequences of failure.
- In the aftermath of the crisis, add your character's reactions to what he or she just went through. Show the angst!

Stage 3: Crises culminate in a climax.
☑ Problem 1: Subplots' problems left unresolved.
Solutions:
- Bring any unfinished subplots to a climax, resolving their problems directly before or during the main plot climax.

☑ Problem 2: Crises like any other scene; punches pulled, intensity tamped down.
Solutions:
- Make obstacles worse, drama more intense and developed, and longer.
- Give greater development to all elements of craft.

- Make stakes clear and related to overall story goal.
- End by showing protagonist shifting strategy to reach same story goal.

☑ Problem 3: Climax predictable, too pat or clichéd.
Solutions:
- Brainstorm and revise for an original ending, a reversal of the expected.

☑ Problem 4: Climax omitted; story drifts off or jumps to character growth.
Solutions:
- Show the story goal reached, or the impossibility of doing so.

☑ Problem 5: Climax underdeveloped.
Solutions:
- Fully develop final scene(s), showing reactions, thoughts, visceral emotions, sensory experiences.
- Show the final defeat of the adversary, inner or outer, depending on genre.
- Complete the plot.

Stage 4: The problem is resolved.
☑ Problem 1: Unclear resolution of the original story problem.
Solutions:
- Show resolution of the original story problem.

☑ Problem 2: Introduction of new problems or goals.
Solutions:
- After the climax and resolution of the story problem, tie up loose ends but avoid introducing new problems.

Stage 5: The Hero or Heroine Learns Something about Self or Life.
☑ Problem 1: Unclear or absent demonstration of character change.
Solutions:
- Develop protagonist's new understanding about self or life, if ending is happy. Show continuing weakness and wound if the ending is tragic.
- Consider creating a final, post-climax, brief scene where your protagonist is tested for character change. Reveal what the character has learned and resolved. Reveal the theme.

CHAPTER SIX

Whole Book: Journeys and Less Common Structures

Options If you have heard of Joseph Campbell's Hero's Journey and want to know how it is applied to structure, then read on. If you would like to know the basics about the Heroine's Journey, read both structures for comparison. If you believe your novel's structure may be other than the classic five-stage form, then read the whole chapter. If you're certain about your novel's structure, then skip to chapter seven about movement and suspense.

In the last two decades, instruction about writing, especially for genre and mainstream writing, has featured the Hero's Journey. Joseph Campbell, the late mythologist, wrote about the Hero's Journey as part of his scholarly research. His protégé, Christopher Vogler, a story consultant for movie studios, is primarily responsible for interpreting it and introducing it to the writing community. Fewer writers have explored the Heroine's Journey, a version of which was developed by Maureen Murdock, a Jungian psychotherapist who also knew Joseph Campbell. Both journey structures are an elaboration upon the universal five-stage dramatic arc, and therefore offer more guidelines for structuring novels.

These two journeys reference mythology, especially the concept of archetypes, which are patterns and roles so universal that they take on mythic proportions and carry meanings that cross cultures and time. For instance, some archetypal roles are the Mother, the Father, the Mentor, the King, the Villain, the Hero, and the Heroine.

The Hero's and Heroine's Journeys differ, although they share similarities as well. The Hero's Journey is a quest in the external world, out of which comes inner transformation. The Heroine's Journey is a quest into the self, out of which comes self-definition within a male-dominant culture.

Here is a summary of these two journeys, followed by basic problems that have occurred in hundreds of manuscripts I have edited. Following the summary and outline of problems, I'll offer some basic suggestions for revisions.

Summary of the Hero's Journey

Note: Capitalized words indicate stages of the journey.

In the beginning, the Hero is in his familiar Ordinary World when a serious event introduces a problem that is his Call to Adventure. He Refuses the Call because it will mean change, challenge, Separation from the known and familiar, and Departure from home. It may even mean risking his life. He also doesn't know if he is capable of the task. A Mentor assures him that he can do it, must do it, and is the only one who can succeed. Emboldened and committed, the Hero departs. He Crosses the Threshold into the Special World, which is alien compared to his Ordinary World.

He quickly learns the rules, encounters Allies and Enemies, and begins his Descent deep into the Special World, the territory of those who oppose him and where he'll find the solution to the problem. As he continues on the Road of Tests and Trials, the obstacles grow more formidable. He reaches the Approach to the Inner Cave, knowing that at its heart will be the Supreme Ordeal. In the innermost cave, he encounters the biggest obstacles and threats to success. If he overcomes these final challenges, he will have claim to the Reward: He'll achieve the goal that resolves the problem that set him on his journey. After he succeeds (or fails), he Refuses the Call to return home, instead emerging from the cave to regale in his glory or to lick his wounds. Believing his quest is over and he can at last begin his Return home, he is confronted with one last obstacle, the Ultimate

Test. Whether or not he reaches his story goal, if he summons all that he has learned, and releases or heals a wound he was afflicted with in his past, he will let his old self die to be reborn into a new, freer self.

This is his emotional passage, his Initiation. Death and Rebirth allow him to overcome this final confrontation (unless the story is a tragedy, and then he clings to his old ways, weaknesses, and the emotional wound).

At last he can Return with the Elixir, perhaps a treasure, but the true reward is being a new, transformed individual, a Master of Two Worlds, an integrated person with wisdom to share, in the form of the theme reflected by his journey.

Examples of the Hero's Journey abound as the outer quest is very much a part of our culture and many others. Any author writing in any genre may choose to use the Hero's Journey as a whole book structure. Most adventure genres and mainstream novels show many of its passages and stages. Most genre novels do as well, although when the novel is one in a series, as true for many detective stories, the hero may not reflect much "deep" change by novel's end. Literary novels that are fundamentally structured with the five-stage dramatic arc will often emphasize the characterization part of the journey, and might not show all of the plot stages of the journey.

No matter what genre you typically read, to see an application of the Hero's Journey, I recommend The Lord of the Rings trilogy by J.R.R. Tolkien and the Hugo and Nebula–winner *Ender's Game* by Orson Scott Card. Both novels fit and transcend their genres (fantasy and science fiction), and that is what the Hero's Journey does in its best execution—it helps the author create the universal.

Summary of the Heroine's Journey

Note: Capitalized words indicate archetypes recognized in Jungian psychology.

A life-changing event compels a woman to go on a quest to find her own identity, separate from the one she assimilated from the male culture and that was modeled by her mother. At first she adopts so-called male behaviors, thinking that she has denied aggressiveness in the past and that is what she needs. This belief leads her into the world of men, often also growing closer to her father. She often achieves success in the work world as she perfects her Animus, the assertive, competitive, perfectionist, and male-identified side of her personality. At the same time, she challenges, rejects, and even rebukes the beliefs in inferiority, dependency, and romantic love that she now sees as cultural indoctrination of women. She may blame her mother and distance herself from her, but when success in the male world also leaves her feeling hollow, she no longer feels close to her father or male mentors. She feels betrayed by everyone and everything she has known and believes, including God as a male-defined creation of the culture.

Alone, "spiritually arid," as Murdock so aptly calls it in her book *The Heroine's Journey*, the woman begins her turn inward, in search of her unique self. She examines her life experiences and searches for memories that seem to reflect pieces of a lost but authentic self. However long this period lasts, it often involves shedding any accoutrements of what the patriarchal culture deems appropriate and desirable female dress, manners, and friends. Yet, she yearns for an end to the grief and emptiness. She fears she may die without finding her true self and a chance to pursue dreams that she discovers within her.

Little by little, or all at once, she finds that connection, and the courage to receive the archetypal power of the Feminine. She integrates it in her own way; she begins to express her unique and now known self. Now she can also express, as needed, nurturing, relatedness, and receptivity, the positive qualities of the Feminine. She reconnects with her mother or with the archetype of the Mother. If the relationship with her earthly mother permits it, she seeks to heal the former breach.

Instead of rejecting all of the Masculine qualities, she integrates the side of herself that also holds the power of the positive Masculine archetype. Finally, she ends her duality, the split of her self and cultural beliefs about the Feminine and Masculine. She ends the misery of beliefs and behaviors not in harmony with her discovered self. She emerges into her new world and selects her new life as an integrated, renewed, and healed person.

Examples of the Heroine's Journey are plentiful among the "Oprah picks" and other novels. Although the female protagonist is always a good candidate for consideration of a Heroine's Journey, a male protagonist can follow the inward search for an independent self-definition of what it is to be a man in his culture as much as a woman can go on an outward quest. Several books mentioned and excerpted in earlier chapters show Heroine's Journey whole-book structure, as do *Animal Dreams* by Barbara Kingsolver, *The Joy Luck Club* by Amy Tan, and *Divine Secrets of the Ya-Ya Sisterhood* by Rebecca Wells. One of my joys in discovering Maureen Murdock's work is that it answers the structural need of authors wishing to develop a psychological story as the main plot, with secondary emphasis on events. For that reason, it works well when a lot of the protagonist's efforts involve looking back at her life, digging up secrets, and seeking an answer to "who am I really, if not the person 'they' told me I was." If that is your kind of story, I recommend that you read *The Heroine's Journey* by Maureen Murdock, and then revise accordingly.

POTENTIAL PROBLEMS USING THE JOURNEY STRUCTURES

The general problem with using these journey structures is that their added complexity creates more details that can go missing or undeveloped. If you develop only part of a journey but not all of it, the novel risks coming across as uneven; some stages will be developed and flow well and other stages will seem thinly developed and choppy.

On the other hand, if you rigidly adhere to every passage or stage of either journey, you may lose some of the spontaneity and originality of your story and writing. Your novel may come across like a cake made from a box mix. The Hero's Journey has become fairly well known in our culture. If your reader finishes a chapter and thinks,

"Here comes 'Crossing the Threshold,' " that reader is no longer happily lost in your pretend world. The hand of the author is showing.

HOW TO FIX THE PROBLEMS

I highly recommend two books, which should be required reading because they can greatly "inform" the development of your plots. Every fiction writer should read *A Writer's Journey* by Christopher Vogler for full explanation of the Hero's Journey, and *The Heroine's Journey* by Maureen Murdock for full explanation about that journey. You may wonder why I do not suggest directly reading Joseph Campbell's work, *The Hero with a Thousand Faces*. This book is one of Campbell's scholarly works and contains far more than the "bare bones" of the Hero's Journey. In fact, it is dense with details.

To avoid an uneven novel or one where the journey structure is far too obvious, use the basic steps to examine your draft and see if you are missing stages that would enhance your individual story. If the omitted stages seem like a solution to something left out that should be there, all fine and good. If following a journey structure feels "organic," not superimposed, you're in business.

Less Common Whole Book Structures

Although the five-stage dramatic structure will appear as the underlying form to most of the less common book structures, they are still distinctive. The primary less common structures include the following:

- episodic: saga, epic, autobiographical, picaresque
- short story collections/linked/novellas
- vignette/slice of life
- epistolary (letters)
- frame/flashback
- double plots/parallel/hourglass
- experimental structures

EPISODIC: SAGA, EPIC, AUTOBIOGRAPHICAL, PICARESQUE

Mentioned in chapter four, episodic structure appears when a novel unfolds from one incident or episode to another one without a distinct sense of where the story is headed or when it will end. It is a very old form of the novel. *The Odyssey* is one example. A latter-day Odyssey is *Cold Mountain* by Charles Frazier, although the protagonist, an injured Confederate soldier, W. P. Inman, has a clear goal. He leaves the hospital to walk home to his beloved Ada. But that is a very long way home with the situations, characters, and problems common to episodic stories. If the writer's style is fresh and the incidents well enough written, the novel may see publication. Several types of stories are more likely to feature or include episodic structure:

- family saga or multigenerational, epic, historical (including any novel that covers large spans of time, usually with multiple protagonists, if not multiple "books" within the novel or multiple novels in a related series)
- autobiographical or biographical novels
- picaresque

Sagas and epics, usually set in historic time periods, may be episodically structured. Although the epic novel was originally in verse (*Beowulf* in the eighth century), it has now come to mean a historical novel with a giant sweep of time and peoples. The Lord of the Rings fantasy trilogy is an epic. Each book follows the lives of several generations. Some contemporary classics include *The Thorn Birds* by Colleen McCullough, the epic *Shōgun* by James Clavell, and the expansive Pulitzer-winning chronicle *American Pastoral* by Philip Roth that recounts the decades in the life of one family and at the same time recounts a collective shift from the zeitgeist of one century to a new one.

In a family saga, the protagonist introduced in Book I of the novel may die. In Book II, her daughter takes over and we read the events

and challenges of her life. In Book III, the granddaughter's life continues, bringing the story of all three generations to an end. Each
part or book may cover that character's lifespan, with the expected
and unexpected travails of the era. When a family saga is well structured, each protagonist in each section, book, or generation has *one
story goal*. There is one unifying element that creates the dramatic
arc and replaces the lower suspense of episodic writing.

For instance, as both an epic and a multigenerational saga, the
Pulitzer Prize–winning *Middlesex* by Jeffrey Eugenides chronicles
three generations of the Greek-American Stephanides family. Of the
many unifying elements, at the core is the quest to answer "Who am
I?" and "What am I?" by protagonist and hermaphrodite Calliope
Stephanides.

A novel based on the author's life, or a biographical novel based
on someone else's life, may include the years from birth or teen years
on, through schooling, into the military and war, back home to
courtship and marriage, through careers and births of children, and
so forth. *A Clearing in the Wild* by Jane Kirkpatrick, winner of the
Wrangler Award, is an episodic biographical novel of the West (or
frontier novel). In a question-and-answer section at the back of the
novel, Kirkpatrick describes using historical research from author
Mary Bywater Cross about Kirkpatrick's protagonist, Emma Giesy.
Cross wrote that Emma Giesy "came as the only woman in a party
of ten from Bethel, Missouri, [and] scouts to find an Oregon site for
their communal society."

Historical novels can be episodic for the whole book or include
substantial portions of episodic writing, especially if they cover
decades in the life of the protagonist.

The picaresque is an old form of episodic structure that draws
its name from a *picaro*, a roguish protagonist who seeks adventure
for adventure's sake, or for some romantic ideal, as is true in *Don
Quixote* by Miguel de Cervantes. Although the protagonists in
these novels may articulate a hope or vague intention rather than a
pressing story goal, reaching that hope or intention is not the point.
The journey itself is the point, and the discoveries about self and life

made along the way. Almost always, the picaresque story is a literal journey: the cowboys in *Lonesome Dove* by Larry McMurtry set out to herd cattle to Montana; the boy and Papa in *The Road* by Cormac McCarthy travel south in post-apocalypse America seeking warmth. But the picaresque is also usually a journey into expanded understanding. The cowboys learn that the journey *is* life and that life is for living in the moment. The boy and Papa are nurtured by their love for one another while moving through a land burnt and wasted from ultimate destruction.

Potential Problems Using Episodic Structure

In contrast to the five-stage structure or the hero or heroine's journeys, the episodic novel offers no obvious singular goal or single problem. Instead of an arc composed of an ever-rising slope that crests at the long-sought climax, the episodic novel looks like an unending series of similar-size hills, too often resembling the Badlands, pun intended! A majority of the time, especially in the twenty-first century where the dramatic arc dominates, episodic structure fails to capture and hold the reader, thus many of these novels go unpublished. A story without a definite destination asks readers to have faith that the author will take them to someplace significant, and along the way create characters and episodes that are themselves gripping. With each problem introduced, the uphill begins again. When the obstacles are overcome, suspense is gone, and your reader must be won over with the next problem. Seldom is this kind of novel salable, especially if the writing is less than stellar.

To my knowledge, episodic structure almost never works with the genre novel. The expectations for the five-stage dramatic arc ensure that the plot will move fast, based on obstacles and opposition to a clear story goal. Notice my qualifier "almost." At the writing of this book, the category romance giant Harlequin has introduced a new line called "Harlequin Everlasting Love," featuring contemporary romances of 70,000 to 75,000 words that may cover the entire life of the couple. The writer's guidelines state:

We are looking for emotionally intense stories with a strong emphasis on well-rendered and psychologically credible characters (who
influence each other's lives over time). The series will be open to
a wide range of plots and situations; each story will require a significant conflict that creates urgency, excitement and momentum.
Structurally, there will be many more options—interesting and
nonlinear ways of structuring the story—than the traditional series
romance typically allows. The narrative can start at any point, can
include diaries or letters, can move freely back and forth in time,
and so forth. Points of view can vary—and first-person narrative
can be used.

Never say never when it comes to creative writing, the evolution
of the novel, and the changing marketplace.

How to Fix the Problems

If you are writing a saga or epic, and you think it is probably episodic, you can strengthen it greatly by doing the following: Emphasize one theme that runs like the Amazon River through all of the
pages. Maybe that theme is betrayal, secrets, loyalty, faith, survival,
unity of family, or search for identity. If you *show* every point-of-
view character working for or against that theme, you'll create a
unity that can give the reader an anchor of meaning throughout the
book.

You can sometimes do extensive revisions to transform your episodic structure into a dramatic one. You probably have all of the five
stages not only present but repeated with each "hill." If your novel
is multigenerational, you may have a climax for the hero or heroine
of one generation, bringing that story and life to an end, picking
up the next family member's life, and so forth. Like runners in a
relay race, you can hand off the baton of one story problem—and
theme—from one generation to the next. The last protagonist, the
last generation's hero or heroine, can finally resolve the problem set
in motion in the long-ago past, and resolve the ancient wound.

Authors of sagas, epics, and episodic historical novels can also overcome the weakness inherent with this less common structure by making the era, the people, and the point-of-view characters come to life through specific detail founded on research. Here is an excerpt displaying such details from *The Namesake* by Pulitzer Prize–winner Jhumpa Lahiri:

> …they adjust once again to sleeping under a mosquito net, bathing by pouring tin cups of water over their heads. In the mornings, Gogol watches his cousins put on their white and blue school uniforms and strap water bottles across their chests. His aunt, Uma Maima, presides in the kitchen all morning, harassing the servants as they squat by the drain scouring the dirty dishes with ash, or pound heaps of spices on slabs that resemble tombstones….

Strong author voice coupled with depth of characterization or theme can render structure nearly irrelevant. Cormac McCarthy does that with *The Road*, as follows:

> …He turned and looked at the boy. Maybe he understood for the first time that to the boy he was himself an alien. A being from a planet that no longer existed. The tales of which were suspect. He could not construct for the child's pleasure the world he'd lost without constructing the loss as well and he thought perhaps the child had known this better than he…. That he could not enkindle in the heart of the child what was ashes in his own. Even now part of him wished they'd never found this refuge. Some part of him always wished it would be over.

Episodic novels that need demolition and rebuilding from scratch are usually autobiographical novels. If you have created a character in your likeness and basically written your life experience for the plot, you are likely to have created too little suspense for your reader. It would be better to revise your story into a memoir and leave it as part of your legacy for family and friends. Then, take one of the most dramatic events or incidences in your life and ask "what if?" and play with fictional possibilities for developing that important event into a strong short story or novel. We have all experienced dozens of these events. As an editor, I find whole novels buried within autobiographical novels: scenes of coming-of-age, mistakes and accidents, falling in love, close calls in military service, loss of friends and family, problems with children, unusual or challenging work experiences, and more. Each one of these major events of life could become the centerpiece of a strong, dramatic novel. And, as a disclaimer for what rarely works, I will say, "It's all in the execution." The success of a novel is only five percent about the structure and ninety-five percent about the quality of the writing.

SHORT STORY COLLECTIONS/LINKED/NOVELLAS

Established short story authors or novelists who enjoy writing short fiction sometimes combine stories into a book. *The Joy Luck Club* by Amy Tan features protagonist Jing-Mei Woo, aka June, who narrates most of the stories in the collection. She is one of four daughters and, after their mother's death, June takes her place with her mother's friends who play mahjong. June visits China to see two half-sisters that her mother was forced to abandon when the Japanese attacked China. What unifies the short stories, now chapters, is not only the narrator, but her attempt to understand her mother and to come to terms with living within two cultures, modern American and traditional Chinese. This search for understanding and reconciliation eventually helps June gain confidence, overcoming lifelong feelings of inferiority.

The Joy Luck Club is considered a collection of *linked* short stories. Other collections are related thematically or by setting, mood, situation, or character. A dark mood, noir, and vividness of disturbing details mark the collection *Coronado* by Dennis Lehane. In *Jesus Out to Sea: Stories*, James Lee Burke selected stories about the courage of ordinary people in harrowing or dangerous circumstances: waiting for help that never comes after Hurricane Katrina; kids getting a mobster to help fight their battle against a bully.

The novella is a difficult form to sell in today's marketplace simply because it is too long for the short story publishers and too short for novels. Lengths of novellas range from as few as 60 to 70 pages to no more than 150 to 160 pages. Established authors will obviously have a better time seeing novellas published. Thomas Wolfe joined with James W. Clark and Ed Lindlof for the publication of their three novellas in the collection *The Lost Boy*. Gabriel Garcia Marquez has his *Collected Novellas*. However, an *unpublished* novella writer with credits and a great story can and have succeeded. If you cannot interest an agent, then market directly to publishers you meet at conferences (where they consider nonagent pitches) or to small presses. In structure, the novella will have classic five-stage structure or one of the less common forms. Its main distinction is an in-between length. Once in a while, an unpublished writer will sell a novella and win the lottery. Stretched to 112 pages, with about one third of them photographs of seagulls, *Jonathan Livingstone Seagull* by Richard Bach not only became a megaseller in the '60s, it is sometimes credited with starting the New Age movement. Another first and bestselling novella of inspirational fiction was *The Christmas Box* by Richard Paul Evans, a mere 128 pages in large font.

Other collections are a mix of short stories and a novella or novellas. Owen King, offspring of Stephen King, debuted with *We're All in This Together: A Novella and Stories,* four short stories. Edmund White published *Chaos: A Novella and Stories*. The difference between a long short story and a novella is an arbitrary matter of page length and a willing publisher.

Potential Problems with Short Story Collections/Linked/Novellas

One problem is entirely practical: Collections of short stories and novellas are difficult to sell, if not written by a recognized author. If you keep track of newly released fiction, which you can do by reading the trade journal *Publishers Weekly*, you'll quickly see that collections and novellas are far more infrequently published than novels. Additionally, a novella may be too small to have a spine wide enough to be spotted on a book shelf—a practical problem of dollar-sign significance.

Another problem with short story collections or novella collections is a weak or absent unifying device or theme. A collection cannot be a potpourri of random stories. As you can see by the descriptions of the three collections mentioned previously, they each have unifying themes, moods, characters, or plights, or all four. For instance, the three novellas in *Right Livelihoods* by Rick Moody are connected with a post 9/11 motif of paranoia. Each of the three novellas, about eighty pages each, features characters who fight against conspiracies, real or imagined.

How to Fix the Problems

If your primary problem is lack of name recognition, then pay your dues by publishing individual short stories, and not necessarily the ones to be included in the collection. You also need a body of related work to pitch as a collection. If you wait to be "discovered talent," you'll be like the characters in Samuel Beckett's play *Waiting for Godot*, and Godot never comes. Instead, concentrate on establishing yourself as a published short story writer and then seek publication of a collection or novella. If you have already done all of this and still haven't succeeded, you may need to revise your marketing plan and solicit small presses directly.

In revision of the short stories that you think are among your best, select those you see as related—and increase that relatedness. Perhaps most have bloodshed, but a few don't. That's easy to fix in one way or another. Your protagonist can cut herself or be a cutter, or your protagonist can drive past a bloody car accident. In a different collection, every story could take place at high noon, midnight, or just before dawn—highly symbolic times that might also reinforce a shared theme.

If you have written a novella, revised it, and have been unable to find a buyer, ask yourself if you can "fill it out" into novel length. This may not be your original vision for the work, but you could end up with a richer and deeper story and up your odds of a sale.

As always, revise short stories and novellas for stronger voice and style, depth of characterization, and originality of story.

VIGNETTE/SLICE OF LIFE

Often the vignette or slice of life is a short story, for good reason: They have limited scope; typically they describe one situation or a relatively short period of time. The terms *vignette* and *slice of life* are often used interchangeably. Vignettes normally describe one or two brief scenes such as "The Gift of the Magi" by O. Henry. They are often light or ironic in tone. The slice of life can include multiple scenes over a limited period of time, like a vignette, but in tone they often depict a realistic, unpleasant, or grim side of life. Two contemporary slice-of-life novels are *Camille's Dilemma* and *A Slice of Life* by D. C. Johnson. They feature incidents in the life of Camille Jenkins, who has given herself the title "Professional Lesbian."

Potential Problems with Vignette/Slice of Life

Because the writer's purpose may be to explore a character, idea, or relationship, these two forms often lack a plot—no rising slope of a dramatic arc. They may be devoid of plotlike conflict or even inner character conflict. They might simply be an author's explorations or observations. Therefore, success is heavily dependent upon strength of voice and style and originality of story. If vignettes or slice-of-life stories are made into book-length collections or novellas, they have the same requirements and problems as described in that section.

How to Fix the Problems

Readers will probably ask, "What's the point?" Therefore, you must work on style, character depth, and vivid and evocative descriptions, if not some take-away meaning. Without a plot, you will have to overcome inertia with stage action (small character actions and gestures) and through emotional movement (shifts of emotions). Take advantage of chapter two on simple outside-in revision techniques to increase the effectiveness and power of your sentences. If your goal is publication of a collection, once again, first seek publication of individual vignettes or slice-of-life stories and establish your reputation.

EPISTOLARY

The term "epistolary" means correspondence by letters—until modern times when e-mail and text messaging came along. It is one of, if not the oldest, form of written storytelling. A novel in epistolary structure uses correspondence as the vehicle for developing characterization and unfolding a dramatic story. In the twentieth century, many of us would select *The Color Purple* by Alice Walker as the premier example of the epistolary novel. While I tend to think of it as a structure for a sophisticated literary story for adult readers, it worked beautifully in *Wenny Has Wings* by Janet Lee Carey, a novel for nine- to twelve-year-olds. The protagonist is Will, who was resuscitated after he and his sister Wenny were hit by a truck. But Wenny died. The novel is entirely composed of Will's letters to her as he comes to terms with his loss.

Effective epistolary novels present their stories through narration, but they have the effect of creating a "now" sense of the story. Here is an excerpt from Carey's novel to demonstrate this tell/show technique:

DAY 12

Dear Wenny,

The truck driver sent us an "I'm so sorry" card. Mom and Dad showed it to me this afternoon. The cover has pink and yellow flowers on it (girl stuff). The card says his brakes went out all of a sudden while he was going down the steep hill. He was honking for us to get out of the way. He swerved and tried not to hit us, and he is so sorry. If there is anything he can do, he'll do it.

The card made Mom cry. She yanked a bunch of Kleenex from my box and made these little gulping sounds....

With the near replacement of letters with e-mail, it's natural that a novel of epistolary e-mails be published. *ChaseR: A Novel in E-mails* by Michael J. Rosen, written for nine- to twelve-year-olds, features a fourteen-year-old protagonist named Chase. When his family moves, he corresponds with his friends via e-mail, e-mail newsletters, and using emoticons (symbols and cartoon figures expressing particular emotions). In 2007, a Finnish publisher released *The Last Messages* by Hannu Luntiala. About 1,000 cell phone text messages, listed in chronological order, relate the story of this 332-page novel for adult readers. What's next in epistolary technology?

Potential Problems with Epistolary

The biggest problem with writing the epistolary novel is creating a sense of a dramatic story. If you are writing in this structure, you would make a mistake if you assumed that you can emulate a real letter. Actual letters are tell/tell, not tell/show. They tell the recipient about the latest family news, sicknesses, gossip, and weather; they suffer from the same problems as any episodic story. To a reader other than the two people corresponding, reading someone else's letters can be boring or make you feel as if you are prying into private matters. When successful, epistolary novels give the reader a feeling of being a confidante, someone trusted with secrets.

The nature of the letter also makes for obvious beginnings and endings, like the low and high points of the hills mentioned under episodic structure. That means the author will have a more difficult time interrupting a scene—and ending a chapter—midstream, at the high point of dramatic suspense. The end of each letter creates more opportunities for the reader to set the book down.

How to Fix the Problems

When you look at your draft of an epistolary novel, write a summary, a synopsis, of the five-stage dramatic arc. Make sure that your letters reveal the skeleton of this structure. Study other epistolary novels—and I highly recommend Janet Lee Carey's novel—to see how to convey action within narration and give the feeling of a novel that is happening in the present. Also notice the re-creation of dialogue. You'll see that fictional letters aren't really like typical letters at all. Here is an example from Carey's novel as her protagonist is visited at the hospital by a youth leader from church:

Well, Mr. James walked right over to my bed and started talking like we were old friends or something. I thought it was pretty strange.

"Hi, Will," he said. "Your mom and dad wanted me to drop by." He pulled a chair up to my bed and asked, "How are you feeling?" When I didn't answer, he said he knew about the truck that hit us....

A superb craft book that offers details on the show/tell technique is *Description* by Monica Wood. Also make sure to review the next chapter in this book on movement and suspense.

FRAME/FLASHBACK

The frame/flashback as a whole book structure is not to be confused with the technique of "flashing back" to the past, which can occur anywhere in the novel. If you visualize bookends, you will easily recognize a frame structure. The novel may open in one time and return to it at novel's end. The most common frame opens in the present and returns to the present; both use the same narrator. Everything that takes place in the novel's interior happens in the past, which makes it a flashback story. In her suspense novel *The Absence of Nectar*, author Kathy Hepinstall opens with Alice, her adult protagonist, who then retells the story of her childhood abuse and the discovery of murders. The end of the novel returns to adult Alice and constitutes a "denouement," a wrapping up of loose ends.

The frame may involve a narrator, one character who is not the protagonist but who begins the story and ends the story. One of the first novels to do this was *Lord Jim* by Joseph Conrad. The frame in Conrad's novel is in a different setting from the interior of the book.

In a frame/flashback novel, the story starts at the end and ends at the beginning. What this means is that it opens in present time, and the character, most often the protagonist, retells the events leading up to the present. Steven Pressfield's historical novel set in ancient Greece, *Gates of Fire*, opens in the protagonist's point of view. Xeo, the sole survivor of the Spartan attack on Thermopylae, has been captured by King Xerxes, who wants to know how 300 Spartans could keep 100,000 Persians at bay for a week. Xeo obeys the king, but begins with childhood and tells the *whole* story in flashback.

A "stock" frame/flashback uses an old woman or old man looking back and talking about a period of life where a traumatic event began, or covering most of the life, to a relative or friend. In *Dinner at the Homesick Restaurant* by Anne Tyler, eighty-five-year-old Pearl is on her death bed when she tells about each of her three children after they were abandoned by their traveling salesman father. In other cases, the novel has the sense of a movie's "voice-over"; that is, you are aware that the older narrator is present even while the author involves you in the younger self's story.

Yet another skillful use of the frame/flashback is to open the novel in the future, in the crisis that begins the climax. This kind of opening makes perfect sense for creating a high-tension hook to draw the reader into the story, to *have to find out what happens*! After the frame opens in the future, the novel flashes back to a significant past when the story problem began, rebuilding to the future time that opened the novel, to be followed by the climax and resolution.

Potential Problems with Frame/Flashback

Any time you open a novel in the story past or story future, you risk a disoriented reader. Most novels I've edited that open in the past and then jump to the present feel like an engine that starts to turn over and dies, then makes that groaning-trying sound and finally catches. The weak beginning derives from many possible problems. You may have loaded up this past with context, which means telling the reader a lot of background information about the events, people, and core conflict. Almost always, if you open with one character present, especially if you don't put that character into a setting, with a goal, conflict, and stakes, the main action of that character will be thinking. Thinking means the burden is on the author to tell well, and that is most difficult as a hook.

Another problem happens when readers confuse a frame in the

past or future for the beginning, especially if it opens in the middle of dramatic action. After all, they don't know it is a flashback until they get to your next section or chapter. If you tell, you can lose them; if you show, you can lose them. The frame/flashback may look easy and a solution to your whole-novel structure, but to open this way requires finesse.

You may also have to revise to overcome the problem of a frame narrator who is not the protagonist. Readers are like ducklings who at birth bond with whatever creature they first see. "Mother" may be a human, dog, or the biological duck mother. Your readers may have become engrossed, settled in to your narrator, the time, and the setting. Turn the page and now they stop reading. The lights come on, the movie stops; the spell is broken. Suddenly they are yanked out of their stadium seats and marched down the hall to a second movie. Although it is related to the first story, now they have to get reoriented all over again. Anything that makes your readers stop and ponder takes them out of the fictive dream, and you want to put them into the story world and keep them there until you release your readers on the last page.

How to Fix the Problems

One of the best solutions is to keep your opening frame brief. Some writers put the frame in a prologue so that the signal of the title "chapter one" helps the reader know that a character, time, and place may and probably will be different. Know that many agents flat out say that they don't like prologues. Many of the reasons have to do with what I've already discussed about the potential problems. If you can escape them, then a prologue may be a good solution. Create clear signals to the reader that you are using a frame and keep the prologue short. Chris Bohjalian's *Midwives* opens in a prologue that is only about 850 words, about three pages of text. Bohjalian signals the frame with the following first paragraph:

> Throughout the long summer before my mother's trial began, and
> then during those crisp days in the fall when her life was paraded

publicly before the county—her character lynched, her wisdom impugned—I overheard much more than my parents realized, and I understood more than they would have liked.

Then, to fully hook the reader into the present story, part one and chapter one begins: "I used the word *vulva* as a child the way some kids said *butt* or *penis* or *puke*."

In *Absence of Nectar* mentioned earlier, Kathy Hepinstall also uses a clear sense of time past to indicate the frame begins in the future and flashes back to the past. She does not use a prologue and her first line reads: "All these years later, there remains a scar on my face." Before 250 words—one page—has gone by, she adds one more reminder of the frame: "...I am convinced that it was the soaring heat of a summer afternoon—together with my brother's betrayal—that made Simon finally decide to kill both of us." The hook is sunk and the story question raised. Now the author can take the reader fully into the past.

Especially in stories where the time jump is great—many decades or centuries later, or earlier—the frame and other chapters will post a date and/or a location: *August 8, 1888, Paris.* Then for chapter one (if a prologue is used) or for a section or chapter two (if no prologue is used): *April 21, 2008, Seattle.* Be careful with relying upon the date alone to signal your frame as many readers skip past them, could get confused and then have to backtrack. Use all of the techniques for making the time and narrator clear.

A peril of using the future, directly before the climax of a novel, as your opening frame is that you can give away too much. Make sure that you leave enough unexplained that readers keep their intense curiosity about the outcome.

DOUBLE PLOTS/PARALLEL/HOURGLASS

If you have written a book with two or more protagonists, you have a double plot structure at the least. Three protagonists would make it a triple plot. When dual protagonists are pursuing lives apart from one another, the plots are said to be "parallel" in structure. They must eventually intersect or have strongly parallel climaxes with similar thematic meaning. If the two plots move toward a convergence point and then continue past it to offer two endings for the two protagonists, it makes the shape of an hourglass; thus the hourglass structure.

Don't confuse the dual protagonist, or parallel plot structures, with having "multiple points of view." Many novels have one protagonist who is fully developed and a number of main characters who hold viewpoints. That means that the writer lets the reader "get under the skin" of these characters, sharing thoughts, emotions, and bodily sensations.

An example of a double plot is *The Book of Daniel*, a National Book Award nominee by E. L. Doctorow. One plot is set in the 1950s and follows the conviction and electrocution of Paul and Roselle Isaacson, accused spies. The second plot is set in the 1960s and shows the problems and consequences of their deaths on their son Daniel, who is a graduate student at Columbia University.

One of my longtime students, Milt Cunningham, has worked a good decade on his magnum opus, *Where Trails Meet*. The novel is a literary frontier novel with an Indian boy, Runs-at-Dawn, and his story problem, and Eck, a poor farmer who leaves Missouri with a wagon train bound for "Californy." The double plots converge at the climax where the two men meet for the first and only time, each one providing resolution of the other one's problem and suffering.

Closer to resembling the hourglass structure, *Not Between Brothers* by David Marion Wilkinson is a historical epic set in nineteenth-century Texas. His two protagonists are likewise a "white man," one of the settlers, and an Indian, a Comanche chief. In contrast to Cunningham's novel, the two men meet in the middle of the novel and continue in their separate but related story lines until they meet again in the last section of the novel.

Time travel novels, including as a subgenre of category romances, often feature parallel plots or a twist on the dual protagonist idea: the protagonist—and sometimes other characters—is another person in the past or future. Eventually, the dual reality is resolved, as it is in the bestselling mainstream gothic romance *Lady of Hay* by Barbara Erskine—or left open, as it is in *The French Lieutenant's Woman* by John Fowles.

Potential Problems with Double Plots/Parallel/Hourglass

Double the story lines and double your trouble. Double the protagonists and double your trouble. You have written *two* books. This structure increases the complexity and therefore also demands greater skill to make it work successfully. One frequent problem is that the reader may find one of the stories, or protagonists, far more appealing than the other. The development, stakes, setting, or personality of one hero may be weak by comparison. For whatever reasons, your writing might come alive in one story and not in the other.

With the requirement of developing two plots, you can end up doing neither justice. Both can seem superficial and beg layering in of greater character depth, more description, and more scenes. If you also have subplots for both story lines, the complexity can create confusion for the reader or weaken the strength of the "throughline," the primary five-stage dramatic arc.

The answer to the reader question, "How are these two plots and characters related?" may come too late in the book, or never! You may also have dual themes; you've written two novellas.

If the two plots follow the protagonist and the antagonist, you can create a divided loyalty. The more that readers get to know an antagonist, the greater is your risk that they develop empathy or even attachment, and then they will feel divided as well by the fate you have designed for the antagonist. On the other hand, this may be your intention, to show two sides of a conflict where there is no clear-cut hero or villain.

How to Fix the Problems

I strongly advise selecting one protagonist and plot as primary, giving them two-thirds of the emphasis over the other "protagonist" and story line. That way, you can more fully develop one story, using the secondary one as counterpoint, for suspense when the primary plot enters a "quieter" part of the story, and as a mirror for problems, issues, and needs of the primary plot hero. Make sure that you have one theme shared by both characters. For example, if one character seeks right use of power and is in a position to effect it, then make the other character powerless and experiencing the result of wrong use of power. Perhaps in the course of the novel, the privileged British prince loses power and the lower-caste Indian man gains it.

Strengthen similarities and dissimilarities between the two protagonists. Perhaps both love children and go out of their way to help them, but that is where the similarity ends. Maybe there are minor things reflected in hobbies, talents, or preferences. Can you create similar events happening in the different worlds or times? In other words, work on parallelism beyond the parallel plots. Think of your novel as if it is a large painting. You want to create some kind of unity that ties in the far upper right-hand corner of your watercolor with the lower left-hand corner. Maybe one color does the trick—a dab of gold here and there throughout a painting that is otherwise using greens and browns.

If you have the feeling, or are receiving feedback, that one story line is more appealing or much stronger than the other, seriously consider dropping one plotline altogether. If you still have the passion to make the double plot work, then in revision strengthen each and every aspect of craft.

EXPERIMENTAL STRUCTURES

Creativity leads writers in every generation to try different techniques. Some work and become one more possible structure and others don't work and vanish to an archive. A definition of an experimental structure is one in which the writer represents story reality in an unusual way or uses innovations in style and technique. Regarding the first, experimenting with "reality," in *Ragtime*, E. L. Doctorow mixes history and fiction to create events that never happened. Michael Ondaatje uses an improvisational method of writing that he calls "radical" and results in the experimental structure present in *The English Patient* and *Divisadero*. He begins with images or a situation. He builds scenes from the images, but it may be several years before he has "a kind of approximate draft." He takes about two years in self-editing during which he moves things around, eventually arriving at an outline when he's nearly done with the novel.

Occasionally, a book will be published in a multimedia form. In the Griffin & Sabine fantasy series, author Nick Bantock created an experimental epistolary form. He included postcards, front and back sides, and letters in envelopes within the book.

Problems with Experimental Structures

The problems are obvious. Any time you break with traditional methods, to succeed you need more than a touch of genius or a huge amount of experience backing you. I recommend that writers always try ideas; that's part of banishing censorship and fighting mediocrity. What do you have to lose? What if your experiment works?

How to Fix the Problems

If you are so fortunate as to have another author's novel or short story to model, you may not be the first to try a structure, but you'll have the student's advantage. For instance, some writers emulate writing a novel within a novel. Others may create a fictional biography—instead of biographical fiction. Some writers have experimented with different fonts, spacing, and punctuation. The long "comic" book, the graphic novel for adults, was once an experimental form.

The five stages of dramatic structure, the two journey structures, and the less common variations offer a way to spot weaknesses and problems in the larger plan of your book. The chapters ahead will guide you through revision of narrower aspects of craft and style, beginning with chapter seven, "Movement and Suspense."

MAKEOVER REVISION CHECKLIST
Journeys and Less Common Structures

☑ Hero's and Heroine's Journeys
- Study *A Writer's Journey* by Christopher Vogler, and *The Heroine's Journey* by Maureen Murdock.
- Add missing stages of either journey, if they make sense to your story.
- Make sure you include the character development accompanying each Hero's Journey stage, not just the plot developments. Make sure you show a corresponding external reflection for the internal developments of character in the Heroine's Journey.

☑ Episodic: sagas, epics, autobiographical, picaresque
- Create one central story problem and theme that spans the entire work, however long and however many protagonists.
- Show every point-of-view character, not just the protagonist, working for or against the theme. This creates unity.
- Add specific details common to the era, culture, social mores, "worlds," and so forth. Intensify the realism.
- Consider if it is necessary to take the strongest stories within the novel and use them, one at a time, to write new novels based on the five-stage dramatic arc.
- In a picaresque, work hard on improving your style and increasing the uniqueness and meaning of the characters the protagonist meets on his or her journey.

☑ Short Story Collections/Linked Novellas
- Seek publication of individual short stories, whether or not they are intended for a collection. You'll need credits, name recognition.
- Check your short stories or novellas intended for a collection to make sure they share a unifying device—a theme, setting, character, etc.
- Examine whether you can turn a novella into a full-length novel.
- Strengthen style, characterization, and originality.

☑ Vignette/Slice of Life
- Intensify any conflict in the vignette/slice of life or other focus of the story, whether a character, idea, or problem.

- Without a plot arc, create take-away meaning.
- Overcome inertia by adding small character actions and reactions, minutiae of facial expressions and body language.
- Use chapter-two techniques to increase the power and effectiveness of your sentences.
- Seek publication of individual shorter vignettes or slice-of-life stories to establish credits and a reputation; then seek publication of a collection.

☑ Epistolary
- Write a summary or synopsis of the five-part dramatic structure imbedded in your chapters and strengthen that arc.
- Turn ordinary letter style into fictional epistolary style by using show/tell and tell/tell techniques.
- Review chapter fourteen, "Character-Driven Narration."
- Read *Description* by Monica Wood.
- Review chapter seven and eight on improving movement, suspense, and scene structure.

☑ Frame/Flashback
- Shorten your opening frame—whether a prologue or chapter one—to six pages or less. Even one paragraph or one page is fine.
- Make sure you open with a hook. Review hooks in chapter eleven.
- Keep the reader fully oriented if you shift characters, times, or settings between the frame and the "now" story. Use transitions such as "Forty years later…" or post dates and locations at the beginning of chapters.
- In flashforward frames, make sure you don't give away too much.

☑ Double Plots/Parallel/Hourglass
- Revise to make one protagonist and plot primary for a strong through-line.
- Make sure all protagonists and plots support and reveal the same theme.
- Strengthen similarities and dissimilarities between the two protagonists.
- Strengthen parallelism with same or similar events.
- If one protagonist and plotline is weaker or less appealing than the other, consider dropping it and revising with just the one.

☑ Experimental Structures
- Take the risk; experiment.
- Use another author's experiments in technique, format, or story-telling as a model to learn from.
- If your experiment seems not to work, toss it or adapt it to a conventional pattern.
- Don't give up.

CHAPTER SEVEN

Movement and Suspense

Options Movement and suspense are at the heart of successful fiction. Sometimes creating them is easy and natural. Other times, incorporating them will be complex in execution, and need close attention in revision. No one should skip this chapter!

If I could persuade the fiction writers of the world to do one thing every year, it would be to read the winners of the Newbery Medal and other awards for best children's literature. Writers of children's fiction know that the apparent simplicity of the novel is anything but simple to write. Yet, their accomplishments offer superb models of all elements of craft.

Children are not an easy sell, and they'll simply stop reading when they're bored. If you think about it, children are almost always in motion. In their developing minds and bodies, their responses to the impinging outer world and lively inner world are immediate. Published writers of children's literature understand the immediacy of the child—and teen—experience. They reflect that understanding by becoming masters of movement and suspense. Read the best of children's novels, and you'll clearly see the well-executed techniques we'll discuss in this chapter.

Everyone knows what movement is; that part is easy. It's action. In fiction, it is certainly that, but it also encompasses the idea of change. Change of ideas, realities, and emotions. These shifts—action and change—create movement of the plot and character, seen and unseen. Your novel is like a brand-new, steam-powered train. If you don't keep tossing coal into the fire, your train will stop and the passengers will never reach their destination. One of your most basic jobs is to keep driving your story forward, through action and change, to its conclusion. Keep shoveling.

Movement and suspense are tied together. Movement raises questions: What will happen next? That is suspense. Some movement is planned and some is unplanned. Suspense is an outcome, a result of movement in plot and character. Creating movement involves far more than the simple ideas of action and change. A whole set of techniques creates movement, vitality, and suspense. Use them when you revise—your writing will be far stronger.

The elements of movement, and therefore suspense, are created by:

- actions, outer and inner
- reactions
- emotions
- reversals
- subtext
- raising questions

Actions, Outer and Inner

Your point-of-view characters take action in two ways: outward and inward; one is visible and the other is known by the reader but not by the other characters. In *Hatchet*, a Newbery Honor–winner by Gary Paulsen, a boy is a lone survivor of a plane crash and must learn how to battle the elements until help comes:

Outer actions: He balanced on the log, holding himself up with the limbs, and teetered out past the weeds and murky water.

Inner action: Here I am and that is nowhere. With his mind opened and thoughts happening it all tried to come in with a rush [implied movement], all of what had occurred and he could not take it. The whole thing turned into a confused jumble that made no sense. So he fought it down and tried to take one thing at a time. [The last line shows inner action.]

This next excerpt occurs while the protagonist is still in the airplane.

Outer action and inner action in one sentence: He did what he could, tightened his seatbelt, positioned himself, rehearsed mentally again and again what his procedure should be. [The last clause shows inner action.]

Reactions

Another form of movement comes from *reactions* in response to actions. Reactions can be shown or narrated through the body, mind, or emotions of your characters. In novels with many characters, they are constantly acting upon one another and reacting to one another, or should be. In the following example from *My First Murder* by Susan P. Baker, I've inserted bracketed comments to indicate actions and the kinds of reactions experienced by private investigator Mavis Davis:

"How did my mother die, Miss Davis?" Catherine asked [action directed to Mavis].

I glanced from her to the others [physical reaction]. Talk about putting me on the spot [reaction implying discomfort]. I didn't know whether I should give them the blow-by-blow or not [reaction—thought/quandary]; breaking bad news was never one of my duties in child welfare or the probation department [narration/informing]. I decided to give them the police version [inner action/thought-decision]. "She was found in her apartment one morning by her employer. She was late for work, and he went up to check on her. It's believed by the Houston Police Department that she was the victim of a serial killer." [Mavis acts intellectually in response to Catherine's question.]

What Can Go Wrong with Action and Reaction
- Protagonist is passive; he or she fails to initiate most actions.
- There is too much outer action and too little inner action or reaction.
- Point-of-view characters react with thoughts alone.
- A character's response precedes the stimulus for it.

In this example, the reactions by the character have been mostly intellectual, and mysteries as a genre are weighted toward the intellectual—solving the puzzle of whodunit. However, developed characterization includes a character's emotions, which are either shown through visceral physical reactions (a lump in the throat) or are told to the reader (she felt sad).

When you were creating your story, I doubt you were analyzing what you were doing and needing to do with each and every sentence and paragraph. In revision, however, it is helpful to look analytically and determine if you are leaving out or overemphasizing anything to the detriment of your storytelling. The late writing instructor and prolific novelist Jack Bickham referred to the sequence of action-reaction as stimulus-response, perhaps because a stimulus may be an unintended action such as a tree branch falling on a person. Whether your characters act or are acted upon by other human beings or nature, this most basic level of movement needs checking in every story, from beginning to end.

PROTAGONIST IS PASSIVE

In revision, look at every page to make sure you included action. This sounds like patronizing advice, but too much musing or thinking can leave the reader in your characters' minds but not in their moving bodies or the environment. I have edited half a dozen thrillers where the primary action was characters sitting around talking. How thrilling is that!

Stories are driven forward by a hero acting to reach a goal. If heroes let others take action and are shuffled forward along the story chronology by outer forces and people, those heroes are less than heroic. They may be *only* passive or worse: They may come across to the reader as victims. Either case makes them unlikable characters if that role continues too long.

Of particular difficulty is an entire novel structured around a defensive story goal. In other words, if the inciting incident presents a problem that *compels* the protagonist to defend herself, rather than *propels* her toward achieving a goal, the story produces a *reac*tive hero, not a *pro*active hero.

In fiction, readers have little tolerance for the passive or victim protagonist, perhaps because The Victim is archetypal and heroes are expected to be go-getter problem-solvers. It doesn't take too much repetition for your victim to come across as a whiner. Since readers tend to identify with—become—the protagonist, no one wants to become a whiner.

A defensive story goal creates a different problem. You might wonder about a fugitive story. If you saw the movie *The Fugitive*, then you may recall that a doctor is sentenced to death for murdering his wife. On the way to jail, he has an opportunity to escape and goes on the lam. The entire story is about him being relentlessly pursued by law enforcement; he is the fugitive. He is in a defensive position, and yet he is heroic. Why? He does not go into hiding or flee the country. His goal is to prove his innocence by finding out who did kill his wife. That means he constantly puts himself in danger, including returning to the hospital where he worked to find evidence about test results of a new drug that he suspects were tampered with. In the process, he eventually finds out who killed his wife and why he was set up as the fall guy. The fugitive is no victim of circumstances; he shows tremendous courage, ingeniousness, and he risks everything, including his life.

I see many variations on the fugitive plot, especially in the form of a heroine fleeing an abusive relationship or being stalked. The suspense category of "woman in jeopardy" is similar to the fugitive plot. A woman is being stalked or pursued by a crazed man such as an ex-husband, a prisoner bent on revenge against a prosecuting attorney (the woman), or her bad choice in a boyfriend. This puts the heroine into a defensive position, which means she must act heroically and courageously to thwart her antagonist. And she must begin those actions soon after the threat becomes known. She must transcend The Victim archetype and become The Hero.

TOO MUCH OUTER ACTION—TOO LITTLE INNER ACTION/REACTION

When a plot involves danger or urgency, action alone picks up the pace and resembles a quickened heartbeat. It's appropriate to write more action than other elements. When emotions run high, outward expressions—reactions expressed outwardly—are more common than internal visceral and unseen responses. As you reread your story, if you notice that you seldom provide external or visible emotions or seldom show internal or unseen body-generated emotions, your characterization will come off as superficial and mechanical.

What are visceral emotions? The body generates responses that match emotions. It's up to the writer to figure out what they may be. For instance, we respond with tight or cramped muscles, gut aches, indigestion, bile, quickened pulse, throbbing headaches, short breath, blurred vision, lumps in our throats, sweaty palms, and so forth. These are visceral emotions. Our ancient biology still creates degrees of fight, flight, or excite responses to just about everything in life, whether we are fully aware of them or not.

Here is an example of how to successfully mix action and different types of outer and inner reactions in a dramatic fight-or-flight scene. *The Golden Compass*, the first book in the acclaimed fantasy series His Dark Materials by Philip Pullman, is for children nine and up. Each character has a "dæmon," a shape-shifting animal partner, like an extension of the self, and yet a separate being. The protagonist is Lyra. Her dæmon is named Pantalaimon or Pan. I have used brackets to identify the actions and reactions below:

"Pan! Pan!"

But the fox dæmon tore at the cat Pantalaimon [action] and Lyra felt the pain in her own flesh [inner physical reaction], and sobbed a great cry [visible visceral emotion] as he fell [action]. One man was swiftly lashing cords around her [action], around her limbs, her throat, body, head, bundling her over and over on the wet ground [action]. She was helpless [narrated emotion], exactly like a fly being trussed by a spider [simile showing and including action and feeling]. Poor hurt Pan [narrated reaction—emotion] was dragging himself toward her [action], with the fox dæmon worrying his back [action conveying emotion]....

Check your novel throughout and layer in reactions to actions, using the full range of possible human responses: outer expressions of emotion and physical discomfort, inner and unseen body-generated emotion, narrated emotion, and narrated thought.

CHARACTERS REACT WITH THOUGHTS ALONE

When I edit unpublished novels, the most frequent action-reaction sequence is action followed by thought—to the exclusion of any other response. This may be the norm more than the exception in some types of novels that are more intellectual as a genre. Mysteries and legal thrillers demand the intellectual skills of deduction. Science fiction is frequently an exploration of ideas and theories. Literary novels often emphasize author philosophy and historical or sociological interpretations embodied in characters and story.

Yet, a character who responds with thoughts alone throughout a story lacks dimension. Characterization is typically superficial. Reader engagement may weaken. Often, the draft reads like an outline. Novels that emphasize thought but exclude visceral responses and outer emotional reactions also tend to skimp on other elements: character description, sensory perceptions (sound, smell, taste, touch, and sight), and setting. Narration will come across as an overt briefing rather than a skillful and organic part of the story. It will either be too long or too short. There may be so much dialogue that we editors criticize it as "talking heads."

Yet, the strength of an author with extraordinary skill in crafting suspenseful and high-paced plots may compensate for thin characterization. Usually these novels are predominantly dialogue, dialogue plus blocks of narration. If the protagonist has "attitude"—that is, if he expresses opinions in place of emotions—and if the author has skill with narration, then these plot-driven books can sell, and sell well.

Take John Grisham, a pioneer of the legal thriller, with his reputation for great plots. His characters have "attitude," opinions, and personality, but seldom express emotion. This genre is part of the larger one of crime fiction, which is more oriented toward ideas and strategies than toward expression of emotions. When Grisham does include emotion, it is well placed. He tells well, often providing two or three pages at a time of backstory, character description, and interpretation of the legal maneuverings. Then he returns to dialogue.

Here is a typical example of characterization, with a bit of emotion, excerpted from three or four pages of narration in *The Brethren*. The two characters mentioned in the excerpt are Aaron Lake, a congressman, and Teddy Maynard, the director of the CIA, who has summoned him:

Teddy pushed the button again, and there was Lake's face. For a fifty-year veteran of intelligence wars, Teddy seldom had a knot in his stomach. He'd dodged bullets, hidden under bridges, frozen in mountains, poisoned two Czech spies, shot a traitor in Bonn, learned seven languages, fought the cold war, tried to prevent the next one, had more adventures than any ten agents combined, yet looking at the innocent face of Congressman Aaron Lake he felt a knot.

He—the CIA—was about to do something the agency had never done before.

They'd started with a hundred senators, fifty governors, four hundred and thirty-five congressmen, all the likely suspects, and now there was one. Representative Aaron Lake of Arizona.

Grisham creates intricate plots, with unexpected twists, and taut courtroom trials. His "snapshot" characterizations, like the one of Teddy Maynard, are compact and satisfying enough, I suspect, for everyone who loves this genre.

Look for places to add emotion expressed outwardly, experienced viscerally, and told. Action-reaction; stimulus-response. I've crafted a formula, so to speak, that is a good one to remember and follow most of the time. It describes what order to write that will include all of the aspects of movement and suspense discussed so far:

Action/Stimulus ➔ Reaction/Emotion ➔ Thought ➔ Action

To show this "chain reaction," I've penned the following example with bracketed comments identifying each component of the formula:

> The tree branch cracked and fell on her. [action/stimulus] She yelped [physical reaction] as it carved a deep gash down her arm; [action/stimulus] burning as if fire ants had burrowed under the skin, [physical reaction] and spurting blood with each rapid beat of her heart. [action/reaction] "Just what I need," she muttered and tried to steady herself. [expressed emotion/thought/reaction] What in the hell was she going to do now? [emotion] Camp was a good eight miles. She could bleed to death. [thought/implied emotion] Fighting a world about to go black, [physical reaction] Ella struggled to rip off her blouse to create a tourniquet. [action]

RESPONSE PRECEDES STIMULUS

Nearly all rough drafts have places where a character will react before the reader knows what the action is that prompted it. "Thud!" "Pow!" instead of "Pow!" "Thud." Or, "He heard the bullet whiz past his ear as the hunter cocked and shot his rifle." Or, the response might be an emotion preceding an event: "She felt as if a hand had entered her chest and clenched her heart. She read the letter. Grandpa had died." Reversing the order is a common mistake, easy to correct. Keep an eye out for it in your revisions.

As you can see, handling actions and reactions has more technique to it than the simplicity of the concept. Well written, both of these fundamentals keep advancing movement and contributing to suspense.

Emotions

We've been talking about emotional reactions, externally expressed and internally felt, yet there is another source of movement through emotions. That is when they change from paragraph to paragraph or even from sentence to sentence. If you have a lot of action, you can have a lot of reaction. Emotions are like anchors deep into a character. Changing them frequently, in tandem with changes in the plot, keeps a story vital and moving.

For instance, if you plan to start a scene with a lower emotional response, then you can build an arc of emotional intensity that creates rising suspense with it. Let's say that a character—let's call him Bill—has not kept a promise. Your point-of-view character, Serena, reacts with anger. Not rage; her first response is irritation. He shrugs his shoulders and says, "Get used to it, honey. I'm not your servant." This makes her angrier. Now her blood is beginning to boil. Her stomach twists and she shouts at him, "You promised. You're not my servant, you're supposed to be my fiancé!" He laughs, retorts, "Not anymore." Now she blows her top. One "Serena" character might show icy rage and walk over to him in determined steps, bore holes in him with her eyes, spit in his face, and scream an invective. Another Serena character might explode in a tirade and throw any nearby object. Yet another Serena character might decide that revenge is a dish best served cold. She might say in a cloyingly sweet way, "Why, Bill, it has been such a pleasure knowing you."

In developing her point of view, you would also provide the reader with her visceral emotions, thoughts, and plans and actions.

What happens when you vary the emotions in response to the outer environment is that you create movement. This can be in addition to the movement created by actions and the suspense when goals are thwarted.

With more than 560 million copies of over seventy novels in print, Danielle Steel is one of the most popular contemporary writers. She especially excels at movement through emotions. Usually her characters simply report their emotions, but one page may include half a dozen or more. In two pages taken from the middle of her novel *ImPossible*, in a mother-daughter telephone call, her characters name the following emotions, in this order: happy, morbidly depressed (backstory), relieved, happy and excited, panicked, relieved, annoyed (backstory), loving, ecstatic, envious, empty.

While showing constantly changing emotions is another source of movement, and building them in an arc adds suspense, there are schools of literary fiction that believe doing so is less artful. The belief is that the reader will supply the emotion from the context of the story, that the strength and originality of the literary writing will create an accumulating impact, intellectually and emotionally, as the reader progresses in the novel. Often, an author of literary writing will use imagery and symbolism to express emotions. Here is a longer excerpt from the Pulitzer-winning novel *A Thousand Acres* by Jane Smiley. The first paragraph conveys emotion through symbolism and the second through metaphor. The protagonist, Ginny, is a farm wife with two children. Her husband has just left to check the fields:

> While they were cooking, I went out to check my garden. Something that always has amazed me is the resilience of the plants. My tomato vines showed no ill effects from the onslaught of the storm, weren't even muddy, since I had made it a point to mulch them.... Some of the tenderest marigolds had been beaten down... but all the greenery sparkled with new life... but I stood off to the side and took it all in as if it were a distant promise.
>
> ...I felt another animal in myself, a horse haltered in a tight

stall, throwing its head and beating its feet against the floor, but the beams and the bars and the halter rope hold firm, and the horse wears itself out, and accepts the restraint that moments before had been an unendurable goal. I went back in the house and flipped the sausages. Pammy and Linda were sitting sleepily at the table.

You could not have two styles of writing further from one another than Danielle Steel's and Jane Smiley's, yet both have loyal and admiring readers. Once more, your decisions about how to revise for movement via changing emotions should be considered in light of your genre.

Reversals

Readers develop expectations based upon where you lead them. A wonderful movement technique is to pop reversals of the expected, which operate to change action, change emotions, or change goals. Taking my soap-opera-like example of Bill and Serena in the emotions section, what if at the end of Serena's surge of anger she broke out laughing, even doubling over. Bill joins her and they fall to the floor kissing. That's a reversal of the expected. And then, what if when the laughing and kissing stops, he says to her, "I'm still leaving." Another reversal. The reader is kept in a state of anticipation, not expectation, delighted by the surprise and wondering what will happen next. Reversals keep story movement going until the reader finds out.

Reversals are a powerful way to break clichés, which are the penultimate example of the expected. All of us have moments when we blank out and write clichéd events, outcomes, dialogue, character traits, reactions, and emotions. A "loose cannon" is a character who can't be trusted to act according to expectations. Therefore, that character might do the reverse of what everyone expects. An "unreliable narrator" is a protagonist who might not be telling the truth to the reader. Rusty Sabich, the prosecuting attorney accused of killing his mistress in *Presumed Innocent* by Scott Turow, is someone the reader doesn't know whether to believe is innocent or guilty until the end. Paradoxically, the reader anticipates a reversal, which supplies constant suspense.

In his Newbery Medal–winning novel, *Bud, Not Buddy*, Christopher Paul Curtis shows his mastery of all of the techniques of movement and suspense, including reversal. In the following excerpt, Bud's new caretakers have locked him into an unlit shed for the night. Notice the skillful mixing of action, reaction, emotion, thought, and reversal:

> I reached my hand toward the gray doorknob and quick as that I went from kind of calm to being in that stand-in-one-place-with-spit-drooling-down-the-front-of-your-shirt kind of scared.
>
> Halfway up the door were three little flat monster heads guarding the doorknob. Each head had two little round eyes staring right at me. The eyes were the only thing in the shed that weren't gray. They were a bright yellow with a big black spot right in the middle.
>
> I dropped my blanket and pillow and back-stepped until my legs hit the woodpile behind me. From all the fast breathing going on you'da thought the five other scared people had come back and brought a couple of scared friends with them.
>
> Each head had a wide-open mouth with a sharp set of pointy teeth and lips smiling back ready to bite. It felt like the shed was getting smaller and smaller and the little mouths getting closer and closer.
>
> Then I knew what I was looking at. The doorknob guards were three dried-out fish heads that someone had nailed to the door.

WHAT CAN GO WRONG WITH THE USE OF REVERSALS

Only a few things can interfere with your effective use of this wonderful technique of reversals, and they are more cautions than items requiring a lot of explanation or examples. Make sure your use of reversals doesn't fall err to these three cautions:

1. You can overuse them such that the reader feels manipulated.
2. A reversal at a time when you have been working hard to build a mood or suspense can release suspense at the wrong moment.
3. A reversal can be out of character.

Subtext

To new writers, the terminology of fiction craft has several mysterious words in it, and "subtext" is one of them. Literally, you have the text and you have what is below—that is, sub the text. Everything hidden from the awareness or observation of characters other than your point-of-view character is a form of subtext. Here is a simple example from everyday life you are sure to have experienced: You are somewhere in public and you have to relieve your bladder as soon as possible. A friend spots you and a long conversation ensues. What is going on beneath the surface is mental and bodily control over key muscles, restless need to "go," desperate need to go, and finally necessity to find a bathroom quick. That's subtext—if you don't tell your friend. Once you tell the friend, the need is no longer *sub*text.

I believe that subtext is a part of every situation and scene in a book or could be. Most of the time, you can show it as private thoughts and intentions, a "hidden agenda." Another common use of subtext is feelings of some kind—sexual attraction, jealousy, disdain—between two characters, unexpressed but perhaps becoming a dawning awareness. Although everything unseen that is going on within your point-of-view character can become subtext, the kind that especially contributes movement and suspense is subtext filled with rising tension.

In *The Jury Master*, Robert Dugoni takes full advantage of building subtext in the form of sexual attraction between his protagonist, attorney David Sloane, and Sloane's secretary of ten years, Tina, who has given notice. In this scene, it is a windy and cold early evening in

---

Here are some possible sources of subtext, if they are used to create beneath-the-surface tension:

- the point-of-view character's internal state: feeling faint, feeling an intense need to say something, a welling up of threatened sobs, sexual attraction
- nature: a storm brewing, night falling, a mountain lion seen in the area
- human-made environment: a heavily laden bookshelf pulled partway from the wall, a patched raft with a slow leak, a hot stove burner left on
- other characters' body language: someone playing with a revolver, a toddler with no caretaker in sight who wanders in the direction of a busy street

---

San Francisco's Financial District. Sloane is keeping Tina company while she waits for a cab. Sloane has a date with a woman named Melda and has just called her on his cell phone, to tell her he'll be a bit late, and reaches her answering machine.

"Everything okay?" Tina asked.

"I'm just surprised she's not home yet."

"Go ahead. I'll be fine."

"No. It's all right." He put his hands in the pockets of his leather coat and hunched his shoulders to protect his neck from the cold. "She probably stayed to have a cup of coffee with a certain gentleman she's been talking about."

"Another man? She stood you up!"

Tina grinned, turning her head slightly to allow the breeze down Battery Street to blow the hair from her face. He had always thought her eyes blue, but now, in the ambient light from the building lobby, they were more the color of a high summer sky, with flecks of gray and yellow. She leaned toward him, as if being pulled by an invisible string, and for a moment he thought she was going to kiss him. But she stepped past him to the newspaper bin behind him, studying the paper through the plastic casing.

[They spot a headline with a name they recognize, relevant to the thriller plot, and Sloane buys the newspaper. Together, with Tina leaning over his shoulder, they read the article about the death of this person. Her cab comes and after some tête-à-tête, she gets in. Continuing:]

"You okay?"

"I'm still in shock that you're leaving."

"Maybe not." She reached for the door handle. "I told you I'd stay for the right guy. You just have to find him for me."

She pulled the door closed, leaving him standing alone on the sidewalk.

Raising Questions

Readers ask questions from the moment they enter a book: Where and when does this story take place, who is the main character, what is the conflict, and what is the story goal. The story goal is turned into a question: Will he or she reach the goal and resolve the problem? The kind of raised questions in this section on movement and suspense are different ones, highly targeted to individual sentences and paragraphs. If you end a sentence or paragraph with an unanswered question, readers must go on to the next one or several to find the answer. This "going on" creates another type of movement and suspense.

In this next example, taken from *The Good Children* by Kate Wilhelm, Nebula and Hugo Award–winner, I have used brackets to identify the raised question.

On Tuesday I was in history class when the principal, Mr. Karel, came to the room and spoke with the teacher, Mrs. Jesperson. [Why did he come? What did he say?] They went out to the hall together, and when she returned, she came to my desk and said I should get my things and go with her. [What's wrong?] Her eyes were teary. [Why is she upset and why does it involve the hero?]

In the corridor, Mr. Karel put his arm around my shoulders and walked me to his office. [What is the bad news that affects the hero?] Kevin and Amy [brother and sister] were there, both of them as afraid as I was. [What happened that affects all three siblings? Parent or parents died?] I thought at first we were all in trouble again, but this was different. [Continued question—What's wrong?] Mr. Karel said he would take us home. [What's happened to their parents?] Someone had gone to get Brian [preschool brother] and he would take us all home. [Seems repetitive—same question] There had been an accident at Dad's work. [Question partially answered, but still—what happened? How bad was the accident? How is Dad?]

Wilhelm intentionally draws out the suspense through this paragraph and a next one when the children arrive home to a distraught mother. The last line of the paragraph is "They killed your father! My poor babies! They killed him! They killed him!" The question of what happened to the father is answered but Wilhelm has only done so after giving the reader a chance to empathize with the hero through the build-up of suspense. And the mother's response raises more questions: "Who killed him? How did he die?"

A less experienced novelist might have compressed this dramatic event into a short narrative statement: "Mr. Karel, the principal, called me out of my history class and laid a hand on my shoulder, saying, 'Son, I'm sorry to give you this news. Your father was killed in an accident.'" You can use the rule of thumb that the greater the dramatic event, the more you should keep from immediately answering what it is.

What Can Go Wrong with Raising Questions

The primary craft problem with raising questions is missing opportunities and not using this technique to full advantage. Instead, the writer may raise and answer a question in the same sentence. Even when there is no looming big event, you should revise your sentences to maximize movement through raised questions. For instance, here is a typical compound sentence: "She looked out the window and saw people in their morning rush to work." Not very interesting, do you agree?

How to Fix It

Cut the sentence in two. The first one raises the question, while the second one answers it—and raises another one. For example: "She looked out the window." [What did she see?] "People rushed to make it to work on time, but none of them would make it." [Why?!] Since I just made this up, all I can say is that we have just entered *The Twilight Zone*. But isn't it true that your curiosity rocketed, and you would have to read on if a novel you were reading had that sentence?

Sentence by sentence, paragraph by paragraph, chapter end by chapter end, examine what you have written. Catch and revise places where you deflate reader interest and end movement by answering the raised questions too soon. One part-of-speech culprit is the coordinating conjunction or other parts of speech used as conjunctions: and, but, nevertheless, otherwise, consequently, so as, then, only, still, yet, hence, thus, therefore, as a consequence, as a result, so that, so then, since, because, though, in order that. Any of these conjunctions can serve as the bridge between a question asked and an answer provided. They are often the bandits robbing suspense. Delete them, divide your one sentence into two, and now you retain the question and the reader interest.

Movement and suspense are critical in turning a ho-hum draft into a compelling, exciting, salable, and deeply satisfying novel or short story. The next chapter demonstrates how these elements also depend upon your successful manipulation of time and pace.

Movement and Suspense Techniques

☑ Actions include:
- outer actions—physical
- inner actions—implied action in thought

☑ Reactions include:
- actions in response
- thoughts/quandaries
- narration/informing
- actions within thoughts/decisions
- visceral emotions expressed by the body

☑ Problem #1: Protagonist is passive.
Solutions:
- Increase the hero's actions.
- Add goals.
- Avoid prolonged victim role.
- Reduce expression of character weaknesses.
- Amplify character strengths.

☑ Problem #2: Too much action—too little reaction.
Solutions:
- Integrate body-generated (visceral) emotions.
- Show outward reactions—body language.
- Add narrated emotion and thought to reveal reactions.

☑ Problem #3: Characters react with thoughts alone.
Solutions:
- Break up thought or "talking heads" dialogue.
- Weave in other elements of craft: backstory, character description, emotion, dialogue, and action.
- Frequently use the following pattern: (1) action/stimulus; (2) reaction/expressed emotion; (3) thought/quandary; (4) decision; (5) new action.

☑ Problem #4: Response precedes stimulus.
  Solution:
  - Check order and revise to place stimulus first.

☑ Emotions—depending on genre:
  - Reveal emotions through visceral/physical expression or narrate them.
  - Show emotions change—within a paragraph, from paragraph to paragraph, and/or from page to page.
  - Build a crescendo of emotional reaction throughout a scene or section.
  - Convey emotions through imagery and symbols.

☑ Reversals
  - Reverse expected emotion with unexpected emotion.
  - Reverse expected outcomes of events.
  - Reverse anticipated character action or reaction.
  - Revise to create a mercurial or unreliable character or "loose cannon."

  Avoid:
  - Overuse or reader will feel manipulated.
  - Breaking a mood or a buildup of suspense at the wrong time with a reversal.
  - A reversal that is unsupported by the characterization.

☑ Subtext
  Sources of subtext (what lies beneath—the unseen):
  - internal state of the point-of-view character: body, mind, emotions
  - hidden agendas
  - nature
  - human-made environment
  - other characters' actions and reactions, or body language

☑ Raising questions
  - End sentences, paragraphs, scenes, and chapters with raised questions.
  - When you answer one question, raise another one.
  - Use foreshadowing to raise questions.

Avoid:

- Missed opportunities—read closely and revise.
- Examine coordinating conjunctions (and, but, so that) and compound sentences. The second part often answers the question in the first part.
- Answering the question within the sentence, scene, or chapter without also raising another question.
- Replacing moment-by-moment suspense-filled action with narration that tells all.

CHAPTER EIGHT

Time and Pace

Options Knowing how to order story time, manage its sequence, handle tense changes, and vary pace is fundamental to successful fiction. Read on. If your revision needs lie in areas other than with handling shifts of time and pace, then review the Makeover Revision Checklist as needed.

When you picked up this book, you probably didn't think you would enter an Einsteinian world. Welcome. In writing fiction, you not only get to play with time and space, you must gain skill in manipulating them. Time is one of the most malleable and important aspects of movement. You are Master of Time's Relativity. In one sentence, you can have your readers settled into downtown Chicago, year 2008, and in the next they will follow you to "On Lake Michigan, two hundred years ago..."

Three aspects of time directly affect pace and can create problems that need checking during revision:

- shifting time
- grammatical tense/immediacy of time
- pace/rate of time's passage

Shifting Time

In the relative universe of storytelling, time can be drawn out or compressed, skipped or repeated. We can even create multiple scenes that happen simultaneously—in story time.

When writers are just getting their sea legs, they do a lot of falling while trying to learn how to balance. Some novices err by providing every event in chronological order. Others give two sentences to one of the biggest events in the life of the character and then draw out something minor like taking a shower. When you shift from one character's viewpoint to a different one, you also have a decision about shifting time. Basically, you have four options for shifting story time:

- overlapping present
- immediate future
- flashforward
- flashback

OVERLAPPING PRESENT

Not to be overused (perhaps once in a novel), repeating one character's experience in the same time and place as you just finished with another character will give your readers a surprise. You're supplying something that we can't do in reality: overlapping the story present. The first viewpoint character may or may not be present in the second scene. There are different ways to do it. Unless you are writing a version of the movie *Groundhog Day*, where the same character repeats the same day, this shift of time will always involve two characters. You may wonder, why do this at all? The answer is: for emphasis. Something of significance must have happened to revisit it.

For instance, in *Island of Dreams*, bestselling romance author Katherine Stone uses the overlapping present in the prologue to establish an inciting incident that happened thirty-six years prior to the present story that begins in chapter one. In this prologue, Gabriel Rourke and his son Liam decide to honor the day of the death of Gabriel's wife, Liam's mother, that evening. In Liam's point of view, he awaits his father, who is upstairs dressing, when the doorbell rings. A pregnant woman and her husband, as well as her

father (Edward) and mother all arrive. Liam knows nothing about
why these people are here on this of all days. The woman has never
met Gabriel, yet he saved her life when she was ten. The scene ends
thus, beginning with Liam's question:

> "Why are you here?"
>
> "Your father asked us to be," Edward answered. "*Me* to be. But
> Lilah and Val and Thomas insisted on coming, too. They wanted to
> meet you. And of course your mother."
>
> But Eileen Pierce Rourke had died.
>
> Been killed.
>
> On this date three years ago.
>
> Shortly before four.
>
> "*No.*"
>
> Liam was halfway up the stairs when the gunshot thundered
> overhead.

The overlapping present begins after a soft hiatus (four line spaces):

> Gabriel Rourke had been suicidal in the way the genuinely suicidal
> are: calm, methodical, determined, clear…at least possessing a
> clarity which to his anguished mind made perfect sense.
>
> He needed to be with Eileen. He had needed such reunion since
> the day she had died.
>
> But Gabriel had survived for his son, loving Liam, caring for
> Liam, until the time came when his boy was old enough to go on
> without him—when, Gabriel's altered thinking assured him, Liam
> would be *fine* without him.…

Several pages continue in Gabriel's point of view until he takes his
life, continuing seamlessly with a viewpoint shift to Edward (father
of the girl Gabriel saved) and to Liam, within a few paragraphs, and
then reaching the end of the prologue.

Examine your story for a dramatic event where this powerful technique might be more dramatic than what you have already written.

IMMEDIATE FUTURE

When a second character picks up where a first one left off—in time—or when a first character continues in a next section or chapter, with the time unbroken, the time shift is to the immediate future. There are many places in a novel where you will want to break off midscene or to end a chapter but continue it in the immediate future. Why would you do that? In bigger scenes, for instance, where important challenges and changes will take place, a break gives readers a chance to take a deep breath and catch their wind. But you don't want to let them go long enough to forget the character, feel cheated by the author, lose interest, or close the book. Let's say you have built suspense and are in the middle of a crescendo. By starting a scene or completing a chapter and beginning a new one in the immediate future with a same or different character, you can actually boost suspense.

In *Wolf's Rite* by Terry Persun, an obnoxious New York advertising executive is visiting clients in New Mexico and, through unusual circumstances, forced to undergo a Navajo vision quest. The executive and protagonist, Lew, is renamed Wolf by the Indians who are with him. The excerpt that follows ends chapter four, just prior to an important scene, and the beginning of chapter five in the immediate future. Notice, too, how expertly Persun deals with time's passage in the viewpoint of his protagonist.

End of chapter four:
"Come with me," Night Walker said, and Lew followed him to his own hogan where Night Walker shoved Lew's suitcase aside. He sat crosslegged and told Lew to do the same. Running Rabbit was behind them and sat also. When Strong Elk returned, he had wood for a fire, some of it green, Lew noticed.

While Strong Elk built a fire, Night Walker left, then returned with a long-stemmed pipe. "I must call Wakan," he said.

Beginning of chapter five:
Lew had difficulty breathing in the thick smoke that filled his hogan. The burning green wood smelled sweet, and the bark strips used as tobacco for the pipe tasted unusual. He wasn't sure whether his light-headedness came from the fire smoke or the tobacco smoke, but his ears became more sensitive to Night Walker's chants as he drifted off. At one point during the ritual, Night Walker and Strong Elk each placed their hands on his shoulders. They did the same to Running Rabbit, who did likewise to them. Lew copied their movements and felt the strength in their bodies, the resonance of their chanting. What seemed like minutes one moment felt like hours the next. Time seemed to have no bearing on what they were doing, yet time did pass as Lew moved in and out of clear-headedness.

What Persun did not do, and you will want to check your own manuscript for this mistake, is tell us how Strong Elk piled the sticks together, how many times he had to try to light the fire before it blazed, or what Night Walker drew from his pouch or canister and put in the pipe, or where the others sat and how they sat, who started the chant and what it sounded like—before the smoke grew thick. Persun could have done all of that—if it was important to focus upon, for plot or characterization reasons, and *if it fit with the shift of time that he wished*. His chapter opens midscene in the immediate future absent extraneous details.

When writers fill in all of the small actions leading up to the heart of a scene, agents or editors might criticize it, labeling it "too much 'business.'" Part of managing your choices in time (order, sequence, and shifts) has to do with keeping your literary balance on the log going downstream—sticking to what matters and staying aware of movement. Many people think that log-rollers, as they are called, find the one ideal spot and stay there. In reality, they are always moving their feet, compensating with small or larger movements to keep in sync with the river and their body equilibrium. That's exactly what you need to do to create the right timing in your novel. Stick with each mattering moment.

FLASHFORWARD

Many writers are afraid of making a big leap in time and instead end up with a lot of slow-moving "and then this happened, and then this, and then this, and finally..." Don't hesitate to cut out interim time, whether it is an hour, day, or decade, to get the story to the next mattering moment. To keep the reader on track, you will need to signal the shift in time. That can be done as easily as "an hour later," or "ten years passed," or by posting a new date and place—for example, "December 7, 1941, San Francisco." When you go over your novel and find places where you are dragging the reader through time, and the story tension lags, existing primarily to cover chronology, here is what to do: cut, cut, cut; then flash forward to what will advance the plot.

FLASHBACK

Flashback is a technique for filling in necessary information and events that occurred in the past. You can supply this need by narrating the past in summary or by creating a scene, a dramatization that re-creates the events. In effect, this latter kind of flashback makes the reader experience the past event as though it is happening in the present.

Some writing authorities will tell you never to use flashback, but there are three occasions where summarizing the past or re-creating it are ideal:

1. interspersing narration of the past into and between scenes in the present
2. in a prologue or as a first scene in chapter one, often followed by a flashforward
3. as the primary story in a frame structure

Other than these three uses, early flashbacks in a novel rarely succeed. They stall forward motion. When you begin a novel, your primary duty is to launch the plot, invite readers to bond with the primary characters, show characters ensconced in first conflicts that reveal stakes and raise suspense, and lay the foundation for the five-stage dramatic arc. Flashbacks slam story motion into reverse. They force-feed readers with exposition—backstory—and with author briefings about the characters, their history, their lives, and their motivations. *Readers don't care*, not until they have become involved and invested in your protagonist and the story.

The reason writers often succumb to narrated flashbacks, even beginning as early as page one, first paragraph, is that readers need orientation and understanding, and the author doesn't know any other way to do this except by narration, often supplying blocks or pages of "telling." The second reason is that it is difficult to discern what your readers will absolutely need to know versus what they can wait to know.

Another temptation is to create flashbacks within flashbacks as the need to explain takes the author from the near past into the longer-ago past. Before you know it, you're back at the Pleistocene era when all the reader really wants to know is what the heroine will do next now that she's been served with divorce papers.

Can a flashback beginning on page one, line one, ever work? Not in *narration*; at least I haven't seen this done. Instead, authors provide at least a first paragraph of the protagonist in the present before they enter a flashback. In contrast, a re-created flashback scene can open a novel, especially in a prologue.

Flashback is a technique to master, along with the other elements of craft, one you will need to use correctly throughout your novel, either by summarizing the past or by re-creating it. As a general rule, avoid blocks or chapters of narration—which will have to be told well—as well as fully developed, re-created flashbacks until you have entered the middle of your novel, and after at least one big crisis or scene of high drama. Wait until you are certain you have captured your reader and know how to skillfully narrate.

Within the technique of dealing with the past, develop versatility with four types of flashback:

- narrated
- re-created
- a mixture of narrated past and re-created past
- a mixture of story present with the narrated or re-created past

Narrated

Based on my experience with aspiring novelists, about one-third will include narrated backstory that is unnecessary on page one *and* a page or pages of narration within chapter one. As a result, most momentum into the main story is lost and the novel sinks from the weight of it all. A big problem is that narrated flashbacks do occur in abundance in published novels. What's the difference? I see strong style, with concrete descriptions and unique details of character, place, and the past. The writer uses techniques of movement covered in chapter seven. Embedded in the flashback summary may be the novel's theme or the central character conflict. For instance, here is a successful, narrated flashback from *Middlesex*, Pulitzer Prize–winner by Jeffrey Eugenides:

I was born a week after New Year's, on January 8, 1960. In the waiting room, supplied only with pink-ribboned cigars, my father cried out, "Bingo!" I was a girl. Nineteen inches long. Seven pounds four ounces.

That same January 8, my grandfather suffered the first of his thirteen strokes. Awakened by my parents rushing off to the hospital, he'd gotten out of bed and gone downstairs to make himself a cup of coffee. An hour later, Desdemona found him lying on the kitchen floor. Though his mental faculties remained intact, that morning, as I let out my first cry at Women's Hospital, my *papou* lost the ability to speak. According to Desdemona, my grandfather collapsed right after overturning his coffee cup to read his fortune in the grounds.

This narrated flashback continues another few paragraphs, ending chapter one. A narrated flashback, well-placed, can be very efficient to compress backstory, also called exposition, freeing you to continue with active scenes in the story present.

Re-created

Re-created flashbacks feature scenes or portions of scenes replayed as if in the present, although the event took place in the past. It is one of the fascinating manipulations of time that authors can make: from the story present, flashing back to the past and re-creating an event then as if it were happening now—what I think of as a mini-flashback, a film clip with a voice-over. Here is an excerpt from *Suspicion* by Barbara Rogan, which follows several paragraphs of narrated flashback. Emma is the protagonist.

> ...Alicia watched her approach with an assessing eye and a faint smile.
>
> "Well," she said as Emma stood before her, "one sees how. What remains to be discovered is why."
>
> "Why what?" Emma asked; and if Alicia had known her better she might have taken heed of her tone. Instead, Alicia smiled as if the answer were too obvious for words and said, "Have a seat, my dear."
>
> Emma saw herself turning and walking out, and for a moment she was tempted. Maggie would have done it, and thrown in a few choice words to boot. But this was Roger's mother. Alicia must care for him. There must be something here to salvage.

The re-created flashback scene is fully developed and continues for two more pages. In total Rogan includes nearly ten pages of narrated, re-created, and a mixture of narrated and re-created flashback. The reader, however, is well into the book, to nearly page 100, and fully hooked into this suspense ghost story.

A Mixture of Narrated Past and Re-created Past

A mixture of narration and re-creation can give movement to a flashback. When well written, the reader becomes absorbed in learning about the past. This setup creates an immediate understanding of character that the reader doesn't have to wait for or have parceled out. As a technique, it would probably be used often if more writers knew how to "tell well," incorporating a sense of movement, conflict, and suspense into explanation, techniques you'll learn or improve by reading about "tell-well" in chapter fourteen.

Continuing with the excerpt from Rogan's *Suspicion*, Emma's future mother-in-law disapproves of her marriage to her son because of class.

Narrated flashback first:
For two years, there was no communication between the Koenigs elder and younger, but when Zack was born, Emma took it upon herself to send Roger's parents a birth announcement. Three weeks later, to her amazement, a large parcel arrived containing a complete layette from Saks and a note penned in Alicia's elegant hand. "To Zachary, from his grandparents. God bless."

Then, a re-created flashback:
That night at dinner she showed the gift to Roger. "We should call and thank them."

"Send it back," he said. "I can't imagine how they even heard."

"I sent them an announcement."

Roger looked at her. "Did you," he said.

"Roger, they're your parents. And the only grandparents Zack has."

She fished Alicia's note from her pocket and passed it over the table. "'To Zachary, God bless.' You don't think they're reaching out?"

"To him, not us. You notice not one word's addressed to us, the proud parents."

A Mixture of Story Present and Narrated or Re-created Past

After they hook the readers with their openings, many authors, published and aspiring, successfully mix the present story and the past story, using narrated or re-created flashbacks. In *Sharmila's Book* by Bharti Kirchner, chapter one begins *in medias res*, in the middle of action. Sharmila, an educated American woman of Indian descent, newly arrived at Indira Ghandi International Airport, prepares to meet Raj, the man her mother arranged for her to marry.

> I still can't believe I agreed to an arranged marriage. I, Sharmila Sen, a thoroughly modern, thirty-two-year-old Chicago-style woman. I wear a power suit by day and teach aerobics evenings in skin-tight Lycra that my sari-clad mother says are both shameful in the eyes of the gods....

Chapter two supplies backstory narration of Sharmila's teen years, college, and dating. Then Kirchner makes a transition into several re-created flashback scenes. In one, Sharmila has lunch with her mother to quiz her about her arranged marriage to Sharmila's father—and about love. At the end of chapter two, Kirchner makes a smooth transition from the past to the present:

> My friends were shocked by my decision. "You're doing what?" said one. "You haven't even met him. You don't know what you're getting into."
> Now standing at the passenger reception area of Delhi airport, I think to myself that maybe I should have listened to her warning. Here I am all alone in a strange land, thousands of miles and several oceans away from home....

In chapter three, the author returns the narrative to the present and into active scenes.

Even though a mixture of the present and the narrated and/or re-created flashback is a common technique, any form of flashback appearing early in a novel can be ponderous and stop the story movement. With skill like Kirchner's, by integrating dialogue, action, reaction, thoughts, emotions, and small stage action, and by taking advantage of these and other techniques of movement, you can make your novel richer for it.

SUMMARY OF SHIFTING TIME

Every story moves inexorably along its time line toward its climax and resolution. Yet, along that time line, every fiction writer must master the skill of shifting time: overlapping present (two scenes, two characters, same time), stepping into the immediate future, flashing forward, and flashing back to integrate a summary of the past into the present, or to replay dramatic events in a scene. Not all techniques need be used in every novel, but knowledge of and facility with them will help you create a stronger revision.

As you revise your novel, the following reminders will help you make best use of manipulating time:

1. Time is putty in your hands; don't hesitate to change it—for greater movement, dramatic intensity, and variety.

2. Find spots in your story that lag and delete them and use a flashforward to a greater mattering moment.

3. Consider a one-time use of overlapping present—the present repeated in each of two character's viewpoints at the same time and place, but reserving this powerful manipulation of time for an event of strong emotional impact and plot significance.

4. Find any place where you have used a narrated flashback or a re-created flashback scene. Ask yourself if you have established enough forward motion, suspense, and character development in the present story to capture reader interest in the past. Study other novels that use a flashback as you have used it and compare whether yours works as well. The safe road is to postpone or delete flashbacks from any beginning sequence unless you plan a frame structure that begins in the present and flashes back for most of the book.

Grammatical Tense/Immediacy of Time

As you have experienced, another aspect of time was your decision about whether to write your novel in present or past tense. During revision, decide if your original decision was the best one, correct common mistakes, and use tense changes to increase impact, as we'll cover next. Although most writing books discuss tense in terms of the present, past, and future, English grammar regarding tense is far more complex. I urge you to review grammar, something good to do periodically, especially before revision. I recommend this website, http://owl.english.purdue.edu/handouts/esl/esltensverb.html# simple.

We use all tenses in the course of speaking and writing, without knowing their technical names. Becoming a grammarian is in no way necessary to becoming a successful author. It's okay if you don't know a gerund from a gerbil. Yet, everything you can learn about the use of language will enhance your command of it.

Some definite opinions have arisen about which verb tense is better or stronger—present tense or past tense. For discussion, let's use the word *jump*. Simple present tense: *I jump* or *He jumps*. Simple past tense: *I jumped* or *He jumped*. Future tense: *I will jump* or *He will jump*. In a popularity contest, past tense wins the day for most novels, by a long stretch. Until the last decade or so, present tense was the territory of literary writers and past tense was the territory of all writers. I believe there was an assumption that if a mainstream or genre writer wrote a story in present tense, he or she was "putting on airs," trying to appear literary. This division of the writing world into literary and everyone else is just the tip of an interesting cultural iceberg worthy of an in-depth essay. Fortunately, the elitism that underlies it is breaking down. Not only are mainstream and some genre writers using present tense, if they feel so inclined, even writers of children's literature are sometimes using both past and present tense in one novel, and mixing first person and third person. Creativity abounds! And where creativity abounds, revision is crucial.

First, what effect in terms of the experience of time do the different tenses produce? Here is how I experience the three:

Present tense	*Past tense*	*Future tense*
Immediate	Some distance	Some distance
Intense	Temperate	Cool
Bright	Light	Dim

There are correct and incorrect uses of tense as well as uses for reasons of aesthetics and dramatic impact. Don't ignore the possibility that changing the tense of your whole book could result in a better book. Throughout writing and revising, you'll constantly select from four tenses:

- present
- past
- a mix of present and past
- future

PRESENT TENSE

When reading the present tense, the reader's sensation is as if the story is happening word by word. Immediacy creates excitement. It creates intensity and action leaps off the page. It's bright. When present tense is coupled with first-person viewpoint, the intensity is compounded, the distance between character and reader the least of all combinations. Notice the "close-up" feeling in this excerpt from *Big Numbers* by Jack Getze:

> My body aches to change position. But I'm not moving. Each ring of the telephone stings my champagne-ravaged head like a swarm of angry hornets. But I'm not answering.
>
> The redhead picks up. "This is Kelly Burns."
>
> I open my eyes. An orange sky blossoms outside Kelly's bedroom window. She's sitting on the bed, a black silk dressing gown tied at

her waist. The place smells like a Nevada whorehouse. Sex, sweat, and perfume.

Now read an example of third-person (omniscient) present tense, in *The Namesake* by Jhumpa Lahiri, a Pulitzer Prize–winner:

But bad luck trails them on the trip back to Calcutta. At Benares station, Sonia asks her father to buy her a slice of jack-fruit, which makes her lips itch unbearably, then swell to three times their size. Somewhere in Bihar, in the middle of the night, a businessman in another compartment is stabbed in his sleep and robbed of three hundred thousand rupees, and the train stops for five hours while the local police investigate.

Do you sense how the change to third-person viewpoint cools down the present tense compared to the same tense in first person? There is some distance between the reader and the character using third person, and more so with Lahiri's omniscient point of view, because of the shifts from one character to another in a more intellectual and objective way.

Using the analogy of the solar system, first person is like Mercury or Venus, close to the sun and hot. Omniscient third-person viewpoint is like Neptune and Pluto—farthest from the beating sun of the human heart and therefore cold. Limited third-person is like Earth and Mars, by comparison warm. Here is an example displaying the "warm zone," using third-person limited (one character viewpoint) present tense, from *Pigs in Heaven* by Barbara Kingsolver:

The humidity rises all week. Friday afternoon feels weighted and endless, like the end of a life. By six, Cash feels desperate. He is back at the Trading Post again, waiting for Rose to finish up. Maybe they will go to a movie. Something to take his mind away from here for two hours. But Mr. Crittenden still hasn't come to lock up and dole out his beads.

Emotionally warm, third-person limited closes some of the distance between character and reader.

A special use of present tense occurs in statements of truism, whether you write a story in present or past tense. When using past tense, writers are frequently uncertain about these statements and mistakenly put them in past tense. For instance, should they write, "Birth, death, and taxes *were* the only constants" or "Birth, death, and taxes *are* the only constants?" Present tense is correct. Another way to think of truisms is as statements of being. Unchangeable. Therefore always true in the eternal present.

Disadvantages of present tense

Independent of the pros and cons of the viewpoint choices, present tense is not without its problems and weaknesses.

- The reader can get worn out by the intensity. It's as if the verb tense is "louder" than the story.
- It can seem artificial and affected. The reader can't shake awareness of the author's hand.
- It creates more frequent use of passive and "to be" verbs. Example: "The surgical assistant is preparing the instrument tray. Mail is delivered daily. She has been living in the house for ten years."
- It doesn't fit the conventions of the genre or just "doesn't work."

If you have chosen present tense, you are probably too subjectively close to the writing to recognize if your writing is afflicted with any of these problems. Seek opinions from a critique group or astute readers. Or, take a page or two and change it to past tense and ask others to choose which they think works best.

Sometimes present tense may seem like the problem when it is not that as much as coupling it with your viewpoint choice. Using first person, you may create the impression of a self-centered character. It is difficult to provide self-description or expression of emotions without them seeming magnified—because of the intensity of the viewpoint. The prose can come across as "too much," "too intense, bright, and self-conscious." Add present tense and you have no distance at all; instead, you've created intensity and intimacy of viewpoint plus intensity and immediacy of tense.

Past Tense

Past tense is the most common of the verb tenses used in literature and, to my ear, sounds the most natural, although that may be because it is used more often and I'm more accustomed to it. There may also be substance to the fact that at some level of awareness, readers know the author has told (previously written) this story and is not now (present tense) telling it. When a writer is using a re-created flashback, for instance, perhaps in a prologue, present tense seems particularly unnatural. My hunch is that one tense will seem to fit a particular story better than another. Consider these brief examples of past tense used in three points of view: first person (using the pronoun "I"), omniscient (all-seeing, using "he/she"), and third-person limited (one character at a time, using "he/she"), and compare them to my revision of them into present tense:

> *First person, past tense:* I focused very hard on the dead geranium in his line of vision. I thought if I could make it bloom he would have his answer. In my heaven it bloomed. In my heaven, geranium petals swirled in eddies up to my waist. On Earth, nothing happened.
>
> —*The Lovely Bones* by Alice Sebold

> *First person, present tense:* I focus very hard on the dead geranium in his line of vision. I think if I could make it bloom he will have his answer. In my heaven it blooms. In my heaven, geranium petals swirl in eddies up to my waist. On Earth, nothing happens.

> *Third-person omniscient, past tense:* Stamp Paid [a name] abandoned his efforts to see about Sethe, after the pain of knocking

and not gaining entrance, and when he did, 125 was left to its own devices. When Sethe locked the door, the women inside were free at last to be what they liked, see whatever they saw and say whatever was on their minds.

—*Beloved* by Toni Morrison

Third-person omniscient, present tense: Stamp Paid abandons his efforts to see about Sethe, after the pain of knocking and not gaining entrance, and when he does, 125 is left to its own devices. When Sethe locks the door, the women inside are free at last to be what they like, see whatever they see and say whatever is on their minds.

Third-person limited, past tense: She was staring straight at him, and Danny caught a little glint in the corners of her eyes. He suddenly realized that if you scratched that porcelain surface of hers, there was some pretty hard metal underneath, and he guessed life was going to get a lot more complicated for Sterling. Danny felt like laughing at himself for thinking there could have been something between them.

—*Winterkill* by Craig Lesley

Third-person limited, present tense: She is staring straight at him, and Danny catches a little glint in the corners of her eyes. He suddenly realizes that if you scratch that porcelain surface of hers, there is some pretty hard metal underneath, and he guesses life is going to get a lot more complicated for Sterling. Danny feels like laughing at himself for thinking there could have been something between them.

As you can see, choosing a tense is a subjective decision. For me, in the above passages, present tense feels awkward in two circumstances: in the use of "I think" instead of "I thought" in Alice Sebold's excerpt, and in "he guesses" instead of "he guessed" in Craig Lesley's excerpt. In my assessment, the reason I have this discomfort is because both are "self-referencing"; holding the mirror a little bit farther away from the face—that is, past tense—eliminates the awkwardness.

Past tense is also used to refer to events in the past, no matter what viewpoint you choose. The events might be in the immediate past or the long-ago past. They might have been former scenes, now in the story past, or they may never have been scenes and are part of the backstory. We've already mentioned simple past tense such as:

"He drove down the street."

But if you wanted to describe an event before this event, you could write:

"He drove down the street, but the light had already changed."

The helping verb "had," used with a past-tense form of the verb, is technically referred to as past perfect. There is also a change, still within past tense, to refer to a single event occurring long before the immediate past such as:

"He had been given two warnings for running yellow lights."

In this case, the verb "had" is coupled with the passive "to be" verb "been" and a past tense verb "given" to represent the past.

Disadvantages of Past Tense

- Past tense is temperate, it offers some distance that is lacking in present tense, and it is light instead of bright; therefore, it can also seem mediocre. It may not highlight the style and voice of the author as well as present tense. If so, shift to present tense and see if doing so wakes you up and therefore wakes your reader. The immediacy of time in present tense may create some missing excitement in your prose that has been otherwise missing.

- In a similar manner, characterization, especially in third person (omniscient or limited) can come across flat, lifeless. You may have to overwrite, working harder on originality of prose, to project through the comfortable but sometimes too comfortable zone of third-person past tense. Sometimes all you need to do is shift to first person, and sometimes all you need to do is shift to present tense to breathe life into your characters.

- Some writers overuse the past-perfect construction "had" or some of the "to be" verbs: was, were, been. This often shows up when a writer shifts to a flashback and adds "had" to every sentence, or nearly so. The first sentence or two signals that the events took place in the distant past; the rest should be changed to simple past tense.

A MIX OF PRESENT AND PAST TENSE

There are three cases when writers use both tenses in one novel, or mix tenses within one paragraph:

1. within thought
2. for different character viewpoints
3. to refer to events in the story past when the primary story is written in present tense

Each choice alters the sense of time and pace.

Within Thought

Writers can represent thought in two ways: direct and indirect. All present-tense thought is direct: I/They/She think(s) about a vacation. I/They/She hate(s) times like these. Direct thought always uses present tense and lends all the qualities of present tense to it: immediacy, intensity, and brightness. Therefore, it has greater impact than indirect thought. Here is an example from *The Other Woman* by Jane Green. The indirect thought follows the last line of dialogue.

> "One day," she says, "you will have a daughter and she will get married, and then, please God, you will get to have *your* wedding."
>
> "You mean I was right all along?" I shake my head as I laugh in disbelief, not at what she is saying, because words don't surprise me in the slightest, but at the very fact that she makes no bones about admitting it.

Occasionally, present-tense direct thought will be italicized, for a single word, line, or a few lines, but only for emphasis. For example, the word "your" above. Or in this line from the same book: "This child may be growing in *my* stomach, may be *my* child, but as far as she's concerned this is first and foremost *her* grandchild."

Not all thought should be direct (first person, present tense) and not all direct thought should be italicized. Sometimes, fortunately not that often, I cringe to see direct thought overused, often melodramatically so. You will find italicized direct thought on nearly every page of the sweeping bestseller *The Da Vinci Code* by Dan Brown. He uses it for plain old thinking, emphasis of words in sentences that don't need it, as well as for appropriate uses—foreign language terms, important realizations or emotion, remembered voice (of Sophie's grandfather), and writings. The emphasis of first-person present tense along with overuse of questions and exclamations creates a melodramatic feeling. Here are several examples from two paragraphs:

The question startled her. *How would Robert know that?* Sophie had indeed seen the initials P.S. once before, in a kind of monogram. It was the day before her ninth birthday. She was secretly combing the house, searching for hidden birthday presents. Even then, she could not bear secrets kept from her. *What did Grand-pére get for me this year?* She dug through cupboards and drawers. *Did he get me the doll I wanted? Where would he hide it?*

Finding nothing in the entire house, Sophie mustered the courage to sneak into her grandfather's bedroom. The room was off-limits to her, but her grandfather was downstairs asleep on the couch.

I'll just take a fast peek!

I can say without qualification that I have never seen any published novel with the quantity of direct thought, overdone and inappropriate, equal to *The Da Vinci Code*, yet obviously, as a fast-paced, high-concept suspense novel, Brown's skill with plotting more than made up for other weaknesses in the eyes of the public. The moral here is that not every published author should be emulated in every aspect of craft.

Indirect thought is always represented by past tense. I/They/She thought about a vacation. I/They/She hate(d) times like these. Here is an example from the Newbery Medal–winner *Island of the Blue Dolphins* by Scott O'Dell:

> A wave passed over my head and I went down and down until I thought I would never behold the day again. The ship was far away when I rose. Only the sails showed through the spray. I was still clutching the basket that held all of my things, but it was very heavy and I realized that I could not swim with it in my arms. Letting it sink, I started off toward the shore.

A much misunderstood technique is the use of direct thought within passages in third-person past tense. That means you will allow first-person and present tense to enter a passage that is otherwise third-person past tense.

The guidelines for direct thought amidst third-person past tense are to use selectively and infrequently for:

1. strong resolve or realization
2. strong emotion
3. identifying a remembered voice, an alternate internal voice (or telepathic voice)
4. written words such as in a letter

Here is an example of strong resolve from *Ice Drift* by Theodore Taylor, in the viewpoint of his male protagonist, Alika:

> Before drifting off to uneasy sleep, Alika decided on the next day's schedule. As early as possible, they would get settled by a seal hole. Food was the priority. *Food is always a priority.* Exploring and building a larger house could come later. Miak had been right. They must prepare for a long stay.

Next, Taylor uses italicized direct thought for strong emotion. Notice how the author returns to indirect thought for the last sentence, which is more musing than emotion:

> Round-faced, puffy-eyed Miak had spent almost six months on his drifting floe before being rescued. *Six months!* Alika couldn't bring himself to think that would happen again. The good spirits wouldn't allow it, he thought.

In another place in this novel, Taylor uses direct thought to represent a remembered voice of instruction:

> Alika moved over on the sleeping platform to comfort his brother. "After we get a seal, I'll make you *aalu*," Alika said. *Make sure the meat is very lean and clean; cut it into tiny pieces and put them into a bowl, adding a few drops of melted blubber, a few drops of seal blood, and a little ptarmigan intestine, and stir briskly with your fingers.* The sauce was delicious when smeared on seal.

What these examples don't show is that although the author uses third person for his protagonist, Alika, in direct thought, "he" becomes "I." Using the second example above, instead of writing *Six months!*, the author might have written *Six months! I'll die sooner than that.* The shift to first-person present tense when an author is otherwise writing in third-person past tense creates a jolt to the reader. It has impact. It communicates, "Wake up! This is important!"

For Different Character Viewpoints

With fewer cardinal rules against using present and past tense, and first- and third-person in one novel, writers have more creative freedom to experiment. Like all experiments, some work and some don't—and the success is a subjective judgment. The most common mixture is the use of first person for the protagonist's viewpoint and third person for all other characters' viewpoints. Sometimes, present tense accompanies first person and past tense accompanies third person. In this way, the protagonist is the peacock with the most brilliance, intensity, and immediacy of story. Seldom, but it's an interesting choice, first person, *past tense* is used for the protagonist and third person, *present tense* is used for other characters. The question: Do your choices work well? Are they the best for your novel?

In the following examples from *Animal Dreams*, Barbara Kingsolver has chosen the latter: protagonist—first person, past tense; father—third person, present tense:

> *Protagonist:* I dragged my bags to the edge of the street. Carlo, my lover of ten years, whom I seemed to have just left, would be sending a trunk from Tucson when he got around to it. I didn't own very much I cared about.

> *Father:* For a long time he stands gripping the door frame, which is exactly the width of a newborn's skull and curves similarly against his palm. He watches his daughters, though there's nothing to watch....

A particularly risky and creative mixture of viewpoints and tense appears in one children's book for ages nine to twelve. In *Crooked River*, author Shelley Pearsall chose *first person*, past tense for Rebecca, her protagonist, and *first person*, present tense for her only other character viewpoint, a captured Chippewa Indian. Two first-person viewpoints! In *Crooked River*, Pearsall met the challenge of creating an authentic voice for the thirteen-year-old settler girl, the young Chippewa, and the year 1812. The excerpt that follows is in the first-person, past-tense viewpoint of Rebecca:

> I saw Augustus Root stand up and move toward my Pa. He was a lawyer from the East who had been living in our settlement for nearly two years. But I must confess, me and Laura never took much of a liking to him. Mr. Root seemed to think more highly of himself than a person should and was terribly fond of listening to the sound of his own voice.

He was also the only man we knew who still dressed in knee breeches and stockings. And truth to speak, Mr. Root's legs were nothing to look at neither. Scrawny old bird legs in white stockings....

And here is the first-person, present-tense viewpoint of Indian John. His viewpoint appears in two- or three-page sections, in italics, at the end of nearly every chapter. Formatted more like stanzas in a poem, the lowercase letters that begin lines are intentional:

when I hear the name Semo,
i laugh
inside my mouth.

the men who caught me
wanted the name
of the young Indian
who ran.
i told them
Se Mo.
shame and dirt.
the gichi-mookomaanag
wandered in the woods
for hours
calling out
shame and
dirt. Shame
and dirt.

while my son
Little Otter,
slipped away.

inside my mouth
i laugh.

Disadvantages of Using Both, or a Mix of Present Tense and Past Tense

- According to entirely subjective opinions, using two or more view-points in different tenses simply may not work. This is a less common choice and thereby will be noticed for the technique itself. That spotlight adds risk of failing, but also kudos for success.
- If you duplicate viewpoint choices, as in writing two first-person viewpoints (or even more), in addition to using past and present tense, you could easily confuse readers, not only by the double first-person viewpoints but also by changing the readers' orientation in time.
- A common mistake is to overuse direct thought, especially for thinking or musing. Too much first-person present tense within a story that otherwise uses third-person past tense creates an amateurish tone. It's as if the author is calling "wolf," pointing reader attention to italicized content that does not deserve the emphasis and may be, in fact, unimportant.

FUTURE TENSE

Just as language provides tense changes to refer to the present and past, it also provides verbs to signal anticipation of the future. Present tense is used to represent events scheduled for the future: "The flight departs at 3 p.m." We also use present tense to indicate intent to act on a state of being we have in the present: "I'm starved. I'm going to get a bite to eat." If that intent is less firm and might or might not happen, then the verb "will" is added: "I'm getting hungry. I'll get a bite to eat." Or a promise such as "I'll get the money to you tomorrow." If there are more teeth in that intention, the verbs "will" and "have" reflect that assurance: "You'll have the money by tomorrow at 9 a.m. or my name isn't Jimmy." If you're a faceless phone worker answering customer service calls, you might use a passive form of future tense, "will" plus a "to be" verb: "You will be receiving the check by Thursday."

Another case of future tense reflects the possibility or potentiality of a future action. The verbs are "conditional," including "can," "could," or "would," such as "I would if I could but I can't." Since these verbs appear in just about every story, a typical sentence might read: "She would tell me bedtime stories, and I would listen, although sometimes, I would fall asleep or wake up later and I would hear my parents talking in low murmurs."

Problems with Future Tense

Like an old-time record player with a stuck needle, writers get caught in repetition of the verbs "will," "could," or "would." Although either construction has its place in the nuances of meaning, incorrectly used or repeated they add words and therefore distance from the greater force of a strong verb. In nine out of ten cases, fewer words create stronger prose than more words. For example, look at the before and after revision of the sentence used previously:

Before
She would tell me bedtime stories every night, and I would listen, although sometimes, I would fall asleep, or I would wake up later and would hear my parents talking in low murmurs.

After
Every night, I listened to her tell me bedtime stories, although sometimes I fell asleep or woke up later to hear my parents talking in low murmurs.

In terms of story time, "would" and "could" make actions seem distant, less substantial. They are hesitant, as if the viewpoint character is ambivalent, not willing to commit. The simple past-tense verbs are direct, immediate, and carry conviction. And they use fewer words.

SUMMARY OF GRAMMATICAL TENSE/IMMEDIACY OF TIME

The reader's experience of immediacy and urgency varies according to the verb tense an author uses. Present tense holds the greatest sense of "right now," past tense gives the sense of a small time lag, and future tense conveys a comfortable "sometime" feeling in most of its forms. Although past tense is commonly used, you may prefer present tense or even a mix of tenses. Problems occur when tense choices ring falsely, flatten style, confuse, or don't fit the expectations of a genre.

Pace/Rate of Time's Passage

Most of us are familiar with the gears of a car—whether that vehicle is a five-speed manual transmission or an automatic—and how they affect speed (and even direction). You shift from a lower gear to a higher one to move faster. The concept correlates to the idea of pace, the rate of a story's progress. When do you speed up and when do you slow down? How do you show a faster pace? A slower pace? Like the options in a car, the passages you write can be very slow, slow, average pace, fast, very fast, reverse, neutral, or park—i.e., stop.

REVIEW—PUNCTUATION AND PACE

Punctuation can become one of your greatest aids to signaling speed changes. What if the writer added ellipsis points to this word repetition? "Dead...Dead." In terms of pace, ellipsis points signify a pause, and can allow the word, as in this example, to resemble a sustained note in music. The meaning of the word "hangs around" longer to permeate the atmosphere. In this case, the pause lets the meaning of "dead" soak in.

Of course, a period means to stop motion, the comma to pause, the semicolon to pause longer—a busman's stop sign. The colon means to stop but to prepare for motion within what follows. The exclamation point is a stop as well, but with the oomph to reach out and send a zinger to the reader's emotions, one way or another. The question mark is more like a pause than a stop in that it is supposed to prod the reader to go to the next sentence to learn the answer. The dash, formally called the "em dash," provides a pause that adds an aside before continuing with the original thought. Quotation marks that close a line of dialogue or set off the special use of a word are decorative, a convention of American rules. They are not used in other countries in the same way, and they have no meaning for pace. A line space such as a line break (in manuscript, a double-spaced line before continuing text) is called a soft break. It signals a pause, and usually a change in time, most often a jump to the near future. A hard break is presented as three asterisks centered in the middle of a line and preceded and followed by a double-spaced line. It signals a full stop and preparation for a change in time, forward or backward, and usually a change in character viewpoint. Even though punctuation is one of the tools of pacing, we have less freedom to use it as we wish due to punctuation rules.

STOP

One-word sentences tell a reader to stop; they equal pulling back the reins on your horse. Maybe there is a snake ahead. They stop motion and have the power of putting the reader on alert. Word repetition creates emphasis, drives home meaning, but it also elongates the moment, which can build great suspense in certain contexts: "Hurry up! Hurry up or the train will hit us! Hurry up!" The elongation of the moment through word repetition can also deepen meaning. "Published. Published!"

Disadvantages of Stop in Pace
Overuse of one-word sentences, or short sentences, leads to the feeling of an inexperienced driver pressing hard on the accelerator and then hard on the brakes and giving passengers whiplash. If you overuse any aspect of craft that should intensify impact, you sacrifice some degree of that impact. If you under use or never use the one-word or short sentence to create sudden stops in the flow, you're missing opportunities for impact and emphasis. Your style will be weaker.

SLOW PACE

Slow pace facilitates character development. With more time, you can develop interior thoughts such as memories, wishes, fears, dreams, and concerns. You can develop feelings, either by showing them as body language or by describing them. You can open up a section of your story with riff-writing and explore development of plot, character, and imagery.

When a character reacts to events, you may wish to slow pace to explore feelings and options. A developed section that explores a character's feelings, thoughts, dilemmas, and decisions is called a *sequel*, according to the late Jack Bickham, a master teacher of fiction technique. In this context, sequel means what follows; specifically, what follows a scene. Scenes are actions directed toward goals. Sequels are reactions directed toward new strategies to reach those goals. Because sequels are reactive and reflective, their pace is often slow, at least slower than scenes.

Specific types of sentences slow pace: Typically, the longer the sentence, the slower the pace. Compound, complex, and compound-complex sentences slow pace. One element of craft—narration—slows pace. It involves telling information, backstory, or context, and narration also includes description.

Here is an example of slower pace from *Beach Music* by Pat Conroy:

Interior character development: I was deeply aware that I was walking beside one of the lives I had refused to live. Once our pasts were entangled in such complex ways that it seemed we were meant for each other if we allowed ourselves to surrender to the simplest lures of inertia.

Sequel: When I arrived back home it was not yet three in the afternoon; I saw Ruth Fox sitting on the veranda of my father's house. I turned off the motor and laid my forehead against the steering wheel of the car. I felt bruised and exhausted to the point of insensibility. Closing my eyes, I did not think I could bear one more confrontation or ghost from my complicated past.

Narration—character description: She had the same doe-eyed self-conscious beauty that in Shyla was edgy and explosive. In Martha, it held its breath, tiptoed into view, took one by surprise whenever she released that tightly coiled spring that controlled the nerve centers of her own quiet uncertainty. Even makeup could not hide the trapped, distracted girl masquerading with pearls and a black dress as a woman of the world.

As you can tell from reading the prior excerpts from Pat Conroy's writing, his style inclines toward slower pace; it's languorous.

Disadvantages of Slow Pace

To imagine what it's like to overuse a slow pace, recall what happened to Dorothy and her friends when they crossed the field of poppies in *The Wizard of Oz*. Their motions became slower and more ponderous. Finally they ceased moving and fell asleep, drugged by the flowers. Don't let that happen to your readers. They can shift from alpha brain waves into delta brain waves. Before you know it, no matter where you live, you'll hear them snoring. Too much slow-paced writing is hypnotic. At best, the reader is lulled; at worst put to sleep or utterly bored. Pat Conroy has an amazing style, great originality in every aspect of his writing, and he is known for his development of his characters. Although I have chosen excerpts that present less movement within narration, *Beach Music* is replete with passages of "show/tell" where narration contains movement within it, turning static telling into vibrant forward motion.

FAST PACE

Simple, short sentences create fast pace. The shorter the sentence, the more it approximates an accelerated heartbeat. That means fight, flight, or excite—adrenaline. If shorter sentences are interspersed with occasional one-word or two-word sentences, the stop can act like a power booster to propel the sense of pace to a higher level. Likewise, one-sentence paragraphs can signal faster pace, the sentence standing in for what in slower pace could have been a page or at least a paragraph.

Because scenes are goal-directed action, they *move*. Depending upon the type of action, the movement varies. If your character is in mortal danger, pace is typically fast. Besides the obvious (action increases pace over narration), remember that dialogue is an important form of action. It, too, increases pace, unless it gets weighed down with information. Kill-and-thrill genres often have a greater proportion of dialogue to narration. To heighten drama, increase pace. Piling conflict on top of conflict increases pace.

The example that follows shows fast pace in dialogue. The hero, Garth "Garv" Carson, is being tracked and pursued. The novel is a "wacky" humorous mystery, *Tailed*, by Brian M. Wiprud.

> I dialed again, this time to home. Otto picked up.
>
> "Alo. This is Garv Carson Critters. Please, tell to me if help."
>
> "I miss you, too, Otto. Put Angie on."
>
> "My Got, Garv! Must come home before soon! Very, very important to come before soon. KGB vas here…"
>
> "KGB?" That was Otto's word for bad guys or the police, which on occasion had been both.
>
> I heard the phone change hands.
>
> "Garth?"
>
> *"Nicholas?"*
>
> "Do exactly what I say and don't ask any questions. Get away from where you are, as far as possible. You remember the bar where I last saw you?"
>
> "What's going on? Where's Angie?"
>
> "The bar. Do you remember?"
>
> "Yes, the—"
>
> "Don't say it! Just call me there in an hour. Stay off the interstate. And don't call back here."
>
> The line went dead.

Although short sentences emphasize quickened pace, sometimes extra-long, compound sentences can represent faster pace through the accumulation of short actions. Again, from this same novel:

I was racing across the parking lot, jacket and shoes cradled in my arms, dodging cars at the pumps, leaping over fuel hoses, headed for where I last saw the Pixie dry-cleaning van, my bare feet slapping the macadam. In my half-dressed state, I must have looked like a boudoir interloper on the skedaddle.

Disadvantages of Fast Pace

Continuous fast pace can exhaust all but your adrenaline-junky reader. If a novel is primarily action, danger, and dialogue, what suffers is characterization, which offers a great complement—and rest station— to an action-adventure novel. Too much fast-paced writing can have the unintended effect of melodrama and slapstick. Instead of reading a thriller, you feel like you're watching an old reel of the Keystone Cops. Or, for anyone who is too young to remember seeing these old clips, you feel like you've overdosed on a triple Godzilla espresso drink.

SUMMARY OF PACE/RATE OF TIME'S PASSAGE

Nearly all of our punctuation marks directly relate to pace, and a review of the section in this chapter as well as chapter two on outside-in style will help you use those tools to full advantage in revision. Deciding on the rate of time's passage, which is directly affected by pacing, is a learned and intuitive skill, and is all-important in terms of movement and suspense. In one of your revisions, use the basic options for pace—stop, slow, and fast—matching them with your story for impact, character development, and action.

Success in holding your reader's interest and satisfying your promises to them by way of the kind of book you are writing depends greatly on your skill with movement and pace. Even though you will eventually need to integrate the many revision techniques, take on a few goals at a time with each revision, rather than trying to find and revise everything at once. Certainly, every effort you make toward bolstering impact and suspense through all the techniques of movement and pace will strengthen your present novel and improve your chances of a sale.

MAKEOVER REVISION CHECKLIST
Time and Pace

Shifting Time
☑ Avoid:
- Strict chronological order; some or many time shifts are typical.
- Details of every little action, i.e., "business"; only include what matters.

☑ Overlapping Present—same time and place; two scenes, two viewpoints
- Use sparingly, perhaps once in a novel.
- Always use a different point-of-view character for the replay of the time.
- The setting may vary.
- Use overlapping present to emphasize an event of dramatic significance.
- Consider the consequences of using this powerful technique at your story beginning.

☑ Immediate Future
- Break off midscene—when tension is high, or start next scene or chapter in immediate future.
- Use a same or different point-of-view character.
- Immediate future excludes minutiae of insignificant actions.
- Use this technique to build momentum and forward thrust.

☑ Flashforward
- Use to cut out interim time of less or no significance.
- Flash forward to a mattering moment.
- Orient reader with a transition or post a date and place.

☑ Flashback
- Avoid flashbacks, in general, at a story beginning, except when you have chosen a whole-book frame structure.
- Avoid flashbacks within flashbacks.
- If you need to present an event in the past—a viewpoint character who will not appear in the novel or who will come in much later, or

have other good reason—re-create a flashback scene in a prologue.
- Provide a signal to the reader such as a transition to mark entry and
  exit from a re-created flashback.
- Weave in brief threads of flashback narration (information, character
  and setting description, events and motives, wishes and dreams,
  family and ancestry—whatever the reader *must* know) amid
  forward-moving scenes.
- Integrate active verbs and narrated movement into narrated flashbacks.

Grammatical Tense/Immediacy of Time
- Do: Review grammar before revising.
- Don't: Let the review intimidate you. Whatever soaks in soaks in.

☑ Present Tense
- Rewrite several pages of any past-tense novel using present tense.
- Change your viewpoint in present tense—from first to third, or vice
  versa.
- Choose what feels most natural to you and gives greatest vibrancy
  to your writing.

Advantages:
- It's the closest to our real-time experience of the "now."
- It carries the excitement of a story unfolding before the reader's eyes.
- It may be thought of in some quarters as stronger stylistically.

Disadvantages:
- Its intensity and immediacy can wear a reader out.
- It can come across as artificial, affected, and awkward. The reader
  can't shake awareness of the author's hand.
- It creates more frequent use of passive and "to be" verbs.
- It may not fit the conventions of your genre, or it may just "not work."

☑ Past Tense
- Rewrite several pages of any present-tense novel using past tense.
- Change your viewpoint in past tense—from first to third, or vice
  versa.

- Choose what feels most natural to you and gives the greatest vibrancy to your writing.

Advantages:
- It is the most common choice and may seem more natural.
- It may better match the reality in the relationship between the author and the story—that is, he or she has already written (past tense) the story we are reading, and the reader senses this.
- It offers a slight distance between the viewpoint character and the reader, which provides more "room," ease, for the writer.
- It won't wear the reader out because it is "warm" not "hot," "light" not "bright."

Disadvantages:
- It may seem mediocre, too indistinct and stylistically flat compared to present tense.
- Dramatic events may lack immediacy and excitement.
- The past-perfect construction that uses "had" may be overused.
- Flashbacks may be overused.

☑ A Mix of Present Tense and Past Tense Thought
- Direct thought is always in first person and present tense, except when there is a reference to the past.
- First-person viewpoint already communicates direct thought, although you can use present tense (if the story is in past tense) for emphasis.
- Reserve direct thought for emphasis of a word or phrase, strong emotion, realization, resolve, a remembered voice or other voice, or for reading written material (subvocalizing in the mind). Use direct thought sparingly.
- Avoid adding "I thought" or "He thought" after the clause of direct thought, if possible.
- Underline direct thought for later italics.
- Avoid using direct thought for low-key thinking, musing, or puzzling.
- Indirect thought retains the past tense if a book is written in past tense. It retains the first- or third-person pronouns that the rest of the story uses.
- Indirect thought has no special punctuation.

☑ Viewpoint Combinations
  ▪ Typical combinations are first-person protagonist and third-person other point-of-view characters, or dual first-person points of view, rarely three or more first-person viewpoints in one novel.
  ▪ Tenses may differ along with viewpoints—suh as first-person present with third-person past, or vice versa.
  ▪ Risks: The combination may simply "not work," seem awkward or contrived, or confusing, especially dual or multiple first-person viewpoints.

☑ Future Tense
  ▪ Read for overuse of the verbs "will," "could," and "would." Where possible, replace with past-tense verbs, usually already within the sentence.

Pace/Rate of Time's Passage
☑ Review of Punctuation and Pace
  ▪ Period—stop; comma—pause; semicolon—pause longer; colon—stop and prepare for motion; exclamation—stop with emotion; question mark—pause and ponder; ellipsis points—pause for the unsaid; dash—pause for an aside or interruption; quotation marks—unrelated to pace; soft break—pause for shift to immediate future; hard break—stop and jump to future, past, or change of viewpoint.

☑ Slow Pace
  Advantages:
  ▪ Facilitates character development—interior thoughts (memories, wishes, fears, dreams, concerns); feelings (describing or showing with visceral physical reactions)
  ▪ Opens up any aspect of story—a chance to use riff-writing
  ▪ Develops imagery and symbolism
  ▪ Can develop a sequel—reaction to events through feelings, thoughts, working through a quandary, reaching a decision, and acting.
  ▪ Can use slower pace in between sections of fast pace, for contrast and to provide reader with a breather.

  Sentence types:
  ▪ Longer sentences
  ▪ Compound, complex, compound-complex

- Longer paragraphs
- Longer chapters

Elements of craft:
- Narration slows pace (supplying information, backstory, description).
- Flashback slows pace by directing reader to the past.

Disadvantages:
- Reader loses interest.
- Plot suspense can't overcome inertia.

☑ Fast Pace
Advantages:
- Can develop scene structure—introduce goals, stakes; show effort toward goal and opposition or obstacles; show character trying different approaches and finally succeeding or not, ending with a disaster or twist.
- Keeps reader interest high.
- Adds zip to style.
- Creates movement and heightens suspense.
- Builds momentum toward big turning-point scenes and climax.

Sentence types:
- One-word or a few-word sentences—stop the reader; arrest attention.
- Simple, short sentences match fight, flight, or excite—adrenaline.
- Occasional one- or two-word sentences operate like a booster rocket.
- One-sentence paragraphs—give visual movement; sense of compression and propulsion.

Elements of craft:
- Clear goals, high stakes
- Scene structure
- Greater use of dialogue
- Greater use of action
- Delete all extra words

Disadvantages:
- Exhaust reader
- Short-change character development
- Can backfire and create melodrama or slapstick humor

☑ Summary:
You can have a brilliant plot and fascinating characters, but problems with time and pace can undermine success. In addition to doing your own revisions, find a friend who is a writer, and ask for critical feedback about these areas.

PART THREE

Characterization Endures

CHAPTER NINE

Viewpoint

Options Viewpoint can be a hazy concept even for writers who think they understand it. To learn about viewpoint "slips," including why and how to avoid author intrusions, read on. Even if you feel certain about your handling of viewpoint, in this chapter you can double-check the effects of viewpoint on the level of intimacy you establish between your characters and your reader. If you see your problems as having more to do with "anchoring" and deepening characterization, then review the checklist at this chapter's end, and go to chapter ten.

When you wrote your novel or short story, you had to make decisions about your character cast, including who was to take the starring role and from what psychic distance. What does that mean? Psychic distance refers to the nearness of the reader to a character. The term viewpoint refers to which character is relating the story and from what distance. I'll never forget one writing class I taught at the community college. I had given a homework assignment to craft a novel beginning. When I asked for a volunteer to read aloud, one woman eagerly raised her hand. Teachers are always grateful for such students. As she began, however, I broke out in a sweat and kept watch on the class reactions. To tell the truth, I feared I might get fired if someone was offended and filed a complaint. The woman opened her novel with a graphic sex scene. The psychic distance was far too close to open a novel in this way.

Like picking a setting for your camera lens, you can tell your story as a "close-up" or as a "landscape." You might have decided to mount your camera on yourself or another person to capture what it is like to be one person viewing outward. The choice you made has a profound effect on the reader's vicarious experience, and you may need to revisit who you chose to tell the story and from what psychic distance and viewpoint.

Nearly every writer unintentionally and occasionally slips out of one viewpoint into another one. Nearly every writer has places where he or she "zooms" out to a distant viewpoint or zooms in too close for what the character would be experiencing. Either by a sudden viewpoint change or by misusing it, a writer can shift reader focus too quickly or erratically, giving the reader whiplash.

Not only do your viewpoint choices directly affect characterization, they also directly affect movement and your manipulation of time. Change a viewpoint from one character to another and you automatically create a shift. Change a viewpoint and you head in a different direction. That's movement.

Viewpoint Choices

When you decided to grant a viewpoint to a character, whether you knew it or not, you made a commitment to develop that character's thoughts, feelings, and physical responses. Readers also vicariously experience what the character sees, hears, smells, tastes, and touch-feels. Viewpoint, not just action, directly affects the distance between character and reader. To know whether or not you need to make a change, consult the review below, which covers the four basic viewpoints and one special case, and the pros and cons of each one:

- Single
- Dual
- Limited—multiple
- Unlimited—omniscient
- Omniscient opening only (special case)

Single Viewpoint

If you wrote your story through the viewpoint of your protagonist and that's all, you chose a single viewpoint, whether you decided on telling the story from the first person—I/me—or the third person—he, she/him, her. That means that your entire novel will stay in the perspective of the protagonist. Any question about sequence, what comes next, will only involve questions of managing time shifts, not viewpoint changes. Here is a brief example of a single, first-person viewpoint, followed by a single, third-person viewpoint:

> *First-person:* My heart whacked against my rib cage, and every few seconds, I hiccupped. I didn't know what else to do, so I clicked and scratched around the lot. I wrapped the light poles and pulled the tape tight. I encircled the body and the potential getaway car.
>
> —*Briga-doom* by Susan Goodwill

> *Third Person:* Before dark Sam went up to the attic window in the rear of the house and carefully searched the hillside with his binoculars. He wished it were not so heavily wooded, that there were not so many huge gray boulders, so many deadfalls.
>
> —*Cape Fear* by John D. MacDonald

ADVANTAGES OF SINGLE VIEWPOINT

The greatest advantage is that you can develop your protagonist in depth, because the hero is involved on every page of the novel, and you can keep the reader completely focused on the story goal. Because short stories are short, a high percentage of them feature a single viewpoint. Otherwise, the protagonist risks being two-dimensional, even if the story adds only one other character viewpoint.

DISADVANTAGES OF SINGLE VIEWPOINT

Several disadvantages dog the choice of a single viewpoint. Too much of one voice can tire readers out—or bore them—for lack of diversity. You'll have a more difficult time creating plot complexity that comes from subplots or action not involving the protagonist. You will be missing the "color" and personality offered by diverse points of view. A genre such as category romance may favor dual viewpoints, or one like thrillers may favor multiple viewpoints.

Dual Viewpoints

Two-character viewpoints allow development of your protagonist and one other character, whether the relationship between the two is as relatives, friends, lovers, work partners, or as protagonist and antagonist. Viewpoints in children's literature are almost always confined to one or two characters—or to the author's viewpoint (unlimited/omniscient described below). That means that you will have to decide if you selected the best character for each scene when you wrote your novel. It also means that you should have signaled readers of your plan to use more than one viewpoint soon after beginning the story.

In my experience, faster-paced novels work best opening with a brief scene in one character's viewpoint immediately followed by a brief scene in the other character's viewpoint. This plan helps the reader become immediately attuned to the dual viewpoint format. Most of the time, the first character in a novel is the protagonist. Later in your book, you may create a sequence like a Ping-Pong game, bouncing between viewpoints from paragraph to paragraph or page to page—within the same scene. This is common in the middle to last parts of category romance novels, but it is not exclusive to them either. Or you may establish a pattern alternating chapters or parts of the book by viewpoint.

In *Getting Rid of Bradley*, Jennifer Crusie has written a fast-paced, humorous romance story. Two and a half pages into her novel, she switches from her heroine to the hero, who also receives two and a half pages for his introduction. After that, the scenes in each character's viewpoint differ in length and development, but the viewpoints alternate throughout the novel.

Dual viewpoints can use third person for both characters (the most common), first person and third person, or first person and first person. Amy Tan uses first- and third-person viewpoints for her dual viewpoints in her novel *The Bonesetter's Daughter*. She also uses a far different sequencing of them for her literary novel than Crusie used for her genre novel. After a six-page beginning in LuLing Liu Young's first-person viewpoint, Tan introduces part one, in Ruth's third-person viewpoint, Ruth being LuLing's daughter. Part two shifts back to LuLing, and part three finishes the book in Ruth's point of view. Because Tan explores a mother-daughter relationship, cultural and historical complexities, and identity, the scenes and chapters are far longer than in a light, humorous romance. Both the sequence of viewpoint changes and the depth of story and character development differ from novel to novel and from genre to genre.

ADVANTAGES OF DUAL VIEWPOINTS

An immediate advantage of dual viewpoints is the development of two characters and their relationship in depth. The reader stays stimulated with two different voices and the greater complexity of relationship of two lives. If one of the viewpoints is the antagonist, the chance for constant conflict, accompanied by understanding of motivation, is greater.

DISADVANTAGES OF DUAL VIEWPOINTS

The disadvantages of dual viewpoints are few. If the writer creates a pattern of alternating chapters, the pattern in itself can seem too contrived or forced. Another possibility is that the character other than the protagonist is more interesting and "colorful" than the protagonist. If one of the characters is an antagonist, depth of development can create too much empathy for the antagonist and a split loyalty. In any case, it's important to have a clear protagonist with a five-stage dramatic story line and to use the other viewpoint character as a polishing stone. And the hero or heroine should have more scenes than the other character.

Limited—Multiple Viewpoints

Technically, any number of viewpoints greater than one is considered "limited" multiple viewpoints. Most novels with multiple viewpoints rotate them among the characters, depending on their roles and importance. Thus, if you created five character points of view, then you'd share scenes and chapters among those five characters, and no more.

A limitation on the number of characters with viewpoints provides control, definition, and structure. Your hero or heroine should always have the most "face time," the term used in the TV industry for time in front of the camera. Your protagonist should have more scenes, more pages, than any other character. Some novels have a second character so involved with the protagonist that he or she may be like a secondary protagonist, and have nearly as many viewpoint scenes. Other characters have bit parts. You can bring in their viewpoints when your hero and another main character (or two) cannot be present to view the action or cannot be in the location you need. Use a character's viewpoint on a need-to-know basis—when the reader must know that perspective for the sake of the plot and forward motion.

Frequently, thrillers and suspense novels use limited multiple viewpoints, either beginning in an antagonist's point of view or in the protagonist's point of view. An antagonist opening is popular because it introduces the threat and begins the adrenaline surge that is part of the enjoyment of thrillers or suspense novels. Similarly, a victim's viewpoint sometimes opens mysteries, ending with the victim's death or disappearance. Not only does this make for a dramatic beginning, but the reader gets to know the victim to some degree, which facilitates caring that the person who did them harm be punished.

In the paranormal thriller *The Seventh Sense* by T. J. MacGregor, the antagonist is one of the story's five, limited, multiple viewpoints in part one, with more introduced in parts two, three, and four. He—Frank Benedict—a frustrated lawyer, opens the novel in a substantial, seven-and-a-half-page first chapter. In itself, that length signals that this character will be a well-developed antagonist. The reader will share a lot of time in his reality.

Although five characters hold viewpoints in part one, chapter one is split between Frank and the protagonist, Charlie. She is an FBI agent who is the sole survivor of Frank's hit-and-run accident that took the lives of her husband and unborn child. Then, Mac-Gregor devotes chapter two to Frank and introduces his wife as a third viewpoint character in chapter three, before returning in chapter four to her protagonist—briefly—for just a page or so. Giving this much development early in the novel strongly establishes her primary characters in depth and creates the "setup" that will allow her to provide shorter scenes for these characters later. Interestingly, her protagonist in real-life would be grieving deeply, perhaps "out of it" due to injuries and loss of the baby. In terms of sequencing and pace, the author wisely did not reduce suspense with hospital scenes of an inert, shocked, and drugged protagonist. Instead, MacGregor introduces all four other viewpoints, not returning to truly develop the protagonist until part two, when the opening line is, "On the tenth day after the accident, Charlie surfaced from the black ocean that had held her captive."

ADVANTAGES OF LIMITED MULTIPLE VIEWPOINTS

Novels are more complex and potentially more interesting with a cast larger than one character. Two viewpoints define a novel as centered in some way on the relationship. A three- or five- or ten-viewpoint novel opens the door to a story about more than relationship or inner-personal psychology. Through the many characters, readers vicariously experience a variety of subjective societal, generational, or geo-political forces and problems. Multiple-viewpoint stories have more scope.

DISADVANTAGES OF LIMITED MULTIPLE VIEWPOINTS—AND SOLUTIONS

There are three common weaknesses in all multiple-viewpoint stories that you should double-check during revision:

1. Granting a viewpoint to a character who doesn't require one.
2. Creating a number of viewpoints beyond your skill to develop them.
3. Failing to develop the psychological arc—the wound, need, and weakness—of each viewpoint character.

It's easy to create unnecessary "extras." Ask yourself, can the "work" done by that character be accomplished by another viewpoint character? For instance, let's say you're writing a contemporary mainstream novel about a family faced with constantly adjusting their expectations and strategies for survival in our ever-changing and contradictory (if not chaotic) society. You've cast viewpoints to the husband, wife, two teens, the husband's boss, and a minister. Do you need separate viewpoints for the boss and minister? Do they have vital scenes separate from the presence of the other family members such that you must give them each a viewpoint? Can you pare away a viewpoint of one of the teens? If the husband is your protagonist, can you give the wife a viewpoint and not the kids? Tightening is sharpening. No viewpoint or sequence should be gratuitous or extra.

Few writers can carry off a "Russian" novel with one hundred characters and their names and nicknames. I'm exaggerating, but if you believe your novel requires seven or ten viewpoints, knowing that each one must have enough development for three dimensions and uniqueness of personality, consider putting this grand idea aside until you have written several novels with fewer viewpoints. That's what T. J. MacGregor did before writing a novel with a dozen view-point characters. If you feel up to the task, first determine how many viewpoints you have and what proportion of the novel is told from each one. You can accomplish this in several ways: Use a story-board—a large piece of paper or giant marker board—and make a blueprint that maps out all of your scenes. Use color markers to dif-ferentiate the viewpoint characters. Step back and look at the pro-portion of each character's scenes. Or use color-coded index cards or sticky notes, one color per character. That makes your quantity of writing devoted to each viewpoint immediately visible. Then, examine where and how you can cut some viewpoints, melding two into one, or redistribute emphasis to three main characters, relegat-ing the "leftover" viewpoints to non-viewpoint minor characters.

Remember: You have an obligation to develop each viewpoint char-acter's psychological arc as well as actions and reactions to events.

That means revealing an inner problem, wound, universal need, weakness, hope, fear, attitudes, backstory, and emotions. Choose to keep viewpoints for characters whose psychological needs most reflect, parallel, or are opposite to your protagonist's. This lends more unity of theme and meaning to the protagonist's struggle.

Unlimited—Omniscient Viewpoints

Omniscient means all-seeing and unlimited. On the surface, this choice looks ideal. You can do anything you want, any time! But the reality is that without the "container" of one character's view-point within one scene, one section, or one chapter, the majority of novelists have a far more difficult time keeping their readers oriented and interested. Because omniscient viewpoint creates the most awareness by the reader of an author telling the story, a writer with particularly original style may choose it. Where the unlimited viewpoints, called omniscient (all-seeing), is in its splendor is in the hands of gifted writers, usually writing in the literary genre. I doubt that these writers give any thought to sequence. The transitions are so seamless, they seem natural.

Elizabeth Strout is one such writer. In her novels, the impact occurs from pages of narration about the characters, with interspersed dialogue and partial scenes, as well as from fully developed scenes, and the accumulation of author storytelling in the organic whole of the novel. Her paragraphs tend to be longer, but here is a shorter paragraph from *Amy and Isabelle* that shows the distant omniscient viewpoint, used by a master writer:

> While the other women tended to sigh a great deal, or make trips back and forth to the soda machine, complaining of backaches and swollen feet, warning each other against slipping off shoes because you'd never in a hundred years get them back on, Isabelle Goodrow simply sat at her desk with her knees together, her shoulders back, and typed away at a steady pace. Her neck was a little peculiar. For a short woman it seemed excessively long, and it rose up from her collar like the neck of the swan seen that summer on the dead-looking river, floating perfectly still by the foamy-edged banks.

Literary writer Elizabeth Strout and legal thriller writer John Grisham make strange bedfellows, but the thriller in its many forms is another genre where many authors write in unlimited multiple viewpoints. Whereas literary writers use the freedom and distance of omniscience to create a whole world and, through dozens of angles, depth of characterization, thriller writers use the choice to place emphasis on the intricacy of powerhouse plots. But when you change viewpoint as often as TV channels, characterization can be thin in plot-oriented stories. Both genres rely heavily on narration—author telling. The following excerpt from *The Brethren* by John Grisham captures the style and focus of thrillers, a complete contrast from the use of omniscient viewpoint in Strout's literary writing:

> Defensepac, or D-PAC as it would quickly and widely become known, made a roaring entry onto the loose and murky field of political

finance. No political-action committee in recent history had appeared with as much muscle behind it.

Its seed money came from a Chicago financial named Mitger, an American with dual Israeli citizenship. He put up the first $1 million, which lasted about a week. Other Jewish high-rollers were quickly brought into the fold, though their identities were shielded by corporations and offshore accounts. Teddy Maynard knew the dangers of having a bunch of rich Jews contribute openly and in an organized fashion to Lake's campaign. He relied on old friends in Tel Aviv to organize the money in New York.

ADVANTAGES TO MULTIPLE UNLIMITED OMNISCIENT VIEWPOINTS

The advantages of writing with unlimited multiple viewpoints are many for the writer capable of using it. For writers with strong voice and original style, why should there be limits? You can write epics that mirror whole eras in society or generations and histories of people. Your canvas can cover a thirty-by-sixty-foot wall in the Metropolitan Museum of Art. For an exceedingly complex story, perhaps one that also spans a multiple book series as is common in fantasy and science fiction, omniscient viewpoint creates the elbow room for the diverse number of characters and subplots. This challenging selection may be the only one that works.

DISADVANTAGES TO MULTIPLE UNLIMITED OMNISCIENT VIEWPOINTS

Rarely is the unlimited viewpoint written well. In fact, it creates the most distance between story and reader, and the least emotional involvement and character depth. Characterization is spread too thin over too many characters to develop any in depth. Unlimited omniscient fosters abrupt shifts and transitions, a bland voice, over-reliance on "telling," and author intrusion. Without the tight focus on one character pursuing an important scene goal, suspense can be diluted, readers' identification with any one character sacrificed. I estimate that about a quarter of the novels I receive for editing have these problems, most of which disappear with changing to a limited multiple, dual, or single viewpoint.

Omniscient Opening Only—A Special Case

Even though a writer might choose first person, third-person limited, or multiple limited viewpoints, a widely accepted convention accepts an opening in omniscient viewpoint, usually that of the author/narrator. It is still a risky choice, because omniscient viewpoint is more distant, an overview, and therefore may prove difficult in hooking the reader. The writing must be outstanding. Frequently, such openings focus on setting—geography, an aspect of nature, or a town. They may describe a family or couple. Or they may discuss a philosophical concept, often related to the theme. After a brief omniscient opening, extending anywhere from a paragraph to a page or two, these omniscient beginnings then narrow into a limited viewpoint—first person or third person (limited or multiple).

Here is an omniscient opening to a novel featuring an outstanding description of setting from *Way of the Wolf* by E. E. Knight:

Northern Louisiana, March, the forty-third year of the Kurian Order: The green expanse once known as the Kisatchie Forest slowly digests the works of man. A forest in name only, it is a jungle of wet heat and dead air, a fetid overflowing of swamps, bayous, and backwaters. The canopy of interwoven cypress branches shrouded in Spanish moss creates a gloom so thick that twilight rules even in midday. In the muted light, collapsing houses subside every which way as roadside stops decay in vine-choked isolation, waiting for traffic that will not return.

With the exception of an omniscient opening, my advice to you is to avoid unlimited multiple viewpoints, unless you are a highly skilled, naturally gifted, or powerhouse plot writer. If you are not persuaded, given the disadvantages I've listed, revise a scene in a limited, subjective viewpoint and compare with omniscient. And seek the honest opinion of another writer, astute reader, or professional editor. Then choose.

What Can Go Wrong Managing a Viewpoint

Although the last section addressed advantages and disadvantages of each choice, other problems occur in the nitty-gritty of each viewpoint. Among the most common are the following:

- Overuse of "I" in first person
- Too much focus on the self in first person
- Author intrusion in third person
- Viewpoint slips in multiple viewpoints
- Hovering viewpoint
- Abrupt viewpoint changes

OVERUSE OF "I" IN FIRST PERSON

Revision is an ideal time for weeding out repetitions of the pronoun "I," which has a way of breeding when you're not looking. I've crafted the following example and followed it with a revision to show one way to reduce the population:

Too many repetitions of "I": I dragged my tired body up the mountain trail. I scraped my shins against pointy boulders, and I slipped on rain-slick wild grass more than once. I stopped and looked up at the dark clouds. I could be struck by lightning at any time, I thought. I had no choice. I had parked my car in the lot at the trailhead, and the only thing I could do was hurry.

Recognize that in first person, you'll have some paragraphs where this many uses of "I" are necessary. As you gaze at your manuscript, you can spot the pronoun leaping off the page. Especially if you see that it is abundant and most of your sentences begin with it, you are probably overusing it.

Revision to reduce number of uses of "I": I dragged my tired body up the mountain trail, scraping my shins against pointy boulders and slipping more than once on rain-slick wild grass. I stopped and looked up. Dark clouds swirled in angry clusters. The prospect of being struck by lightning increased with each passing moment. But there was no choice. The shelter of my Honda awaited me in the lot at the trailhead. The only thing I could do was hurry.

TOO MUCH FOCUS ON THE SELF IN FIRST PERSON

When the focus stays on a character who is too self-reflective or self-reacting, the effect is narcissism or neuroticism. The same amount of focus in third person will not create the same preoccupation with self as in first person. Frequent repetitions of "I" are partly to blame. But the effect also has to do with the immediacy and intensity of first person. Here is my example:

Too much focus on the self: I recoiled at her insult, belittling me, making me feel worthless, incompetent, and worst of all stupid, and in front of my peers. I was reminded of the time in high school when I'd sat on some gum in the bleachers and didn't know that it had stuck to the back of my skirt. Everyone who passed me laughed and I didn't know why. It was the worst day of my life. My body shook and tears threatened. I felt ashamed. I felt angry, and then angry that I felt ashamed. And she did it in front of three other call center workers. And then just walked away as if she hadn't told me my call volume was too low.

Although it is more difficult to create this self-preoccupied world than to spot it when reading and editing, the effect will be of an immature person and of too much or too many emotional reactions, either narrated or shown in the body.

Revision to reduce sense of self preoccupation: When my supervisor expressed her unhappiness with my call volume, it sent me rocketing back to high school and the embarrassment of the day when everyone laughed at me because I had gum stuck on the back of my skirt. At the time I thought of it as the worst day of my life. Amazing that small events like that can make you feel bad years later. I felt my hot cheeks and glanced at my three nearest coworkers. They must have overheard her.

Although I expected them to be stifling laughter and sharing little jokes about me, they weren't. In fact, one rolled her eyes at the receding figure of our boss, and the second one just shook her head. The third girl leaned toward me and whispered, "Like she doesn't have anything better to do. Don't let her get your goat."

AUTHOR INTRUSION IN THIRD PERSON

Because third person includes use of the pronouns "he," "she," and "they," there is more likelihood for intrusion by the author, which is technically an omniscient viewpoint, into a character viewpoint. Usually, the writer has a goal—to inform, describe, or offer an opinion—which temporarily replaces the character-driven scene goal.

Outside-in description of point-of-view (POV) character: Her blue eyes sparkled in the Caribbean sun, the rays making her dark red hair glow as if on fire. It was so good to be alive. Ella felt like dancing.

In her viewpoint, she can't see her own eye or hair color, or the special effects. Almost every novel has a few places where the author jumps outside and provides something the POV character wouldn't see or know.

Writers want to keep setting present, along with a sensory experience of it, or they want to make the scene more atmospheric, and setting is a great way to do that. In example one, the author has entered to do this such that the intrusion of setting is unnatural; it breaks the flow and is not organic to the character's experience at the moment.

Example one—intrusion of setting: Bruce had never seen a dead body, except at the funeral home, and never like this—lying in a pool of blood on the sidewalk, mouth agape, flies buzzing. Bruce stood there, fascinated and shocked at the same time. A fall breeze of the onshore wind reaching inland brought a chill to the air, helping maple and oak and birch leaves depart from their branches. Bruce felt in his pocket for his cell phone.

Readers enjoy novels where they learn history, details of careers and industries, and how things are created. The trick is to work these details into your writing through the natural thoughts of the character, coloring them with the opinions and personality of the POV character, and including them in places where the POV character would be reflecting on them.

Example two—intrusion of author wishing to inform: It was the first time Llew had stepped foot in a courthouse, and this one was old, dating back to 1845. After the county fathers argued through one bitterly cold December night, they decided that the courthouse should be located in Springfield due to the population base. Llew paused in the rotunda and admired the inlaid designs on floor tiles and wished she had brought her camera. She'd like to capture that design and work it into one of her paintings. After the courthouse was built, everyone agreed that a wise decision had been made.

Most of us can spot a lecture or sermon a mile away. The purpose of some novels seems to be that the writer needed a soapbox to get something off his or her chest. Let story and a character's passion, based on a need rooted in that character's personal history, drive your story, and offer your opinions only when they are directly relevant. Often, a long section of dialogue is also suspect for pontificating. If the dialogue is especially long, it must be called a monologue. A short, emotionally powerful statement of conviction will have more impact than a long argument. "My dear, I don't give a damn," said Rhett Butler (changed by Hollywood into "Frankly, my dear..."). Catch these types of author intrusions and avoid the temptation!

> *Example three—author intruding with beliefs or pontificating:* After Jerry watched from the Al Gore documentary, he stopped for a Ben & Jerry's, then walked back to the parking lot. If the politicians didn't stop bickering and start acting, the planet was going to make itself uncomfortable or uninhabitable for human beings. Everyone should write their congresspeople, regularly, and send letters to the editor, and of course conserve, conserve, conserve.

In this next example, the last clause is in high diction associated with higher education or the use of language common to the established (versus nouveau), upper-income class. The sentences prior to this last clause are in informal diction and may correspond to someone with less education or lower-class upbringing.

> *Example four—diction doesn't match character:* Like his pappy and his grandpappy before him and, Billy Bob supposed, like his greatgrandpappy before him, he got the touch. Touch the sick people and they get well. He glanced at his watch; if he were going to arrive at the Dickinson's by their dining hour, he had better leave now.

Throughout your revision process, keep an eagle eye out for author intrusions. Every novel I've worked on has some, in one form or another.

VIEWPOINT SLIPS IN MULTIPLE VIEWPOINTS

Because you get to know all of your characters intimately, it's an easy mistake to slip from one to another in the same scene, even if briefly. What's so bad about that? You're breaking a rule to develop

one character's point of view per scene, unless your chosen viewpoint is unlimited. Sometimes, of course, breaking a rule works and
sometimes it doesn't. Nearly all writers slip up sometimes.

> *Example of slipping from one viewpoint to another:* Chris hefted
> his end of the television, being careful to keep the weight balanced
> and his back straight. He resisted the urge to wipe sweat on his
> sleeve. Louis knew how he felt. Together they carried the monster
> TV down three flights of stairs to the truck.

> *Correction of viewpoint slip:* Chris hefted his end of the television,
> being careful to keep the weight balanced and his back straight. He
> resisted the urge to wipe sweat on his sleeve. He saw Louis twitch
> as a bead rolled into his ear, and knew he wasn't alone. Chris made
> sure not to hold the monster TV too high for Louis's sake and led
> the way down three flights of stairs to the truck.

Notice, too, that when the viewpoint slip is corrected, the POV of
Chris has more development. These kinds of slips are common and
need correction in revision.

HOVERING VIEWPOINT

This problem is slightly more difficult to spot, especially in your
own work. The feeling for the reader is that the character is moving through the action and setting almost like a ghost. The point of
view is like a helium balloon tethered on a string to a kitchen chair,
or what I call "unanchored." Here is an example I've adapted from
one of my student's works:

> Brittany hardly noticed her mother's church friend, Mrs. Rodriquez,
> and her husband. It was the awesome guy who caught her eye.
> Even in the dimmer light of their entry hall, his skin looked as if
> he had spent eighteen summers surfing, although by his curly black

hair and caramel-colored eyes, she guessed he might be one of the Puerto Rican guys from Franklin Street.

The women embraced and her father shook hands with Mr. Rodriquez. Brittany remained seated as the cute guy approached her. "Hey," he said, "I'm Felipe." His smile showed dimples.

This is a fairly short example to detect this problem, but what makes it a hovering viewpoint is the lack of clarity about where Brittany is relative to the guests arriving at the door, as well as the surprise of her sitting. When the reader reaches that piece of information, they'll wonder where she is sitting, whether she was standing and is now sitting, and other details that would put Brittany into the setting. Also missing is any of Brittany's sensory experience to anchor us in her physical body. The passage contains no sounds, smells, taste, touch, or visceral body experience in reaction to seeing this handsome dude. We see only a few visuals and hear a bit of his dialogue (and no other sounds), and share Brittany's thoughts. The point of view has not yet landed.

ABRUPT VIEWPOINT CHANGES

This problem can take place from section to section or chapter end to chapter beginning. It is different from a viewpoint slip in that the writer is intentionally changing viewpoints, having completed a section or chapter. It is primarily a problem of a missing transition. Below I've made up an ending to one chapter and a beginning to the next:

End of chapter: Alone in his tiny office, Otto could no longer stare at the computer screen and finish Crawford's audit. Nor could he do what he most longed to—forget this job, go home, and take his beloved Sophie into his arms. He pushed his chair back, folded his hands behind his head, and closed his eyes. At least he could visit her in his daydreams.

Beginning of next chapter: Mrs. Blackstein frowned at her. "Are you certain you want to take a second job when your first one already consumes your weekends?"

"It will help the time fly," Sophie said, grabbing her shoulder bag and briefcase. She turned away from her mother-in-law and hoped she had not read Sophie's irritation with her.

If your reader has not previously met Mrs. Blackstein, or perhaps has not yet had a scene from Sophie's point of view, the transition is abrupt. If your readers pause and mutter, "Huh," then you've lost them—and you never want to lose your reader. One of the problems in the example of the chapter beginning is that it is out of viewpoint. Readers can't identify the main character until they reach the last clause in the line I created for Sophie: "...hoped her mother-in-law..." Everything prior to that is objectively seen and heard. To go from Otto's longing for Sophie to Mrs. Blackstein in dialogue (even assuming the reader has "met" Mrs. Blackstein in prior sections) may be too abrupt. Here is one possible smooth transition for the example:

For the three weeks that Otto had been gone to work on the Crawford audit, Sophie had successfully bit her tongue. She wasn't sure she could continue much longer against her mother-in-law's harping at her.

Another abrupt viewpoint change occurs when an author is writing in omniscient. A shift within a paragraph from one character's subjective viewpoint to another character's subjective viewpoint can send a reader "OOB": out of body.

Some of the mistakes mentioned above can contribute to lack of dimensionality of your characters. The next chapter introduces the pillars of deep characterization and the importance of defining and developing your theme.

MAKEOVER REVISION CHECKLIST
Viewpoint

☑ Viewpoint Choices
- Single—using first person or third person
- Dual—two characters
- Limited multiple—more than one but a limited number
- Unlimited multiple omniscient—no limit, including author's viewpoint
- Omniscient opening only—special case for a novel beginning

☑ Single Viewpoint
Advantages:
- Protagonist developed in depth
- Hero involved on every page
- Reader kept focused on story goal

Disadvantages:
- One voice tiring, can bore the reader
- Plot lacking in complexity or "color" supplied by subplots and other viewpoint personalities and action
- Single viewpoint may not fit genre preferences

☑ Dual Viewpoints
Advantages:
- Development of two characters in depth
- Two different voices, complexity of relationship of two lives
- With one viewpoint that of antagonist, chance for constant conflict, depth of reader understanding about antagonist's motivation

Disadvantages:
- A pattern of alternating chapters can seem forced, too "even."
- Character other than protagonist may be more interesting or developed
- If other character is the antagonist, development of a viewpoint may create too much reader empathy, splitting loyalty to hero

☑ Limited Multiple Viewpoints
Advantages:
- Greater control, definition, and structure offered for writer
- With many viewpoints, the novel is more complex, potentially more interesting, greater scope.
- Focus can turn outward on societal, generational, or geo-political forces.

Disadvantages:
- May be too many and unnecessary character viewpoints
- May exceed writer's level of skill
- Obligation to develop each point-of-view character's actions and reactions, and inner story arc: story goal, backstory, needs, wishes, fears, hopes, and emotions

☑ Multiple Unlimited—Omniscient Viewpoints
Advantages:
- Writer can take on a giant story, a large cast.
- Story can mirror large societal movements and eras, cover generations, span countries and worlds and time.
- Facilitates writing multiple subplots, dozens of character lives, and complexity of ideas and overall story
- Fits genres with many books in a related series such as fantasy and science fiction or multigenerational epics
- Can showcase author's style and unique writing

Disadvantages:
- Loss of "container" of one character, one viewpoint per scene
- Reader can become disoriented, distanced, and uninterested.
- Awareness of author writing the story can distract reader.
- Characterization can be spread too thin, not enough development of hero and main characters.
- Prone to author intrusion, especially blocks of narration for information, character description, and backstory
- Precludes tight scene structure based on one character's goals and needs
- Shifts of viewpoint can be abrupt, transitions needed or inadequate.
- Overview voice can be bland.

☑ Omniscient Opening Only—A Special Case
- An accepted option for opening a novel—often used for establishing setting, geography, country or world, era, sociopolitical or familial backdrop, or author philosophy
- A risky choice requiring outstanding writing

☑ What Can Go Wrong Managing a Viewpoint
- Overuse of "I" in first person
- Too much focus on the self in first person
- Author intrusion in third person
- Viewpoint slips in multiple viewpoints
- Hovering viewpoint
- Abrupt viewpoint changes

CHAPTER TEN

Character Dimension and Theme

Options If you worry that your characters lack dimensionality, and you aren't sure of your theme or how it connects to characters and plot, you're in the right chapter. If you want to create more personality, an edge to your characters, start here and read through part three. If you are seeking ideas for strengthening descriptions and character narration, skip to chapter fourteen.

---

know a few people, very few, who can spout plot summaries of novels on request. What most people remember, I contend, are their favorite characters. Mystery writers seek to create a series character so strong and unique that he or she will carry a series and a readership who loves that character. Who are some of your favorite sleuths? Nero Wolfe? Amanda Peabody? Kay Scarpetta? Jim Chee? Easy Rawlins? I'm just scratching the surface, I know. Which other famous characters rush to mind? You could probably fill a page with names.

Many literary agents reject manuscripts saying things like, "It just didn't excite me," or "Characterization superficial." Of course, your story may need work on style, plotting, and suspense, the kinds of improvements covered in the prior sections. However, I have seen a nearly universal phenomenon in the manuscripts I work on: Almost every novel that is finished in the eyes of the writer still needs work on characterization. To begin with, the following components of characterization are frequently missing or underdeveloped:

- Backstory wound
- Universal need/personal yearning

- Strength and weakness
- Clarity of theme

It's common for plotting to eclipse character development. Most published authors come back in revision to "layer it in." This makes great sense since novelists know the characters far better after completing the early drafts.

Backstory Wound

You're bound to have revealed quite a bit about your protagonist and main characters through action, reaction, thoughts, goals, and description. Although these areas can be underdeveloped, I also see little backstory that bears directly upon the psychological story.

The types of past events that mesh best with the inner characterization story tend to be those that have left emotional wounds. The idea is that until protagonists come to terms with their pasts, they will always control them. Resolving the past supplies deep motivation for their actions. To be free of the wound means they will be able to transform themselves and their lives. In most books, the critical past event has taken place before the present story. However, in some novels, the inciting incident that begins the story *is* the significant wounding event.

Let's take a look at a few characters, their backstory wounds, and their motivation to change. For instance, a death of the protagonist's parents is a common trauma leaving a wound, often supplying motivation for the character's profession or passion.

In Patricia Cornwall's Scarpetta series, Dr. Kay Scarpetta, medical examiner and forensic pathologist, watched her Sicilian father die a slow death when she was a girl. Since then, she has chosen to work around death, solving crimes. She once had a serious relationship with Mark, who died in a London bombing. Scarpetta is a perfectionist and has few close relationships. Might her career, her need to create as ordered and perfect a world as possible, and her few close relationships have something to do with the backstory event?

In the Harry Potter series by J. K. Rowling, Harry's wizard parents were killed by the Dark Lord Voldemort, although this antagonist was left in a state that is neither dead nor alive. He is obsessed with killing Harry. And Harry wants to find out exactly what happened to his parents and put Lord Voldemort out of existence and fulfill the special destiny that is his parents' legacy.

Mother-daughter conflict, the need for the daughter to separate and define herself, is a common source of backstory trauma in many novels.

In *White Oleander* by Janet Fitch, when Astrid, her protagonist, is twelve years old, her beloved mother, Ingrid, a famous poet, murders a man who scorned her. The rest of the story is about Astrid's miserable life. She gets shuttled in and out of foster homes. She's raped, she's shot by a stripper, and, as she grows up, needs to find evidence of her mother's love, to punish her mother for abandoning her, and especially to claim personal power and a life of her own.

In *The Divine Secrets of the Ya-Ya Sisterhood* by Rebecca Wells, Siddalee, called "Sidda," is a successful play director in a life that is fulfilling her dreams. But she isolates herself with doubts about her plan to marry after her narcissistic mother, Viviane, or "Vivi," has a full-blown temper tantrum over what Sidda has been quoted as saying about her childhood in a major feature interview. Vivi's elderly women friends, the Ya-Yas, give Sidda her mother's scrapbook photo album to help Sidda put together the puzzle pieces of memory. She faces the realities of her childhood with an alcoholic mother and an abandoning and alcoholic father. She recognizes how she and her siblings suffered from her mother's physical and emotional abuse. These realizations result in a confrontation between Sidda and Vivi, and in Sidda's eventual decision that she can continue with her successful and happy life and marry the man she loves. She is not her mother.

A legitimate question is whether a character must have a wounding event in the past to become dimensional. And the answer is no. In some of our greatest literature, the story problem is sweeping, of such magnitude that it becomes the defining motivation for all of the characters. Freedom from bondage—of any type—defines

The Adventures of Huckleberry Finn by Mark Twain. Survival and family unity define *Grapes of Wrath* by John Steinbeck. Justice and racial equality define *To Kill a Mockingbird* by Harper Lee, and the lack thereof in *The Invisible Man* by Ralph Ellison. Yet these and other "Great American Novels" have developed characters based on an author's skill in etching them as unique individuals within the larger context of society and history. These characters have a past; they may not have an individual wound that defines the dramatic arc as much as they experience the greater problems afflicting all of the characters—and often their readers.

List or summarize the references you made to your protagonist's past, even if that past begins the novel. Then write a summary of which events in the past are significant to your character and your genre. What have you already written, or could construct, that can serve as the primary backstory event that leaves a psychological wound on your protagonist? How can you use that backstory wound to supply need, illuminate character, *and* drive the plot? This is a critical question to answer in revision.

Universal Need/Personal Yearning

Showing your protagonist struggling to fulfill a universal need such as respect, justice, or even revenge adds to the creation of a dimensional character. While nearly all of us in real life struggle to fulfill most of the universal needs over the course of a lifetime, fiction is selective. *Choose one need for one novel.* I call the traumatic or dramatic event in the past the "hole in the soul." The protagonist and main characters will always be seeking to fill it, to heal. That's how important these universal needs are—for love, family, community, identity, leaving a legacy/making a difference, trust, faith, and so forth. The protagonist's quest to fill the hole in the soul creates the internal or psychological story. This character arc is all-important in *driving* the character's actions in the external story.

Why can't the protagonist get that need met? Because of the wound, the hero has a blind spot. He has not been able to let the past go, and the wound makes fulfillment of the need always just beyond reach. I have long believed that thinking in terms of a "universal need" is too abstract. The hero experiences it as a personal yearning, and suffers for want of it.

These deeper aspects of characterization are not frivolous; they provide the unity and coherence of one theme. For instance, if you're a geeky kid with a lightning bolt etched on your forehead, and your parents have died and you're living with some abusive moronic relatives, you not only grieve the loss of your parents, you need to find "your people"; you yearn to belong. How do you do that? You have to find out who you are—a wizard—and go find other wizards, but you are different from them, too. You still have that lightning bolt scar on your forehead and an evil force that keeps stalking you. You're singled out; you belong, but...

Once you know what your character suffers, you can name the yearning and show it in the foreground or background of every page. A death in the near past means your protagonist will be grieving and need healing to move on into a new life without the loved one. A death in the long-ago past can create different yearnings, depending on the nature of the loss. An unsolved murder can give a yearning not only for justice but also for understanding. A mistake with dire consequences drives a yearning for redemption, for self-forgiveness. Any one of these and the myriad other universal needs, as experienced deeply and personally, should consume your protagonist, while at the same time, they are compelled by the plot. Consumed, compelled, and in conflict. Dramatic intensity. Any backstory wound with any universal need can work in any genre, from humor to tragedy, from L'Engle's *A Wrinkle in Time* (need: self-confidence) to Clancy's *The Hunt for Red October* (need: freedom).

Jennifer Crusie, author of nearly twenty humorous women's romance novels, opens *Getting Rid of Bradley* by revealing the backstory wound:

> "I've never known anyone who was stood up for her own divorce before," Tina Savage told her sister. "What does it feel like?"

You gain dimensionality as soon as you begin to build the scaffolding of the psychological side of your characters. Once you are certain of your protagonist's yearning, go through your novel and make sure you show it, within scenes (action events) and sequels (reactions and processing), and in dialogue and narration. When given the opportunity of filling that need, show instances when your character seizes the opportunity, sometimes to the detriment of gaining an important scene goal. In that way, your protagonist's yearning can become an obstacle to your plot and another source of conflict.

"Not good." Lucy Savage Porter tried to smooth her flowered skirt with a damp hand. "Can we go? I'm not enjoying this." She gave up on the skirt and clutched her lumpy tapestry bag to her as she glanced around the marble hallway of the Riverbend courthouse. "Bradley signed the divorce papers. We don't even need to be here."

Her protagonist, Lucy, is introduced as a victim of her ex-husband's truancy, and we're given a subtle clue about her problem when she *asks permission* to go from her sister. Throughout the three-page opening scene of Crusie's novel, protagonist Lucy Savage identifies her psychological problem and yearning that will unite the internal story of the novel. In one place, she thinks, "Maybe the problem was that she wasn't an independent kind of person." To make sure the reader is in sync with the protagonist's inner goal, Crusie ends this first section of chapter one as follows:

Lucy closed her book with a thump. *Nobody's ordering me around anymore. From now on, I'm going to be independent even if it is illogical. I'm going to be a whole new me.*
    That's it.
    I'm changing.

Once you realize that the protagonist's yearning is a driving force in the plot as well as within the character, you will also see that it creates personal stakes. If a hero has made a terrible mistake, it would be devastating not to be forgiven or find redemption. If a hero has been told by authority figures that he is a good-for-nothing failure, it would be devastating not to achieve self-respect or self-worth. Make sure you have two stories and two sets of stakes in your novel: the outer stakes of the plot goal and the inner stakes of the universal need.

To produce unity and coherence, as well as one theme, don't give each point-of-view character a yearning divergent with the protagonist's yearning. Craft yearnings that are supportive and parallel, or opposite but related. One agent called this "the master effect." For instance, if a character yearns for freedom, then the antagonist should act to deny that freedom. Other characters can be allied with one side or the other. That's part of the success of Tom Clancy's *The Hunt for Red October*. Jack Ryan, CIA analyst, will fight to the death to ensure freedom and the American way of life. Marko Ramius, captain of the *Red October*, seeks his freedom by trying to defect to America from the Soviet Union. He is being pursued by the entire Soviet Atlantic fleet under the command of Marko's one-time student Viktor Tupolev. Everyone is acting to defend freedom or deny it. The highest plot stakes are an all-out war between the Soviet Union and the United States.

Strength and Weakness

As you revise, look for one of the following three problems of inadequate character development:

1. the absence of a strength or a weakness
2. the over-amplification of a strength or a weakness
3. too many strengths or weaknesses and none primary

By strength, I am referring to one quality of character that is more prominent than any others present in your protagonist (and each point-of-view character). Because all heroes show courage, what other strength is unique to your protagonist? And not overused? For instance, I think of independence and determination as among the most overused strengths and therefore not very distinguishing.

If you don't have a noticeable or unique strength for a character, one starting point is the classic "seven virtues." Translate them into modern terms and think of synonyms. Here they are:

1. Chastity—pure, right-minded
2. Abstinence—self-controlling, mindful
3. Liberality—generous
4. Diligence—industrious, careful, persevering
5. Patience—peaceful, receptive
6. Kindness—sympathizing, compassionate
7. Humility—respectful, selfless

Of course, there are hundreds of other qualities that can be outstanding strengths: brilliance, reasoning power, intuition, humor, charisma, cleverness, tolerance, leadership, inclusiveness, resourcefulness, inventiveness, and so forth.

How did your character come by his or her strength? Sometimes, it works to make a tie-in between the traumatic backstory event and the emergence of the strength. Whatever doesn't kill you makes you stronger. For instance, if your character was orphaned, she might be a super-nurturer, giving to others what she was deprived of. Or, if your character had strict, punitive parents, she might become a defender of rights or perhaps a creativity coach! She'll aim to fight suppression or cultivate potential.

If you gave your protagonist and other main characters a strength but no weakness, or if that strength is a super-strength, then your characters will be superheroes, two dimensional and ultimately cartoonlike. Since fiction aims at verisimilitude—an approximation of real life—we human beings are flawed creatures. Depth and authenticity of character mean showing weaknesses as well as strengths.

Once again, make sure you have singled out one weakness as primary. If you give any character a hounding pack of weaknesses, he will come across as tragic, comic, or both. The weakness, like the strength, may have its origins in the backstory trauma. The weakness may be the "flip side" of the strength. Faith may become piousness.

If you haven't given your characters a weakness, there are, of course, countless possibilities in human nature. For a jumping-off point, consider the "seven vices" and some of their synonyms:

1. Lust—desirous
2. Gluttony—excessive
3. Greed—insatiable, avaricious
4. Sloth—lazy
5. Wrath—raging, furious
6. Envy—covetous
7. Pride—haughty, aggrandizing, self-centered, arrogant

The antagonist should also have a strength and weakness. The "vice" should be prominent, the "virtue" minimal. Without a virtue, your antagonist becomes a Black Bart, a cartoonlike bad guy. The antagonist, too, should be three-dimensional.

Overemphasis of a protagonist's weakness makes readers not want to identify themselves with the character. You want a reader who will commit as soon as possible to the worthiness of the character, his or her heroic qualities, and the importance of the story goal. The weakness may have carved itself into the fiber of your character because of the intensity of the backstory event. The weakness is also important to show as intruding upon the efforts of your protagonist to reach the goal. That way, your point-of-view characters will sometimes oppose the very goals they seek to reach. Opposition comes from without and from within. You pick up another and necessary source of conflict—the character in conflict with the self.

Clarity of Theme

Some writers have a definite theme in mind before they begin writing. That theme may or may not be the one actually reflected by the completed story. Other writers figure that the theme will become evident as they reread the first draft. Simply put, *theme* is your novel's message. Less simply put, theme is the abstract equivalent of the protagonist's universal need fashioned into a statement of what he or she has come to learn. The theme states the personal growth or character change that completes the inner story arc. It has not been separate from the plot but has entwined with it.

You may reread your novel and still find yourself unable to articulate your theme, or you might come up with a bushel of themes. In either case, you'll need to dig deeper into your understanding of your hero to figure out one primary need and one primary theme.

What often confuses writers about knowing their novel's theme is the seduction of story. If you've done your job, your story will have captured your reader (and you!) and produced the entertainment you wished. Now someone is asking you what your novel is about. Start with an easy one-word answer—one of the universal needs, say love or healing. Then create a more sophisticated answer such as "You can't bring back a lost loved one, but you can open your heart to new loves." Or, "Life is for the living."

Sometimes, a hero must pursue a series of needs to reach the primary one. For instance, a heroine may yearn for love and family, but she won't be able to fill that need until she deals with the trauma in her past that made her feel unworthy of love. So the novel's theme will be about self-worth. The reward for claiming self-worth is love and family.

The central conflict that defines your story, your plot, and the theme that defines your character's deepest need have all been "done" before. You may have heard references to the existence of fifteen or fifty plots, with all others being a variation on them. For consideration of your present novel and for the others you intend to write, the list on page 214 may help you.

When you know the underpinnings of deeper characterization and its relationship to your novel's theme, you can diagnose many of the problems in your present draft. Follow the "bones" of backstory wound, strength, weakness—and the way those factors impede and propel the plot goal—and make sure you show and tell your character's personal yearning of one universal need throughout the story.

With these fundamentals of deep and satisfying characterization, the next chapter will give you the tools to make sure your story is character-driven, from page one on.

Time-Honored Conflicts and Themes

Basic Four

Person vs. Person (person vs. human-made forces comes under Person vs. Person)
Person vs. Nature
Person vs. God/Goddess or Immortal
Person vs. Self

Common Conflicts and Themes

Adultery
Adventure *(expeditions, quests)*
Ambition
Betrayal
Conquests *(war, occupation)*
Deliverance *(by rescuer or savior)*
Disaster *(defeats, catastrophes, falls)*
Discovery *(secrets)*
Grief *(loss)*
Hate *(relatives, non-relatives)*
Insanity
Jealousy
Love *(filial, platonic, heterosexual, homosexual; incestuous, adulterous)*
Misjudgment *(false accusation, assumption, or suspicion; mistake)*
Murder *(homicide, genocide, infanticide, of enemies)*
Persecution
Pursuit *(fugitive, the chase, persuasion)*
Puzzle *(mystery, enigma, riddle)*
Rebirth *(recovery, renewal, start-over)*
Redemption
Remorse
Revenge
Revolt *(conspiracies and revolutions)*
Rivalry *(malicious, competitive, survival-based)*
Sacrifice *(for another, for one's kin or group or country, for an ideal or belief; and sacrifice of another or an ideal or belief)*
Sex *(involving people, animals, objects; adultery)*
Supplication *(appeals and requests for assistance)*
Survival
Victimization *(the unfortunate, prey, slave, kidnapped, forgotten)*

MAKEOVER REVISION CHECKLIST
Character Dimension and Theme

☑ Backstory Wound
- Create a traumatic event in the hero's past that leaves its mark and that fits with your story, character, and genre.
- Show hero's repeating desire to resolve the hold of the past.
- Show how emotional wound interferes with character change.
- List or summarize what references you've made to the past in your novel.

☑ Universal Need/Personal Yearning
- Decide what universal need (the "hole in the soul") your hero is deprived of, due to the traumatic past.
- Show the universal need as a personal yearning and make sure your character demonstrates that yearning throughout the novel, in subtle and overt ways.
- Make sure that main characters' needs in some way mirror, oppose, or parallel your hero's need.
- Show yearning as a driving force through the story, sometimes overwhelming the drive to reach the plot's story goal.

☑ Strength and Weakness
- Check your hero's development for three problems: absence of a strength or weakness, over-amplification of a strength or weakness, or too many strengths or weaknesses and none showing as primary.
- Choose or hone one primary strength and one primary weakness. They may derive from the traumatic backstory event. Avoid overused strengths and weaknesses.
- Make sure your antagonist has a primary "vice" and "virtue" so that he or she will have three dimensions. Consider whether your antagonist and protagonist are mirror opposites in this regard.
- Show the weakness interfering with scene goals, in places in the story; thus, the hero creates obstacles through internal conflict as well.

☑ Clarity of Theme
- Translate your character's yearning, the universal need, into a statement of theme, the message of your story.
- Make sure you have one theme, not many, and that it is reflected throughout your novel.

CHAPTER ELEVEN
Character-Driven Beginnings

Options Every writer must revise a novel beginning, usually multiple times. Beginnings are complex and your decisions are many. There is wisdom in the old saying, "Well begun is half done." Read and reread this chapter, using the examples as models for your own book. Try different ways of starting your novel. Poll your friends. Then use your best version.

As you revise your novel or short story, expect to revise, rework, rethink, or otherwise fuss and fume over your beginning. Most writers do, and must. Beginnings are the most difficult to write well, and success in getting to first base with a literary agent or publisher hinges on them. There is a good reason for the difficulty: beginnings have more "jobs" than any other part of the novel. Although other chapters have addressed aspects of these functions, this chapter will pull everything together.

Just as the term "movement" is far more complicated in execution than the simple definition of "action," the term "beginning" means far more than first words. It encompasses all of the setup events of your novel, and those may span a first 60–75 pages. In the parlance of plays and screenplays, the beginning is referred to as Act I. It usually includes a first time that your hero changes direction toward continued pursuit of the story goal. That change of direction marks the end of the beginning and the beginning of the middle.

Your beginning must establish larger story elements. To use a house-building metaphor, you know you're going to need a foundation.

As you prepare to do that, you'll need to first address larger issues: the environmental assessment of the soil, the city permits, the location on the lot relative to sewer, water, powerlines, and electricity as well as to sunrise and sunset, proximity to other homes, protection of trees, home owner association guidelines, and the purchaser's aesthetic preferences. All of these matters fall under larger issues. To lay the foundation, you'll need how-to skills, tools, and materials, in accordance with the physical properties of the building materials and the laws of nature. These are smaller, but equally important requirements to build a house. Beginning your novel or short story involves a similar two-stage process. When you planned and wrote your first draft, you made decisions about big-picture concerns and how to implement them. As you continue with the revision process, step back and become a home inspector prior to a sale: check your decisions and execution of them, from foundation and setup through your full novel beginning. Your list should include:

Larger elements: your genre, the tone and atmosphere, setting and time period, the protagonist and antagonist, other characters, the story problem and hero's goals (outer and inner), what's at stake in plot and character, what the reader can expect intellectually and emotionally, and the theme

Smaller elements: time and place of opening, first viewpoints and sequence order; hooks; first scenes, sequels, or summaries

Larger Story Elements

The following discussion will help guide you in your reexamination and revision of these critical story elements related to beginnings. Because many of the above elements and techniques have been touched upon or developed, I'll offer a summary and review of each one and offer greater depth for those that have not yet been discussed.

GENRE

Chapter four listed the way that fiction is categorized for purposes of selling and shelving your book. There is no substitute for being a reader of the genre in which you are writing, and for reading in other genres for contrast and inspiration. One problem to spot during revision is what I call the "animal, vegetable, mineral" problem or, "What is it?" If you mix too many genres, instead of an adorable mutt, you can end up with a disease-ridden mongrel. Novelist-musician Charley Snellings wrote a spoof on this problem in a song, "Dear Agent": "It's a fiction horror romance novel with quite a different look." Make sure your beginning makes your primary genre clear.

TONE AND ATMOSPHERE

Every novel is an original, every story is imbued with an atmosphere, and every genre has a distinctive tone. The worst possible case occurs when a novel has none of these qualities. That's why you should examine your beginning and see if you can now, with some objectivity, give a description that distinguishes your novel in these ways. Like the old program *Name That Tune*, even a first paragraph of your novel, perhaps as little as one line, can communicate all of these qualities, as these examples demonstrate:

> Driving into Chicago at five o'clock on a Wednesday is like entering a circle in hell—possibly one sandwiched between the Pit of a Hundred Thousand Root Canals and the Fiery Baths of Microwaved Cheese. It was a crisp blue June afternoon, and there the Lincoln and I were stuck in hell's Canyon of Interminable Cross Merges. New York is no treat at that time of day, either, but it's merely a stroll through bunny-soft purgatory by comparison, believe you me.

Originality? I give high marks on this author's style—described variously by reviewers as "demented and fun," "audacious and always original," and "wicked." Although there is no way to tell from this first paragraph that author Brian M. Wiprud's novel *Tailed* is a caper mystery, it's clear that his tone is humorous, worldly, and sarcastic. The atmosphere he draws here is harried and cynical.

To improve your tone and atmosphere, work on your style, per the instructions in part one, and read chapter fourteen on narration.

SETTING AND TIME PERIOD

The reason so many novels start with setting and time period is to get the reader oriented and "grounded" as quickly as possible. Using the example above, notice that Wiprud immediately establishes all of these basics in his first few words: "driving" (twentieth or twenty-first century), "Chicago" (setting), "five o'clock Wednesday" (time/day). The reference to "Microwaved Cheese" fine-tunes the time period as modern.

Make sure your beginning orients the reader to your story's time and place, but is in keeping with the tone and atmosphere you seek to create.

Protagonist and Antagonist

Although the first pages of a novel need not begin with the protagonist or reveal the antagonist, the extended beginning of your novel should make those roles (although not necessarily the actual identity in the case of the antagonist) clear. More novels than not do begin with the viewpoint of the protagonist, which facilitates the reader's entry into the story and identification with the hero's quest at the earliest possible time. Most of the larger elements of beginnings are shown through the viewpoint of the first character on stage.

OTHER CHARACTERS

Again, for the sake of reader orientation and accomplishing your setup work, introduce all or most of your viewpoint characters and as many of your minor characters (not counting unnamed "bit" characters such as "the waitress," "the traffic cop," and so on) within your first several chapters. Don't introduce a new viewpoint character for the very first time in the middle or last part of the novel. Even just naming this person early on and/or giving the character a brief scene in his or her viewpoint can resolve this problem.

Avoid a common mistake that can occur on first pages: introducing too many characters and character names. How many is too many? Probably any named character in excess of three is too many. You might have other characters referred to by role—"his brother," "the fisherman"—but don't overwhelm the reader with a playbill.

Once again, this rule of no more than three named characters depends upon author finesse and genre. For instance, readers expect to work hard and learn from historical novels. Take *Shōgun* by James Clavell, the bestselling Asian saga set in seventeenth-century Japan. On the first page of the prologue, Clavell names but two characters and their roles, John Blackthorne, Pilot-Major, and Salamon the mute, anchoring the reader in Blackthorne's third-person point of view. On that first page as well, Clavell names the ship, the *Erasmus*, and lets us know that it is the sole surviving ship of five, with "eight and twenty men" left alive out of one hundred and seven, and only ten of them walking, due to starvation and scurvy. Thankfully, Clavell does not yet introduce more names because the rest of the first page sets up the historical context, the countries involved, and the purpose of the Dutch expeditions before this one, "to ravish the enemy in the New World." By the end of the prologue, however, Clavell has introduced a dozen names, mostly of crew members, and provided short dossiers of characters that will become important. He's given readers a history lesson, all within the context of high drama on the open seas: Blackthorne fighting a storm "like a madman."

If you have named or introduced more than three characters, change some names to roles or postpone entry of other characters until later, even a page later. Parcel out the readers' work so they can assimilate the setup of your novel. The last thing you want is to create confusion.

STORY PROBLEM AND HERO'S GOALS

Chapters five and six provided extensive discussion of the story problem and outer and inner goals—the former referring to the plot and the latter referring to the protagonist's need, also discussed at length in chapter ten. Although these two jobs are critical to the reader committing to your story and knowing what and who to invest in, the author may not reveal them on page one. Yet, some authors reveal the story problem and hero's goal in paragraph one. And nearly all published novelists make them evident by the end of the first couple of chapters.

The techniques for introducing the story problem and hero goals in beginnings will be taken up again later in this chapter under hooks, scenes, and sequence.

STAKES IN PLOT AND CHARACTER

Stakes correspond to story goals and character needs. When you read or hear someone ask, "What's at stake?," the answer should state what will be gained if the hero succeeds in reaching the story goal and what will be lost should he fail. The inner stakes mean the success or failure at fulfilling the universal need that is the "hole in the soul" of the protagonist and that has its origin in a past event, usually a trauma.

Your job is to know what these stakes are and describe them in concrete terms. This means being able to state stakes such as finding the abducted child and putting the kidnapper behind bars, instead of just "securing justice." It means landing the job with AlphaMaleInc as the first female CEO, not just "finding work"; otherwise, an application at Taco Bell assures work. Buying a dream home *and* finding Mr. McDreamy to share it is concrete; "finding happiness" is not.

The concrete definition of goals, stakes, and needs allows the reader to take frequent soundings of how close your hero or heroine is to achieving them. Buying the dream house, for instance, is only one half—and the easier half—of the joint goal that includes finding Mr. McDreamy to share it. What's at stake? Perhaps not enough in this latter goal—externally—but what if the personal yearning is to fill the need of having roots for a single mother who has been homeless or in shelter facilities? What if she finds one or the other but not both? Maybe that will call for character change as she realizes that self-respect is the *real* need, and now that she has that, she knows that the dream house and man are nice but not required for her roots. That is but one of many possible scenarios for what's at stake.

Define the losses and gains, making sure you know them and, in turn, the reader gets to know them. Can you up the stakes, make them higher, with more to lose and more to gain? The greater the stakes, the more your readers will care about seeing your hero succeed.

WHAT THE READER CAN EXPECT INTELLECTUALLY AND EMOTIONALLY

Novel beginnings are full of promises to your reader. Every one of the larger story elements makes a promise. Particular stories make intellectual promises—that the reader will find new, interesting, or provocative ideas. This seems true for many kinds of science fiction stories: Orwell's *1984* and Margaret Atwood's *The Handmaid's Tale* both present the ideas of totalitarian control of a future government trampling over individual rights.

Other stories emphasize emotional promises, for the reader to be stirred and feel whatever emotion is appropriate to the story—afraid, sad, inspired, nostalgic, entertained, and so forth. You can see in the Wiprud example supplied earlier that *Tailed* is going to entertain.

THEME

All novels have, or should have, a theme, a take-away message. If the novel is strongly character-driven, the theme will derive from the universal need that has been the hero's psychological quest (covered in chapter ten). Some but not all novels make that theme evident in their novel beginnings. Although a theme will emerge out of the story, many writers like to reveal it in various ways in their story opening. In the section that follows, I'll present various kinds of hooks, one of which reveals or foreshadows the theme.

Smaller Elements

At what point in time did you open your story? When drafting, every fiction writer faces the necessity of setting up a time line and then creating the order of events and their locations along it. During revision, take a second look at this time line. A frequent problem is opening a novel at the wrong time in the protagonist's life. Anything you can imagine is possible and probably has been done: follow a character from birth to death; open in old age and flash back to birth, carrying on through the years; open in the present and continue through a day, a week, a month, or longer; start in the future, and then use a flashback. Or sequence the story such that it goes back and forth between past and present or between past, present, and future. It's all been tried; it's all been done, and done well.

Do you have an urge to tell readers: "Wait until you get to chapter three, from there on, the story really flies"? That may be a broad hint from your inner editor, who knows you should start the story in chapter three. Use the following guidelines to help you determine if you're on track or need to make a change:

- Start in medias res/in the inciting incident.
- Open near the end.
- Begin prior to the story problem.

IN MEDIAS RES/IN THE INCITING INCIDENT

The Latin phrase *in medias res* (in the middle of things, or "in the middle of the mattering moment") means beginning in midscene, with characters conversing, fighting, fleeing, or in some other way acting. The background concerning what led the characters to this point is postponed until later. That's how George R. R. Martin opens his fantasy saga, *A Game of Thrones*:

"We should start back," Gared urged as the woods began to grow dark around them. "The wildlings are dead."

"Do the dead frighten you?" Ser Waymar Royce asked with just the hint of a smile.

Gared did not rise to the bait. He was an old man, past fifty, and he had seen the lordlings come and go. "Dead is dead," he said. "We have no business with the dead."

"Are they dead?" Royce asked softly. "What proof have we?"

"Will saw them," Gared said. "If he says they are dead, that's proof enough for me."

Starting *in medias res* with dialogue must introduce a source of tension and movement, both fully supplied by Martin's opening. He establishes setting—the woods, and time—dusk. There is character conflict, the introduction of a possible character triangle with mention of Will, a third character, and the outer threat of "wildlings." With no more to go on than this little bit of dialogue, I see at least one possible theme: "Your survival may depend upon trusting the right person." Because opening in dialogue demands skill to quickly orient the reader as to who is speaking about what, why, and where, many writers begin *in medias res* but they use narration or a combination of narration (telling) and scene (showing).

Take for instance the opening of the paranormal thriller *The Seventh Sense* by T. J. MacGregor, winner of the Shamus and Edgar Allan Poe awards:

Saturday, May 24
12:02 a.m.

The BMW's windshield had fogged up again, reducing the traffic on I-95 to a long, glistening red snake of taillights. Frank Benedict rubbed his palm in quick, angry circles against the glass, clearing a small area through which he could see the road.

Stupid drivers ought to be in bed, he thought, and tipped the flask to his mouth. The scotch burned a sapid path down his gullet and ignited in the pit of his stomach. But it didn't even touch his pounding headache....

MacGregor opens chapter one in the point of view of the antagonist, Frank Benedict, a lawyer who is frustrated and drinking while driving—and then he hits the protagonist's Explorer. Chapter two begins, also *in medias res*, but from the point of view of the protagonist. Frank Benedict has left the scene of the accident: hit and run. Here is the beginning of chapter two, as Charlie, the protagonist, returns to consciousness at the scene of the action:

My baby.

Charlie Calloway lay on her side on the saturated ground, legs drawn up, arms wrapped around her huge belly, and squeezed her eyes shut against a tidal wave of pain. A contraction? *No, please...*

Rain poured over her, running into her eyes, her mouth, into her ear. She heard a horn blaring somewhere and knew that it had something to do with her, but couldn't remember what....

A pertinent question to ask yourself is this: What is "mattering" about the moment of your beginning, if you have begun in medias res? You could open in the middle of almost any dramatic scene and capture reader attention, so why this one? There are three answers to this question:

1. The scene is the inciting incident of the plot that defines the dramatic arc of the whole novel.
2. The scene has meaning to the whole novel by foreshadowing the character arc and revealing a possible theme.
3. The scene is full of inner and outer conflict, character development, and compelling writing.

T. J. MacGregor's novel starts with the inciting incident of the hit-and-run driver and follows with introducing the effect on the protagonist: injured, the fate of her baby and husband not yet known. However, there has been a crime. In due time we learn that both baby and husband have died. The accident sets in motion the story plot and the dramatic arc of finding Frank Benedict and bringing him to justice. It also sets in motion the psychological arc for protagonist and FBI veteran Charlie Calloway as she searches for understanding, if not peace of mind, about life after death and the new life she now faces.

NEAR THE END

Starting near the end of your story is dynamic because your protagonist may be literally at the edge of death. This kind of opening begins *Big Numbers*, a debut mystery by Jack Getze:

> The stench of my own vomit fills my nose. Breath comes in short, shallow gasps. Why doesn't blabbermouth just shut the hell up and get this over with?
>
> "You said you've never been deep-sea fishing, Austin, so I'm guessing you don't know dick about giant bluefin. But when you were a kid, jigging off that pier in California, did you ever hook up with a two or three-pound bonito?"
>
> A muddy green Atlantic Ocean surrounds us, the expanse of gentle swells empty but for the fifty-two-foot Hatteras under our feet and a dozen chum-sucking seagulls screaming overhead.

Getze ends this climactic first scene of the protagonist about to be dumped overboard by his killer as follows:

> Something heavy bumps the half-pound metal lure to which I am fatally attached. The line draws taut, digging deeper into the green, rolling swells. Eternity tugs on my shoulder straps.
>
> "Looks like a hook-up," Mr. Blabbermouth says.
>
> "And I thought life was shitty three weeks ago."

With that transition, readers are prepared to find out how Austin arrived at this fate, but they will have to read the whole book to catch up to the beginning and learn whodunit and how Austin can escape the apparently inescapable. This opening is full of high stakes, conflict, and sharp style. The challenge with opening near your climax is that the high drama could end up being the highest drama in the whole novel; in other words, all other conflicts and crises can pale against the first one, leaving your reader feeling that the actual climax is anticlimactic.

PRIOR TO THE STORY PROBLEM

Although beginning at the end is one option, beginning *before* the beginning is another. In other words, some novels open in the near or far past relative to the presentation of the story problem. The quintessential story that reflects this time choice has a familiar opening: "In the beginning was the Word..." The story problem? In Book I (the Old Testament) of this great epic, you can choose any number of events as the one that presents *the* story problem: Eve takes a bite of the forbidden fruit, Moses leads the Jews out of Egypt and into the Promised Land, Abraham receives the Ten Commandments, or another story.

If you have begun your novel in the long-ago past, then you must have planned to lead the reader, through scenes and crises, to the one central problem that will carry the reader through to the end of the novel. If you start closer to the story problem, those scenes will become backstory—events that took place before the novel begins. A beginning in the long-ago past tends to set up episodic structure. As mentioned in chapter six, episodic plots pull readers through incident after incident, perhaps through years in the life of the protagonist, before they eventually reveal a central, high-stakes problem and story goal. If not handled carefully, episodic plots can leave readers floundering and hoping for life preservers, eager to know who or what is *most* important to latch on to.

If you are writing a multigenerational saga, you may indeed begin with a modern family's ancestor, in a prior era and perhaps a different country. Even so, you will have to decide each generation's story beginning, choosing the age of the new protagonist, setting, and mattering moment. The quality of writing must be very high for big blocks of narration to succeed early in a story. General wisdom advises beginning close to the story problem or the inciting incident that will introduce the story problem. Review chapter six about frames and flashback stories to decide if your story fits one of these time lines.

If you have begun your story in the near past, it may work well, if you have written it skillfully. In the near past, you have a chance to establish context. Context refers to the era, time, setting, situation, immediate location, characters, and conflicts. These supply setup and explanation. Beginning with context also sends up a flare warning of quicksand. The writer's temptation is to dump blocks of explanation or to fail to show any movement. Now your novel joins the *Titanic* as real estate on the ocean floor.

Here is an example of opening in the near past, offering context in a skillful way. *Range of Motion* by Elizabeth Berg opens with a two-page prologue of the first-person protagonist philosophizing about tragedy, hope, hopelessness, appreciation, and gratefulness. This contemporary literary story then begins chapter one with the story context, although this event in the story past constitutes the introduction of the story problem. Notice, too, the words I've italicized that show the terrific movement in this narrated beginning about the near past:

I can *tell* you how it happened. It's easy to *say* how it happened. He *walked* past a building, and a huge chunk of ice *fell* off the roof, and it *hit* him in the head. This is Chaplinesque, right? This is kind of funny. People *start to laugh* when I tell them. I see the *start of their hand to their mouth,* their poor disguise. I *laughed* when I heard. I thought after the doctor *told* me what happened that Jay would *get* on the phone and *say,* "Jeez, Lainey, *come* and get me. I've got a goose egg the size of the world. *Come take me home*." Only what happened wasn't like Chaplin: Jay didn't *land* on his butt with his legs *sticking* out at chopstick angles, *twitch* his mustache, *get back up and walk away*. He *landed* on his side, and stayed there....

Although this opening describes the past, Berg has included the reader in the event by dramatizing it within narration. The voice of the narrator is very much like that of a friend talking to you on the telephone telling you what happened. We are also clued into the time—contemporary, the relationship—a husband and wife, the diction—informal, and the narrator's awareness of how strangely comic her husband's accidental death is. Berg has made the reader completely sympathetic to the narrator and ready to learn what happens next.

To help you find that right time and place, and to know if you need to revise, answer these questions:

- What is your novel about, not the whole genre, but your particular novel? Begin with one word: self-determination, belonging, identity, redemption, justice...
- Where along the time line of your story does this need of your protagonist assert itself? Where is securing this core need most threatened?
- Have you begun your novel with your protagonist at a crossroads or soon to be at one? Write a list of events that may offer answers to these questions. You may find events in the story past or story future.
- What if you began your story at one of these other times, turning your present beginning into a scene later in the novel or moving it into backstory?
- Which crossroad event strikes you as most powerful? Should it become your climax or your beginning?
- Why not craft several openings, at least writing a few pages for each one. Then choose which opening time and place works best. Which version is supported by your intuition and reflects the meaning of the novel and launches your story?

HOOKS

Every beginning must draw your reader into your story and, as quickly as possible, get them to suspend disbelief in your created world and accept it as "reality." Prior sections of this book display a variety of openings, beginning with setting and time, omniscient overview, in medias res—with dialogue or scene, and with frame structure. Some decisions are based upon the best *time* along the story line. There are other possibilities for a hook that include:

- Narrative hook
- Quiet opening
- Dramatic opening

Narrative hook

Many authors begin with a narrative hook that tells the reader something important, often related to the problem, need, or theme. The narrative hook is often *outside of place and time*, and shows off author style and character voice. If you did not start your novel with one, I urge you to try it out. Most important, some narrative hooks signal a time of great change, a turning point, and typically feature one of the great events of life and fiction: *love*, *hate*, *sex*, *birth*, *death*, and *spirit*. The narrative hook can be a powerful way to begin. It ranges from a one-line paragraph to half a page. Consider the impact of these shorter examples.

Narrative Hooks
- "The first time my husband hit me I was nineteen years old." *Black and Blue* by Anna Quindlen
- "The day Kevin Tucker nearly killed her, Molly Somerville swore off unrequited love forever." *This Heart of Mine* by Susan Elizabeth Phillips
- "It was my devil's own temper that brought me to grief, my temper and a skill with weapons born of my father's teaching." *Sackett's Land* by Louis L'Amour

- "Eden." *So Wild a Dream* by Win Blevins
- "I slipped into my first metamorphosis so quietly that no one noticed. Metamorphoses were not supposed to begin that way. Most people begin with small, obvious, physical changes—the loss of fingers and toes, for instance, or the budding of new fingers and toes of a different design. I wish my experience had been that normal, that safe." *Imago* by Octavia E. Bulter
- "Dear Wenny, I died too." *Wenny Has Wings* by Janet Lee Carey
- "Some say that love's enough to stave off suffering and loss, but I would disagree.... But teachings about spirit and kinship require repetition before becoming threads strong enough to weave into life's fabric, strong enough to overcome the weaker strains of human nature. It was a strength I found I'd need one day to face what love could not stave off." *A Clearing in the Wild* by Jane Kirkpatrick
- "Scott Duncan sat across from the killer." *Just One Look* by Harlan Coben

I urge you to try your hand at a narrative hook, weaving into it characterization, the story problem, the theme, and/or something tantalizing from the story that raises questions and suspense. In my opinion, a well-written narrative hook adds class; it predisposes me to expect an author who knows her craft. I believe it may do the same for agents and editors.

I also believe that when the narrative hook alludes to the character wound and need, it reaches into the deepest part of the reader's heart and sets the frame for the entire novel. I have a hunch that many readers choose particular genres, authors, and novels based on the universal needs and yearnings that they have grappled with in life. Crime fiction readers may have had life issues focused on justice or law and order. Readers of love stories may have had the need for love and family most pressing in their lives. Perhaps those who prefer the complexity and less tied-in-a-bow endings of women's fiction have suffered in relationships or experienced less than fairy-tale marriages. The same theory could hold true for what themes writers choose in their novels.

Is it difficult to wrap so much into your novel's first words? Don't let the difficulty prevent you from writing several drafts until you find the combination that captures many if not all of the possibilities of the narrative hook, and offers the best entrée to your book.

Quiet Opening

The "quiet" opening refers to novels that begin with calm. The author may write about setting and time period or offer the philosophy of life of a character. He or she may summarize backstory or supply information. The quiet opening can correspond with showing the characters in their ordinary worlds before facing the story problem. The quiet opening may be in scene or outside of scene. If you drafted your novel with this kind of beginning, know that its success depends greatly on your skill in writing well, with concrete details and specificity, with obvious flair—distinctive style, and with a source of tension and embedded movement, even if in narration.

Every writer who must begin a book two, or subsequent books in a series, faces the necessity of filling in backstory events and introducing characters from the prior book or books. Sometimes the author accomplishes this with a quiet opening. *The Sorcerer: Metamorphosis* is the second book in a series by Canadian bestseller Jack Whyte. Here is the beginning from the point of view of Merlyn:

There is no more important day in a man's life than the day he formally takes up a sword for the first time. At that fateful and long-anticipated moment when a youth extends his hand for the first time, witnessed formally by both his elders and his peers, to grip the hilt of the sword that will be his own, his life and his world are changed forever. In the eyes of men, he has become a man, and his boyhood is irrevocably and publicly discarded for all time, much like the shed skin of a serpent. Far more important and traumatic than his first knowledge of a woman, the commitment of taking up the sword is the last and greatest rite of the passage across the gulf between boyhood and manhood.

A different kind of quiet opening begins a cozy mystery in a long-established series by Carola Dunn. She begins *A Mourning Wedding* quietly, but in scene, as follows:

Lady Eva Devenish capped her gold fountain pen and leant back with a sigh, flexing her beringed fingers. These days her hand was always stiff after writing. Sometimes she even felt the beginning of a cramp, but she wasn't going to let it stop her. Her writing was still tiny and neat, and her eyesight nearly as good as ever.

Dramatic Opening

Opposite in nature, the dramatic opening is almost always guaranteed to hook the reader. It usually starts in the middle of a scene, whether near the climax or at the inciting incident. It holds less risk than a quiet one because of the guarantee of drama. But the peril of beginning dramatically is that after the high drama is over, you have the rest of your novel to keep the reader engaged. You do not want the opening scene to stand apart as a Mt. Everest amidst a bunch of hills. In other words, you can create a tough act to follow. In revision, identify subsequent dramatic crises to the dramatic opening and assess their level of drama. Make sure you build an incline of ever-steeper suspense leading to a climax that is as dramatic as, or more dramatic than, your opening.

A startling and dramatic first chapter to a startling novel that some experts classify in the fantasy genre and others as beyond classification comes from *The Lovely Bones* by Alice Sebold. After the narrative hook, the author provides three paragraphs of exposition—or backstory—and then opens a scene where the narrator is brutally raped and murdered. The excerpt below provides the narrative hook and the first paragraph of the scene:

My name is Salmon, like the fish; first name, Susie. I was four-teen when I was murdered on December 6, 1973. In newspaper photos of missing girls from the seventies, most looked like me: white girls with mousy brown hair. This was before kids of all races and genders started appearing on milk cartons or in the daily mail. It was still back when people believed things like that didn't happen....But on December 6, 1973, it was snowing, and I took a shortcut through the cornfield back from the junior high. It was dark out because the days were shorter in winter, and I remember how the broken cornstalks made my walk more difficult. The snow was falling lightly, like a flurry of small hands, and I was breathing through my nose until it was running so much that I had to open my mouth. Six feet from where Mr. Harvey stood, I stuck my tongue out to taste a snowflake.

As you reread the start to your novel, experiment with writing different beginnings, creating types that correspond to the different beginnings offered in this chapter. Then choose the best as the new start to your novel.

FIRST SCENES, SEQUELS, OR SUMMARIES

Now that you are returning to your novel beginning, determine if your present draft opens in action, reaction, or summary. If you open in action, even if preceded with a narrative hook or a quiet bit of small action, you have begun with a scene. *Scenes,* defined technically, are events propelled by a character goal that occur at a particular time and place. They have forward motion and produce conflict as the character with the goal encounters opposition. You can count on a basic formula: Goal + Conflict = Suspense. You'll use this formula, in all kinds of guises and permutations, throughout every piece of fiction you write.

If you decide that you have opened your novel with your first character in reaction to something that happened prior to the novel's beginning, you have begun in what the late Jack Bickham referred to as a sequel. The word *sequel* means, in this context, what follows. It fits places in your novel where a character expresses emotion and collects thoughts about something that has happened previously. Using a pop psychology term, the character is "processing," figuring out what happened and what to do next.

Summary is exactly what it means in our everyday use of the word. This kind of beginning provides information about the characters, the setting, lifestyle, or background information that sets the backdrop for the subsequent scene when the reader will fully "enter" the novel.

Without reservation, I recommend that you begin your novel with a scene. One reason why is because of the problems inherent with sequel and summary. Sequel means that readers have been deprived of the suspense of the off-stage scene that occurred before the opening of the novel. Now they are held hostage to "listen" to the reaction of the character or characters. It also means that the author will be tempted to narrate too much, to retell the scene that triggered the emotions and quandary, and tell, tell, and tell—everything. More than not, sequel beginnings feature one character alone with his or her thoughts and feelings. I don't recommend that any unpublished novelist begin with one character alone, because the character will inevitably turn inward, which means lots of telling versus action.

Summary means narration. Summary is obviously author-driven. If your writing isn't in and of itself fantastically interesting, then you'll bore your readers. In other words, the author takes over the story to brief the reader and only later does the novel settle into a character-driven story.

Scenes are based on forward-moving action. They operate to get the story launched, to put the characters into situations where they must overcome obstacles and move toward commitment to a life-changing quest. Scenes also contain sounds, smells, temperatures, touch-sensations, and visuals. They create the verisimilitude, the sense of reality that is missing in narrated summaries or thought-based sequels. Scenes are more dynamic than sequels or summaries.

Because scenes comprise about three-quarters of any novel, it is critical that you check your novel for strong scene structure based on strong character motivation, the subject of the next chapter.

MAKEOVER REVISION CHECKLIST

Character-Driven Beginnings

Larger Elements of Story Beginnings
☑ Genre
- Double-check that your beginning is in keeping with genre content and style.
- If your story is a combination of genres, make sure one is primary.

☑ Tone and Atmosphere
- Is your beginning tone deaf? Without distinctive tone or atmosphere?
- Decide what tone and atmosphere you want to convey.
- Work on style per part one and character-driven description per chapter fourteen.

☑ Setting and Time Period
- With the exception of using a narrative hook, in paragraph one, orient your reader in place and time.
- Keep the tone and atmosphere while revealing place and time.

☑ Protagonist and Antagonist
- If your genre and story permit it, open in your protagonist's point of view.
- Make sure you introduce the protagonist within the first few chapters.
- Even if you do not want to reveal the identity of the antagonist, with some exceptions, make clear the threat to your protagonist and pit him or her against this opposition in the beginning chapters.

☑ Other Characters
- Introduce all, or mostly all, main characters within the first few chapters.
- Introduce as many minor characters that play a role in the story as soon as possible.
- Avoid introducing more than three named characters (in general) on page one. Use roles in place of names until it is necessary to formally introduce a character.

- Parcel out the introduction of other named characters, taking care not to overwhelm the reader.
- Beware of density of unfamiliar detail—limit other names and dates, especially on first pages.

☑ Story Problem and Hero's Goals
- Review chapters five, six, and ten.
- Consider revealing the story problem and hero's story goal on page one; aim not to postpone making them clear beyond chapter one or two.
- Define the goals—outer and inner—in concrete terms so that the reader always knows how close or far the hero is from reaching them.
- Review hooks.

☑ What's at Stake in the Plot and Character?
- In the beginning chapters, make clear what of value and importance will be lost or gained, should the hero fail or succeed.
- Make sure the stakes are worthy of reader investment. Can you up the stakes to something of greater urgency or importance?

☑ What the Reader Can Expect Intellectually and Emotionally
- Decide what your reader will expect from your beginning. If unclear, revise.

Smaller Elements of Story Beginnings
☑ Story Order/When to Begin
- Scrutinize your beginning on your time line. Use intuition to feel out other starting points that might be more meaningful.

☑ In Medias Res/In the Inciting Incident
Advantages:
- Hooks reader instantly into an ongoing scene
- Opens in a scene with meaning to the whole novel
- Inciting incident introduces the story problem and plot
- Introduces the protagonist and the inner problem and goal

Disadvantages:
- Without surrounding context the reader may be confused, not hooked.

- Explanation of who, what, where, why, and when can intrude awkwardly.

☑ Near the End
Advantages:
- Captures reader with the high point of conflict and drama
- Shows highest stakes
- Implants knowledge of where the story is headed

Disadvantages:
- The rest of the story may be anticlimactic by comparison.
- You may give away too much.
- Missing setup may confuse the reader.

☑ Prior to the Story Problem
Advantages:
- Able to establish full and rich context and characterization
- Earlier crises contribute drama to eventual introduction of story problem.

Disadvantages:
- Episodic structure saps energy from reader who needs clarity.
- Early scenes seem like warmups for central story conflict.
- Childhood less interesting than adulthood where story takes shape.
- Too many plotlines, multiple themes; many books packed into one

☑ Questions to Answer to Help Find the Best Beginning:
- What one word states what your novel is about?
- Where along the time line does your protagonist's deepest need appear?
- Where along the time line is this core need threatened?
- What are the significant crossroads in your story?
- Does your story open or close at a meaningful crossroad?
- Could your most powerful crossroad work better as the beginning?
- Would the beginning of your climax work best as an opening?
- After writing several pages for several possible openings, which one is best supported by your intuition, reflects the meaning of the novel, and launches your story?

☑ Hooks

Narrative hook:

- Tells something important, usually related to the problem, need, or theme
- Shows off author style and author or character voice
- Signals a time of great change in the life of the protagonist
- Reflects life's most powerful emotions regarding love, hate, sex, birth, death, or spirit
- Raises questions and suspense

Quiet opening:

- Works with accomplished writers whose style is distinctive and whose skill includes using concrete details, specificity, imagery, and embedded movement within narration
- Sometimes used by authors of series to orient new readers to characters and prior story events
- Sometimes corresponds with opening before the story problem

Dramatic opening:

- Usually in medias res, whether near the end or simply with a scene
- Less high risk than quiet opening
- Make sure your dramatic opening doesn't eclipse everything that follows

☑ First Scenes, Sequels, or Summaries

- Determine if your present opening is action, reaction, or summary.
- Create verisimilitude with sounds, smell, temperatures, touch-sensations, and visuals.

Disadvantages of sequels or reaction sequences:

- Deprives reader of off-stage scene, yet must "listen" to emotional reactions
- Usually means the off-stage scene must be recapped, told to reader
- Character often turns inward, which creates more telling versus showing.

Disadvantages of summaries:
- Author-driven narration to brief the reader
- Delays beginning of plot
- Reader will be bored by unskillful writing of information and back-story.

Advantages of opening with action or scene:
- Creates forward-moving action
- Gets story launched
- Puts characters in situations to overcome first obstacles and move toward commitment to quest
- Scenes make up three-quarters of most novels.

CHAPTER TWELVE

Character-Driven Scenes and Suspense

Options A common assumption is that scene = plot. This chapter works to change that assumption and show how it is necessary to make your scenes character-driven, to create full development of plot, character, and suspense.

Scenes are the workhorse of fiction. Characters hold the reins and call out the commands. Because scenes, in the primary story and in subplots, comprise most of the internal structure of novels, you've got to master how to write them. Often left out in writing instruction is subtext. Add subtext—a source of unnoticed or inner character conflict—to scene structure and you are guaranteed greater development of characterization and another source of suspense. If you omit subtext, which is revealed through the thoughts and perceptions of your point-of-view character, it's like leaving your character to control the horse team with one rein.

Developing a Scene in Full

Throughout this book, I've discussed scenes as character-driven action toward a goal that occurs in a particular time and place. You may have one or several scenes in a chapter. They may have the same or different point-of-view characters. Your scenes may occur in the main plot or in a subplot. The structure of scenes is a microcosm of five-stage dramatic structure: a character with a goal runs into opposition, which creates conflict that builds greater suspense through repeated thwarted efforts, until finally the character succeeds and reaches the goal, or fails. The scene ends with change: a surprise, twist, setback, or disaster relative to the goal. Emerging from the scene, the character has an insight—about the plot or himself. Instead of a story goal—to resolve the big problem that defines the whole novel—the point-of-view character creates a scene goal, which will advance his or her cause toward reaching that story goal.

EXAMPLE OF BASIC SCENE OUTLINE

Let's use a simple hypothetical situation, first building a basic scene and then adding characterization and then later, subtext. Refer to the following example to fully develop your most important scenes.

This scene takes place in a living room at 7 p.m. The protagonist of the scene is a teen girl named Brandy. Her stated scene goal is to borrow the older of two family cars. She approaches her father, who is watching TV. She asks for the keys to the car, explaining that she needs to study for a test with her girlfriend Susie, who has the notes from a class Brandy missed while sick. Her father says no, that it's raining and expected to get worse. He doesn't want her out in it.

Brandy has to come up with a different strategy. She launches her second attempt by telling her dad that Susie lives only a mile away and he knows Brandy is a safe driver, and the test is tomorrow. She *has* to get to Susie's to get the notes, or so she tells her dad. He again says no, telling her that she can study her textbooks and notes and use any online homework resources that the teacher has provided, and besides, she can always call or e-mail Susie.

On her third try, Brandy wraps her arms around her father and gives him a hug and tells him that he's got to trust her sometime, that Mom told her she could go to Susie's, and besides, she'll pick up a movie he's been wanting to watch on her way home. Dad caves. He reaches into his pocket and hands her the keys with admonitions to be careful and call him from Susie's so he knows she has arrived safely. Just then, Mom walks in and says, "I never said you could take the car to Susie's." Uh-oh. Disaster. Brandy is caught in a lie, and now she's grounded.

This example offers the bare bones of a scene. It's an okay outline but it's not complete. It's missing depth of characterization. Let's plug the holes with:

1. the foundations of character motivation from the plot
2. deepest motivation supplied by the traumatic event in the past
3. her character strength and weakness, also molded by the past

FOUNDATIONS OF CHARACTER MOTIVATION FROM THE PLOT

What's at stake? On the surface, what's at stake is that Brandy won't get her way. She won't get the notes that will let her study for the test, so she may not do well on the test. That is all visible and, ostensibly, is what her father is being asked to believe. It is apparently not a midterm, final, or SAT test. Should she get less than a great grade, the loss will not be overwhelming. From Dad's point of view, not only is this true but the risk of her driving in a bad storm is greater than a lower grade.

However, only when readers are allowed inside a character's thoughts can they know the real motivations and therefore what the character believes is at stake. Suppose Brandy has planned to drive to a copse of cottonwoods outside her small town where she has arranged to meet her drifter boyfriend who has camped there. She plans to run away, taking the family's old car—after all, her father and mother have just bought a Prius.

How high are the stakes? The answer can't be known until the reader knows how Brandy feels about her boyfriend, Drew. Suppose she thinks she is in love but knows her parents not only would never let her date him, they would freak if they knew he was twenty, she being a mere sixteen. What if she isn't in love with him, but he's convinced her that he knows where there is a sack of money, perhaps discarded by a thief, and Drew found it in a homeless camp and left it there, buried in a different place from where he found it? He needs a ride and he's offered a thief's bargain. And besides, he likes her and she likes him. The hormones are having a field day.

So what are the stakes then? Remember, stakes explain intensity of motivation. Since they are close in age and Brandy believes he likes her, she probably isn't thinking of him as homeless or a danger. The prospect of a treasure hunt might sound magical, an adventure, and maybe she really believes she'll get a substantial sum of money. Of course her parents will get over being mad. And the money might buy her...what? Develop your character's stakes. Make sure they are clear to the reader in each scene, not only showing what the plot offers but what the character has at stake within his or her inner quest for resolution of the past.

DEEPEST MOTIVATION SUPPLIED BY THE TRAUMATIC EVENT IN THE PAST

What does Brandy most yearn for? What has happened in her past that brings this one particular need to the forefront? What if she is desperate for freedom and autonomy? What if when she was six years old, she was struck by a car after she had just stepped off a school bus, and ever since her parents have been like hawks watching her every move?

In revision, look for ways to allude to your scene point-of-view character's yearning, past, and wound, and/or the need that is pushed forward in a particular scene. It is often easiest to weave this information in within the character's thoughts, but you may also see opportunities to convey the information through dialogue.

CHARACTER STRENGTH AND WEAKNESS, ALSO MOLDED BY THE PAST

What is her strength? To claim a tiny space of self-determination in a smothering cocoon of parental fear may have made her *ambitious*. What is her weakness? *Gullibility?* Use your scene point-of-view character's strength to push the action toward the goal. Use the weakness as an obstacle.

EXAMPLE OF SHOWING THE CHARACTER COMPONENTS OF SCENES

All of these possibilities put the scene—the stakes and motivation—in an entirely different light. In the next revision, her motivations, backstory, and character strength and weakness, should be written in, through Brandy's point of view. Accompanying them will be her feelings, reactions, planning, and sensory experience: sound, sight, smell, touch, and taste. Let's develop how these additional components might be shown:

Feelings/Sensory Reactions: anxiety/heart beating fast, excitement/talking fast, fear/feeling hot, hands trembling, love for her dad/giggly, wistful/tear in eye, worry/frown.

Planning: coming up with different things to tell Dad so that he'll give her the keys; alternate thoughts about whether she has everything in her pack that she planned to take; alternate thoughts about whether Drew will be there as promised and what will happen if she is late.

Backstory: To bolster her confidence, she may remember other occasions when she proved to herself that she could take care of herself. She might review her accomplishments and assure herself that when she has her part of the money, she'll be able to do x, y, and z. She may tell herself that her parents will be proud and they'll see that she can live on her own. She may make reference to the accident and her understanding of that event as being why her dad is overly concerned for her safety instead of trusting her good driving and maturity.

Once the scene is rewritten based on adding characterization, it will gain depth, emotional power, and higher suspense. But is the scene done? Not yet. It's missing subtext.

In the hypothetical scene between Brandy and her father, possibilities for subtext abound. During the whole conversation, she might loop her arms around her dad or grab and hold his arm. He

Subtext

Subtext is what is hidden below the surface of a scene that contributes tension or conflict. It includes subterranean forces with origins in (1) the point-of-view character's emotions, needs, and motivations; it may even be a covert scene within the scene; (2) the unexpressed but experienced "vibes" and body language between characters as interpreted by the point-of-view character; (3) nature; and (4) the human-made environment.

tugs against her, until finally, later in the scene, he tells her to let go; she's squeezing his arm like it's a giant toothpaste tube. What's the message from this subtext? You decide; you're the creator. She might find her mouth dry, her voice thinner or softer than usual, belying her inner state. You can show how they lean toward or away from each other, the warmth or teasing in their voices, the winks or laughs or frowns and pouts that are put on. These body language cues relate to deeper realities beneath the surface, ones that communicate as much, and sometimes more, than the surface communications. Perhaps rain changes to hail against the window, or there is thunder or lightning. Maybe the fire in the fireplace spits and flickers from rain coming down the flue. In the human-made environment, what if Brandy picks up a trophy she won in sixth grade, or gazes at a framed first-grade crayon drawing of her dad, mom, and herself with a happy sun face overhead?

Perhaps Brandy gauges some of the success of her attempts to get Dad to say yes by watching his foot tapping or by how he punches the TV remote. All of these possibilities convey subtext. The reader will pay full attention to them because if they are out of the control of the protagonist (the weather, her father's responses) or outside her awareness (gripping her dad's arm, fingering her trophy), then the subtext is like the proverbial "loose cannon." It could explode onto the scene, or interrupt the scene. If what is hidden becomes the focus of attention, it turns the action and suspense inside-out.

What basic scene structure and subtext do is raise questions.

Subtext offers an opportunity to craft tension that is counterpoint to conflict stemming from opposition to the character's scene goal. It is especially worthwhile to "turn up the volume" on subtextural tension when outer scene tension is lower-key.

Will Dad say yes and let her use the car? Will Dad get irritated by Brandy's relentlessness or even get mad? Will the rain turn into such a storm that the streets flood and Brandy will not be able to get out even if she wanted to?

For instance, in one of my client manuscripts, an early scene in the novel featured the common situation of a crime scene. An officer was down, killed. That brings out the big brass. The protagonist is the local, highly experienced detective. There was, however, no clear scene goal. Of the possibilities, the local detective could want to get rid of the higher-ups, ASAP. If so, he would instruct his people to hurry and collect the evidence. I also saw an inherent possibility for subtext. As the detective and the one "big gun," a famous lawman, interacted, I could imagine alpha male instincts. Subtext could involve the protagonist wanting the big gun to recognize his authority, to validate his judgments, and respect his territory. There could be subtle posturing as the men talked, smoked, and issued orders to the lower-ranked men. Readers of such a scene will not invest in the exchanged conversation or information as much as they will in the subtle posturing and one-upmanship between these two men. When the outer scene action is less dramatic, plant goals in your subtext that offer a higher level of interest to the reader.

Every scene can have one source or multiple sources of subtext. What if there's a tornado warning? Now the pressure is on to get the evidence, load the body up, and get the hell out. What if, while the two men are sniffing each other out, the storm hits full force and intensifies? What if the local officer in charge wants to close down and leave, for the safety of everyone, but the mucky-muck wants to stay until the last shred of evidence is collected? More conflict!

Have you developed subtext throughout your novel?

Keep Scenes Fresh

If every one of your scenes had identical structure and full development per the prior advice, you would create a severe and collective yawn from your readers. Faster pace demands less development of interior characterization, description, and fine details and more use of summary and action, including the action of dialogue. A scene may be as brief as half a page or as long as twenty pages. Slower pace creates an opportunity for full development of all aspects of the scene. What I have observed in many published novels is that scenes tend to be more fully developed and longer at the beginning (minus the hook, which may be a very short chapter one) than later when all of the setup is done and the characters known. Likewise, the reactions of the protagonist and other main characters to scene disasters or twists, where they express emotions, churn in a quandary over what to do, reach a decision, and then take their next actions may be fully developed early and abbreviated later. Check the proportion of development in other books in your genre.

Scenes in your novel, as is true in published novels, vary with the degree of development of all of the elements above. If you are like most of the writers I've worked with over the years, you will not have known about some of these essentials of character-driven scenes. Now, in your revision, take an important scene and write it with *all* of the above elements so that you know what you know, and what you don't know. Then, on a case by case, scene by scene basis, layer in the full character dimensionality and higher drama that come from full development.

Diagnosing Scene Problems

Most of the manuscripts I've edited show many of these common deficiencies in scene development. Use the following list as a self-editing checklist to catch yours. Don't feel badly if you have several or many. That puts you in good company with other writers, professional and aspiring, who had these problems in their crummy first drafts (which is normal) and corrected them in revision:

- No clear scene goal
- Scene goal buried too late in the scene
- Scene goal minor; stakes insignificant
- Scene goal unrelated to story goal
- Obstacles and opposition absent
- Obstacles and opposition weak, not sustained
- Obstacles and opposition too quickly overcome
- Conflict is entirely inner
- Conflict is entirely outer
- Stakes greater for another character—wrong POV for scene
- Twist, surprise, or disaster at scene's end missing
- Setting for scene inert, passive
- Little or no internal thought, reactions, or sensations for point-of-view character
- Little or no body language, setting details, or subtext
- Viewpoint slips, scene wanders out of time or place
- Too much thought, not enough goal-propelled action
- Scene is summarized in part or whole and is too critical to do so
- Disaster is contrived
- Scene development is too uniform over many scenes
- Scenes happen in same or similar locations (offices or restaurants especially)
- Important scenes omitted or shortchanged
- Trivial scenes developed

Endings—The Uncertainty Factor

Although a full scene is completed with unexpected twists or reversals, especially setbacks or disasters, any of these endings should have consequences related to the scene goal and story goal. There is another function of ending your scene with the unexpected. That is *uncertainty.* Remember: Uncertainty is the twin of anticipation, the latter created by goals and foreshadowing and the former created by reversals, twists, and disasters.

Ending your scene prior to completion of full scene structure is another important technique. As you examine your scenes during revision, cut some scenes short of their completion, interrupting them with some other scene or development. You may or may not return to an interrupted scene, or if you do, you might pick it up later in its time line or simply summarize how it ended. You might start a scene and then stuff a flashback scene (or flashforward) into it such that you have a scene within a scene. Many time travel novels use this technique. Common, too, is working inner reactions into scene events. Then, at scene's end, the processing of it has already been taken care of and the pace can leap ahead into a next scene. I call this combination of scene and responses to it a "shortcut." This technique is a great pacing technique.

Another way to vary a scene ending is to shift from pursuit of a goal to showing your character feeling, thinking, and sorting things out. You might have begun with a scene, but you'll end with thinking and emotional processing, unless you decide to resume the scene and complete it after the character has made a decision about what next action to take. Then you'll have a sequel within a scene.

Section/Chapter Endings

As you may have guessed from the prior instruction about scene endings, the most effective section or chapter endings are those that force the reader to turn the page. That means ending in the middle of a high point of dramatic suspense, where reaching the scene goal is still in jeopardy, with questions raised, with reader emotions engaged and stirred, and/or with a hook to the next section or chapter, which is often something worse and unexpected.

While your characters won't often be in life and death struggles, when they are, a chapter ending before the reader knows if they will survive is ideal. Here is such a chapter ending from *Seeds of Time,* a time travel adventure for nine- to thirteen-year-olds, by K. C. Dyer. Delaney is the name of a dog:

> In desperation, with the water now up to Delaney's chest, she reached up to grab the rock wall for purchase. As she clutched her arm around Delaney's neck, her hand slipped and both of them plunged underwater. His paw wrenched free, but before she could even feel relief, a sudden sharp shock ran through her body and she found that she could no longer breathe.

More often than ending a chapter at such high drama, you'll want to find a place to end your section or chapter that at least keeps questions unanswered. Even without knowing the plot of *The Getaway Special*, a contemporary science fiction novel by Nebula Award–winner Jerry Oltion, you can appreciate this ending to one of his chapters where scene drama is lower: "'Let's climb to the top and see if we can see any sign of civilization,' she said."

As you check your section or chapter endings, you may be wondering if it is *ever* okay to end them with emotional closure and at the end of a scene. My answer is a hearty yes. The trick is to determine that closure is your *best* choice. If you have raised enough suspense from the prior developments in your story that you are certain your reader will be compelled to continue reading, then you may want to "seal" the section or chapter with a satisfying emotion. You may have decided to open the next one with a different character's viewpoint and you don't want to either finish an incomplete scene for the prior character or return to that action. The main thing is to make your endings intentional. Check all of your section and chapter endings.

Book Endings

Ending a novel is a different story than ending a chapter or section. After all, everything in the plot has been brought to conclusion at the climax, and the character change may have also been shown, before the last chapter, section, page, paragraph, or line. You may have received feedback that your novel ending is unsatisfying, or feels incomplete, or seems unclear. Most novels are not tragedies, nor are they open-ended and intentionally mysterious. Most novels end meeting a number of "specifications":

- They offer explanations or answers to any lingering reader questions.
- They reveal what the protagonist, and other main characters, have realized or learned, about self and life.
- They reflect or state the book's theme.
- They may harken back to the novel's beginning.
- They may reveal a gift or surprise.
- If characters have been brought together or shared the ordeal of the plot, they show them sharing triumph and togetherness.
- Depending on the nature and subject of the novel, the mood will be positive: relief, reflective, uplifting, happy, or playful.
- They may end with a joke or moment of humor in which the reader feels included.
- If the novel will continue as a series, there will be acknowledgment of only one part of the quest that has been completed, but the rest will be left to anon.
- The paragraph and or sentence structure of the literal end of the book will convey completion.

Here is one example of an ending, from *Absolute Power* by David Baldacci. Notice how it matches the above criteria:

Down on the street, Seth Frank stood next to his car for a few moments admiring the simple beauty of the evening, sniffed the air that was more reminiscent of a wet spring than a humid summer. Maybe Mrs. Frank would like to hit the neighborhood Dairy Queen. Just the two of them. He'd heard some good reports about the butterscotch-dipped cone. That would finish off the day just fine. He climbed in his car.

As a father of three, Seth Frank knew what a wonderful and precious commodity life was. As a homicide detective he had learned how that precious commodity could be brutally ripped away. He looked up at the roof of the apartment building and smiled as he put the car in gear. But that was the great thing about being alive, he thought. Today might not be so good. But tomorrow, you got another chance to get it right.

Use the above list and example, and other endings you study, to create the strongest and most satisfying ending for your novel.

Big Scenes

Once you've checked your scenes and made sure that you have correct structure, developed characterization, and used subtext, it's time to check your big scenes, the ones of higher drama. They may be "high" events such as weddings, love scenes, or any other celebratory scenes. They may be crises such as murders or rapes, battles, or any other terrible conflicts. Big scenes differ from other scenes by their intensity and importance, and how the challenges—met, overcome, or failed—result in a turning point.

Out of all of your scenes, identify which ones are big, or have the potential to be fully developed into big scenes. By definition, your climax is one. The inciting incident might be a big scene, but if it begins the novel, you won't be able to offer the foreshadowing development that others require.

Big scenes require special treatment. Because you want drama to be at a higher pitch than for other scenes, you will have to build greater suspense. In *Plot* by Ansen Dibell, he uses the term "set piece," instead of "big scene" and supplies a terrific outline of a way to jack suspense higher. I prefer to use the label "big scene" instead of "set piece" because the latter is a term used more often with plays and screenplays. Simply put, you can set up your big scenes most effectively by using escalating foreshadowing followed by reversal, then offering the big scene itself, and following it with character processing that shows the turning point.

A short story has room for one big scene—the climax. A novel for nine- to twelve-year-olds, for instance, may have two, maybe three. Short novels may have three or more big scenes. An epic saga may have a dozen, in the primary plot and in the subplots.

FORESHADOWING #1

Begin setting up your big scene with subtle foreshadowing. Perhaps your characters casually talk about the future event in one way or another, such that the reader can latch onto it and anticipate the big scene with excitement or dread, depending upon whether the characters know it will be joyous or disastrous. Anticipation creates suspense. For instance, characters would naturally discuss an upcoming wedding. Your protagonist could have a dream about the wedding, but wakes up at some critical early time in the ceremony. This is foreshadowing! In romances, the heroine and hero, if both have a viewpoint, may think about the first time they will make love. Less obvious foreshadowing would be alluding to it through the promise implied in kissing.

Big scenes of terrible events should also be foreshadowed. The protagonist or characters may talk in terms of "when we find the explosive devices," "when I get him in the interrogation room," or "when the killer visits her gravestone." As the plot advances, any time a character mentions or thinks about the wedding, making love, an explosive device, interrogation of the suspect, or the killer visiting the gravestone, it reminds the reader that the story will include this event. Foreshadowing raises suspenseful questions: When will it happen? What will happen when it does? Will anyone get hurt or killed? Will his strength pull him through? Will his weakness undermine his success?

FORESHADOWING #2

An escalation in foreshadowing is a developed scene of a like nature. In romance novels that's easy. The first embrace or hand-holding foreshadows the first kiss; the first kiss foreshadows the first lovemaking. A lesser fight or argument foreshadows violence. Both sex and combat are archetypical situations. But you can fore-shadow any event that you plan to be a big celebration or terrible crisis, even if it is not an exact match. Writers may use a different viewpoint character for this developed scene than they will use in the big scene, for instance. The emotion may be identical—sadness, joy, anger—and the circumstances parallel yet different. The teen-age girl Brandy, used earlier to illustrate a scene, may have caused a bumper-scruncher earlier in the novel—so her father has even more cause not to want her driving on a stormy night. But then Brandy drives too fast when she picks up Drew, which foreshadows not her death in an accident but Drew's, later, when he takes the wheel.

A SCENE OF REVERSAL

Earlier, I discussed the powerful technique of reversal, catching readers off-guard and delivering the unexpected, which then sets them up for the greater drama that lies just ahead. Directly before your big scene, create a short interaction or scene that offers tone or content that is the reverse of that you will feature in the big scene. For instance, a couple quarrels over dinner before they fall passion-ately into bed to make love for the first time. The cowboys drink and tell jokes on the first night of the trail ride in *Lonesome Dove*, before the big scene the next day when they cross the first river and one of them dies (attacked by water moccasins).

THE BIG SCENE

Finally, you'll have written or will need to work on your big scene, developing it in full glory and drama. As you revise, pull out the stops and use all possible aspects of scene development: action, reaction, reversal, raised questions, scene goals, opposition, multiple attempts and opposition, full sensory experience, thoughts, context, and subtext.

TURNING POINT

Last of all, make sure you follow up each big scene, immediately or soon after other viewpoint scenes, to show your protagonist processing what happened: expressing emotions (the big scene should end with a setback, too), reorienting to the whole book story problem and goal, glimpsing some of the truth or the theme, and finally reaching a turning-point decision. After each big scene, your protagonist should continue to seek the same story goal, to resolve the problem that began the novel, but now he or she does so with greater understanding and a new direction.

All of the steps of the big scenes heighten reader anticipation and take suspense to a new and higher level, building what is called "rising slope" that crests at the climax.

Make sure you have many big scenes that are of high drama and are fully developed.

Suspense

Everything discussed in this chapter, and in this whole book, serves the cornerstone of fiction: suspense. Keep the following checklist handy for all of your revisions.

Heightening Suspense
Check your novel for places to incorporate the following suspense-creating elements:

- Create a loudly ticking clock. The story goal—or scene goal—must be accomplished within a stated time framework, or else...like Kay Kenyon establishing three months before Earth will be entirely swallowed up by the crystal-growing network of information in her novel *Maximum Ice.*

- Move your scene or sequel into a dangerous or unpredictable setting. Or, you can make the mundane seem dangerous by turning a jog through the park into an obstacle course—dodging pedestrians, dogs, balls, kids, and sprinklers.
- Add a minion to help the antagonist or make a former ally into a turncoat, both of which make your hero's success more difficult.
- Turn the scene goal into a damned-if-you-do, damned-if-you-don't dilemma.
- Increase the number and difficulty of obstacles in a scene.
- Hamstring your protagonist with a temporary injury.
- Take away a source of your protagonist's power or skill.
- Give the antagonist a secret weapon that the reader knows about.
- Give readers (and the antagonist) knowledge that the protagonist doesn't have.
- Plant an emotional time bomb early in the story—an object of emotional meaning to the protagonist or victim, and light the fuse by presenting it in some form (found, destroyed, given away) later in the story.
- Start some of your scenes at a later point of difficulty—for example, revise to begin your scene where presently it ends.
- End a scene with a decision that is not revealed to the reader.
- When a scene protagonist is about to reach a goal and resolve a conflict, add a complication that makes him or her fail instead of succeed.
- Create times of misunderstanding and mistaken communication between the point-of-view characters and other characters.
- Take away options that were formerly there.
- Close escape routes.
- Replace goals with smaller stakes with ones of larger stakes.
- Bring in a new character (not point of view), event, or problem that is foreshadowed, not contrived, but makes new headaches.
- Raise emotions to out-of-control levels, or raise them to that point just before the character might lose control. Keep the reader on tenterhooks.
- Turn arguments into fights.

- Have an ally die.
- Have news of a family member's death.
- Kill the protagonist's mentor.
- Keep sexual attraction as a tease until you decide on a big love scene.
- Use nature as an ally and enemy.
- Set some scenes at night and use the fear factor of darkness.
- Use non sequiturs and show reactions and actions based on misunderstandings in dialogue.
- Add conflict from greater forces—political, social, cultural, historical—or institutions—government, hospitals, prisons, churches.
- Assign a number between one and five, one being the lowest level of suspense and five being the highest level of suspense. Give each of your scenes a rating. Decide if you have enough scenes of higher suspense.

Use the outlines of the structure of scenes, big scenes, and sequels as guidelines meant to become part of your makeover revision toolkit. Know that in revision, you can let your creativity use these tools for all the impact and special effects you envision. If you need to pick up pace, lop off one scene and begin another with higher stakes. If you need to develop characterization in greater depth, add subtext. If you lose your objectivity for revision, hand your pages to someone else, reader or novelist, and ask that person to mark places where they wish the pace were faster, the suspense greater, the characterization deeper.

With your character at the helm of your story, the next chapter will help you turn your hero, heroine, and main characters into the story people that will make a lasting impression on your readers.

Finally, remember this axiom: "Whatever you can conceive for a scene, you can always make worse." You can quote me.

MAKEOVER REVISION CHECKLIST
Character-Driven Scenes and Suspense

☑ Basic Scene Outline
1. A character with a goal runs into opposition.
2. Conflict builds greater suspense through repeated, thwarted efforts.
3. The character succeeds and reaches the goal, or fails.
4. The scene ends with change—a surprise, twist, setback, or disaster—relative to the scene goal.
5. The character reaches a new insight about the plot or himself or herself.

☑ Foundations of Character Motivation from the Plot
- Make stakes clear.
- Connect character motivation to stakes.

☑ Deepest Motivation Supplied by the Traumatic Event in the Past
- What does your point-of-view character yearn for?
- What happened in the past that brings this particular need to the forefront of your scene?

☑ Character Strength and Weakness, Also Molded by the Past
- Tie strength and weakness to key event in the past.
- Show strength and weakness play out through the scene, using the strength to push the action toward the goal and using the weakness as an obstacle.

☑ Show the Components of Character Stakes and Motivation
- Show feelings as expressed by the body, using sensory reactions.
- Show planning—the different plans developed by the point-of-view characters to reach the goal.
- Show the POV character reflecting and reviewing accomplishments and past events relative to his or her need and the plot or story goal.

☑ Subtext
Definition: What is hidden below the surface of the scene that contributes to tension or conflict

- Sources of subtext: emotions, needs, motivations within the POV character; the vibes and body language between characters; nature; human-made environment
- Make sure that subtext is clear and raises questions and therefore suspense.
- Use subtext to craft tension that runs counter to the conflict in the primary scene, and develop subtext when the outer scene tension is lower key.
- Examine your manuscript to pull out and develop multiple sources of subtext for multiple sources of tension, conflict, and raised questions.

☑ Keep Scenes Fresh
- Vary scene lengths and number of pages of each scene.
- Plan shorter scenes for faster pace, longer scenes and more development for slower pace.
- Model the length of your scenes in your novel's beginning based on what is typically done in your genre. Often beginnings have longer scenes.
- Make your development of your scene "protagonist's" reactions to scene outcomes, showing and narrating emotions, thought/processing, decisions, and actions, correspondingly more or less more fully developed at your novel's beginning and more abbreviated later—per what is typical in your genre.

☑ Diagnose Scene Problems
Use page 250 for a checklist of scene problems.

☑ Endings—The Uncertainty Factor
- End scenes with the unexpected.
- End scenes prior to completion, keeping your reader asking questions.
- Interrupt some scenes with other action.
- Summarize some scene endings at a later time.
- Write a flashback scene into the middle of a scene—or a flashforward—if your story supports that action.
- Work a sequel to a prior scene into a present scene.
- Develop sequel components throughout a present scene's actions as the scene progresses, creating a "shortcut."

- Begin a scene but cut it short to end in a sequel, or to continue after the sequel to the conclusion of the scene.

☑ Section/Chapter Endings
  - End sections and chapters at high points of uncompleted drama.
  - End with questions still raised.
  - To end a section or chapter with emotional completion or a scene ended, make sure you have a good reason to do so and that your story has sufficient suspense from prior development.

☑ Book Endings
  - Answer or explain lingering reader questions.
  - Reveal protagonist's (and sometimes other characters') realizations about self and life.
  - Reflect or state book's theme.
  - May tie in to book's beginning
  - May reveal a gift or surprise
  - Show characters who have shared the ordeal together, sharing conclusion.
  - Show a positive mood, in keeping with your story.
  - May end with a joke or humorous interaction
  - Novels in a series should reveal what is yet in need of pursuing while also concluding the quest of the present story.
  - The paragraph and sentence structure of the literal ending words should convey completion.

☑ Big Scenes
  Definition: Scenes of higher drama, of greater intensity and importance than other scenes, and resulting in a turning point
  Outline of big scenes:
  - Foreshadowing #1: Show characters talking about upcoming event, or in some way anticipate the big scene (a dream, an implication of the scene).
  - Foreshadowing #2: Develop a scene of a like or parallel nature in action, emotion, or subject.
  - Scene of Reversal: Add a short scene that is opposite or different in nature, action, emotion, or subject.

- The Big Scene: Fully develop this scene with all parts of scene structure.
- Turning Point: Follow up big scenes with a sequel, recognizing the "route" to reach the whole book goal has changed.

☑ Suspense
Use the checklist on pages 257–259 to heighten the suspense in your novel.

CHAPTER THIRTEEN
Character Personality and Voice

Options Some of the most lasting impressions of characters come from the most apparently superficial descriptions of them—their physical appearance, mannerisms, and especially how they talk, to themselves and others. When you join their drives, needs, and motivations with these more visible aspects of characterization, you can create characters as endearing and unique as your best friends.

Guaranteed, you need to give your protagonist a more distinctive personality and voice than you have. How can I be so sure? I have read hundreds of novels by writers of every level and talent, published or not yet published. Every one of them had a protagonist and other characters who were not distinctive enough.

It is a strange phenomenon that the last character to become interesting is the hero or heroine. Philosophical discussions aside, you have to do something about it. After you've followed earlier recommendations to develop the depth and dimensionality of your protagonist, you've taken one giant step forward.

Think of your protagonist, and each main character in turn, as a job applicant and you're the employer. How would your character rate in the ten to fifteen seconds of a first impression, before he or she opens her mouth to speak? After you see the first thirty applicants, will you remember your protagonist? What goes into split-second first impressions?

Throughout this book, I've been advising you to deepen character, to tap your own emotions and use them to create the reactions your characters would be expected to have. I've told you to make sure you give your hero or heroine a universal need that came out of a wounding experience. Now, it's time to get superficial! It's time to work on the outside-in impression your character will make and probably be remembered for.

Descriptions

In planning and writing your novel, you surely developed some descriptions unique to your protagonist and other characters. In revision, go through your manuscript, perhaps with a highlighter, and find where you incorporated distinctive descriptions or traits. That way you can see at a glance how often you have—or haven't— presented your character as a distinctive individual in the mind's eye of the reader. Two categories of description and characterization to mine for distinguishing your characters are physical appearance and emotional/intellectual disposition. These two categories include what is most concrete and visible in the comportment and disposition of your characters. Although you don't need to include every item in your novel, you should know the answers to the items on the list on page 266 for any given character in your book.

While I encourage you to draw from the list of physical and emotional/intellectual details to make your characters memorable, I believe that attitudes and passions go to the heart of their individuality. In my opinion, these two are not optional; they are so important that you should specifically work on them in your revision. What is a hero without attitudes or passions? He or she will be a conduit for information and an actor toward an important goal, but will have as little personality as John or Jane Doe. The "affect," as they term it in psychology, of characters with subdued personalities is flat. Not a fun blind date.

Don't let the censoring forces of political correctness keep your point-of-view characters from having attitude. *Attitude*, as I'm using it, broadly refers to strongly held opinions, beliefs, values, biases,

Drawing Your Characters in Distinguishing Detail

PHYSICAL APPEARANCE

Gender, age, height, weight, body build, body hair, race, skin color, skin texture, hair body and style, hair texture and color, smell of hair, head size and shape, facial hair, eye shape and color, shape of brow, shape and fullness of lips, teeth size and color, personal grooming, handshake, hands, nails, body smell, added scents, carriage and posture, activity level (lethargic to manic, focused to attention deficit), deformities, hereditary physical attributes, birthmarks, scars, overall health, habitual stances and gestures, voice quality—volume and timbre and pitch (soprano, alto, tenor, baritone, bass), quality of laugh, head-to-toe clothing (style, functionality, quality), accessories (jewelry, bags, satchels, gloves, scarves, hats)

EMOTIONAL/INTELLECTUAL DISPOSITION

Attitudes (opinions, viewpoints, mind-sets, biases, prejudices), *passions* (desires, keen interests, needs, yearnings, obsessions), emotions hidden or obvious—*most dominant emotion* (sad, mad, glad, inscrutable) and how it is shown or expressed, *sense of humor* and expression of it (jokes, puns, silly humor, slapstick, wry, sarcastic, dirty, wholesome, raunchy, perverse, flirtatious, irreverent, political, racial, sexist), *temperament* (introvert to extrovert), *operating mode* (logical thinker to intuitive hunch-taker; sensate/ empirically based to feeling/emotionally based), *intellectual type* (scholarly/abstract, experiential/concrete, quick, slow, bright, dull, methodical, multitasking), *dominant perception* (tactile, visual, auditory), *orientation to life* (cynic, pessimist, realist, optimist, idealist), *hard-wiring* (compulsive/ thorough, phobic/fearful, vacillating mood/sensitive, impulsive/risk-taking, neuroses/distortions, psychoses/without basis in reality)

judgments, prejudices, superstitions, pet peeves, and preferences— about everything. Out of these attitudes will come moral codes and behavior, political and religious beliefs, personal and lifestyle habits and choices, leisure-time preferences, job choices, favorite channels and programs on TV and radio, games and frequented sites on the Internet, selections of magazines and newspapers and books, and so forth.

What underlies the attitudes that your story people hold? This goes back to the nature/nurture debate. Some attitudes may be fueled by heredity and biology, but characters, like people, are also molded by major outside, or environmental, forces: family, friends, neighbors, community, town, region, country; by particular institutions—religious, educational, political, technological, workplace; and by socioeconomics.

When you offer a self-description (physical, emotional, intellectual), and express an attitude by your point-of-view character, the reader adds to a mental file about that character. When you offer a description of another character, the reader adds to two mental files: the one for your point-of-view character and the one for the character being described. Here is a description of a minor character and the protagonist in a first mystery, *Murder Uncorked*, by Michele Scott. Notice the protagonist's attitude that colors the descriptions and helps create two distinctive personalities:

> Nikki Sands hated her job almost as much as she hated her past. She straightened her crisp white blouse and put on her best smile. She approached the couple at the table she was serving, and couldn't help but notice the woman watching her with that unmistakable glint of self-importance that judged Nikki to be nothing but the peon who was waiting on them. The woman had a glamour-girl theme about her, but that hair needed a good hairdresser. Hadn't she heard that frizzy platinum blonde was passé? Not to mention the Pat Benatar smoldering-eye-makeup look....
>
> Lately, she'd been attempting to try something very anti-L.A. The concept of not judging others—something she found *exceedingly* difficult to do, especially in this case....

The next descriptions, from *Dust to Dust* by Tami Hoag, follow a beginning scene where the protagonist, Sam Kovac, is grousing about nicotine gum:

Kovac scowled down at her from the corner of one eye. Liska made five-five by sheer dint of will. He always figured God made her short because if she had the size of Janet Reno she'd take over the world. She had that kind of energy—and attitude out the wazoo.

"What do you know about it?" he challenged.

"My ex smoked. Lick an ashtray sometime. That's why we got divorced, you know. I wouldn't stick my tongue in his mouth."

"Jesus, Tinks, like I wanted to know that."

He'd given her the nickname—Tinker Bell on Steroids. Nordic blond hair cut in a shaggy Peter Pan style, eyes as blue as a lake on a sunny day. Feminine but unmistakably athletic. She'd kicked more ass in her years on the force than half the guys he knew. She'd come onto homicide—Christ, what was it now?—five or six years ago? He lost track. He'd been there himself almost longer than he could remember. All of his forty-four years, it seemed....

What both of these examples show is anything but a neutral character channeling information. These two characters have attitude; their descriptions of the other characters and themselves are colored with strong opinions.

All well-written novels add to the readers' mental files, accumulating details worked into the story. Often, with literary novels, it is more difficult to pull out a paragraph for example, as I have done above, because the whole story has been soaked in a unique dye distinguishing the protagonist. Every part of the novel contributes to idiosyncratic characterization.

The other emotion I have singled out as essential to memorable characterization is *passion*. Attitude tends to have a pejorative slant of being against something. Passion glows with a positive slant of not only being for something, but being zealously, enthusiastically, fervently, irrepressibly for something. Passion is infectious. Agents recognize it and respond favorably to it in query letters as well as in manuscripts, and readers recognize it, too. And love to experience it vicariously. Then the readers feel passionate about recommending the book to their circle of friends and family and you have word-of-mouth sales—the best.

Heroes and heroines should be passionate about their lives, what they are seeking, and what finding it will do not only for themselves but for the people they care for. Passion is single-minded in that it brooks no reasoning to the contrary, no nay-saying. Scarlett O'Hara will save Tara. Frodo will see that the One Ring is destroyed. Your characters must passionately give their all to finding justice, redemption, understanding, or self-respect, as well as do their equivalent of saving Tara and destroying the Ring. At the beginning of this book, I discussed methods of "deep listening" and harvesting your own emotions using an "inside-out" technique. Endow your protagonist and other characters with passion, and animate them with your own deep feelings, through your prose. Breathe life into your characters. It's okay if they were blue babies in your prior draft. Now see them cry, and laugh, and love with passion flowing in their veins.

Review any character sketches you made and use the list to add to them. Reread your pages specifically for physical and emotional descriptions, attitudes, and passions. The next stand-out quality is how your characters use language—in speech and thought—to make a lasting impression of who they are by their unique voices.

Paradoxically, attitudes are limiting; they draw boundaries. Passions are expansive; they dissolve boundaries. Your point-of-view characters, most especially your protagonist, need to have both sharply defined. Then your characters will be remembered.

Character Voice

In part one, I discussed the importance of discovering and developing your style, to strengthen your unique author voice, which is a constant part of your whole novel. Each character will carry your author voice but should be distinctive in his or her own right. All of the factors I listed in what causes "attitude" are the same ones that contribute to how your character uses language. One of the problems is that writers' language use stems from those same factors in their lives, yet they may have a character as different from them as an extraterrestrial—or their character may even *be* an extraterrestrial. That's why you need to put extra attention into your characters' voices—in narrative passages and in dialogue—to carve them out as different from you. This extra effort is worth it.

Before you dive into a revision to improve character voice, and therefore uniqueness of personality, I recommend that you create a character dictionary. In the future, create a dictionary for each character prior to and as you write your first drafts. Find any and every resource you can that reveals language use of your character. Perhaps you have created a ninety-year-old woman as a character. What race? What religion? Where did she grow up? Put together a profile of these factors and call your area's homes for seniors. Perhaps you'll find someone, within a decade of your character's age, in one of these places. Record her use of language. Add to your character dictionary.

If you can't meet doppelgängers for your characters, then read books by other authors whose characters match yours in at least some ways. Add to your character dictionary. Go online. Rent movies. Keep notes.

One of the most amazing and welcome changes in American publishing is what I see as a renaissance of voices and cultures. Authors of all races and ethnicities are at last seeing publication and gaining recognition for outstanding writing. Consider, for example, *Obasan* by Joy Kogawa, *A Thousand Splendid Suns* by Khaled Hosseini, and *The Toughest Indian in the World* by Sherman Alexie.

You are probably aware of the unresolved and heated discussion in the literary community about whether any writer, of any race or ethnicity, can create and write in the voice of a character from a race and ethnicity different from their own. Creatively, you can write anything you want to. In terms of the politics of publishing, opinions are mixed. I could say, "It all depends," but I think the jury is out.

However, the challenge you face is to make your characters as authentic within their identities and worlds as possible. If you do have a point-of-view character, or even a minor character with a speaking role, who, for instance, has ancestry that is Japanese, Afghani, or American Indian, like the authors quoted above, then you would certainly want to read novels written by these authors, and add to your dictionary for your character's language use.

What if you, and your characters, are white, as in Caucasian (after all, who *is* "white"), of Anglo-Saxon roots, and to boot, your family's religious affiliations are one of the garden-variety Protestant types? In other words, what if you are a WASP (white Anglo-Saxon Protestant)? What is the distinctive language and voice of a WASP? Especially if you also come from, and hold residency by virtue of socioeconomics in, the middle class?

I think writing middle-class WASP (or WAS Catholic) is one of the toughest challenges for differentiating character, especially if the author has the same roots. As I understand Rita Mae Brown, writing in her wonderful book *Starting from Scratch*, the use of language of this group is bland and banal. Because this group has formerly comprised the bulk of the population, middle-class WASP speech defines the primary American language. Brown states, "All government talk is middle-class talk at its worst. A wonderful television documentary is middle-class talk at its best."

You certainly don't want your writing to fall somewhere between government talk and documentary talk. *Bor-ing.* Further, her analysis of middle-class language use describes it as inoffensive, soothing, evasive of issues, great at *telling* about emotions, and absent of offensive metaphors, except when in a crisis and then, to be expressive, includes sexual metaphors. My experience as an editor and writer with WASP, rural, lower- to middle-class roots is in agreement with Brown's ideas, although I think there are more factors that go into our language use. But your origins and class may indicate a need to go to extra lengths not to end up with an author or character voice that is flat, bland, forgettable. If you do have one of the three socioeconomic classes assigned to your characters, I recommend that you read about all three classes and use of language in Rita Mae Brown's book.

I am convinced that giving your characters attitude and passion and finding ways to show these two personality-forging qualities will cross half the distance of the voice problem. To help cross the other half, work hard at adding the following to your character dictionary: individual use of diction and syntax, vocabulary, metaphoric language, idioms, sayings, and dialogue tags.

DICTION AND SYNTAX

For clarity, *diction* is a word choice and *syntax* is sentence structure. Within each, you have a lot of decisions to make on behalf of each character. Formal, complex, and refined? Informal, simple, and colloquial? Or mix and match. Add other diction choices: special use of language due to the period or era and setting, character age (teen talk, for instance), race, ethnicity, region, education, job, and other attitudinal influences. Rita Mae Brown and others talk about word choices that stem from Latin/French or Anglo-Saxon/Old English derivations. Words that have origins in Latin and French have a lot of "ence," "ion," or "ment" endings: commence, position, parliament. Latinate diction pervades our higher education use of language. Because higher education used to be affordable only by the upper class, it is the diction associated with older wealth. Latinate diction and syntax favors longer words and longer sentences and an intellectual distance. Linguists say that about seventy percent of our American English language is derived from the Latin/French, although the one hundred most commonly used words are Anglo-Saxon.

Remember that Greek and Latin were taught in American schools, even in primary grades, but not Anglo-Saxon! The Anglo-Saxon period in English history lasted from 449 to 1066 and the words were primarily of German origin. Those words and sentences are shorter, pack more emotional punch, and seem more authentic as they don't beat around the bush (an Anglo-Saxon phrase). Here are a few comparisons of words that, you can see, would make a great difference in setting apart one character from another.

Latin/French	Anglo-Saxon/Old English
aid	help
story	tale
extinguish	put out
frigid	cold
people	folk

For syntax, you can review chapter two on sentence variety and make some decisions for each character's syntax based on sentence types and parts of speech. Here are some examples of narrative voice (narrated, not in dialogue). Notice how different one character voice—and the personality communicated—is from another.

I knew there wasn't nobody besides me and him she cared much about; not unless you wanted to count Eddie White and I never. Eddie was a shiftless old boy about my age; he worked around the oil patch whenever he felt like working, and when he didn't he hung around Thalia playing dominos or running his hounds. He was too no-count for a girl like Molly to pay attention to. I think she just mentioned him once in a while to keep me and Johnny uneasy.

—*Leaving Cheyenne* by Larry McMurtry

The diction in this passage is colloquial and shows a narrator, Gid, who uses incorrect grammar—"wasn't nobody, me and him, I never, no-count." Even "to pay attention to" is lower diction. Gid is uneducated. The vocabulary is simple and seems rural. The syntax includes several compound-complex sentences. In general they are long (averaging twenty-one words per sentence), and I could imagine him using run-on sentences. Gid has attitude; he doesn't much care for Eddie White.

Here is another example:

> His voice had a deep sexy rumble with a gentleness that stirred her. She had noticed it right from the first. Now she loved his voice, and damn near everything else about him, except the way he behaved. The last thing she needed at her age was to be involved with a self-proclaimed wacky artist who acted like a juvenile delinquent. What she had said to him that morning was true. If she became openly involved with him romantically, she'd be the laughingstock of Paris, and even New York. She had a reputation to protect. Liam didn't.
>
> —*ImPossible* by Danielle Steel

The diction of this narrator is a mixture of formal and informal. Sascha is educated. Her word use is precise, articulate, educated, and sophisticated—"behaved, self-proclaimed, juvenile delinquent, openly involved, laughingstock." The syntax has more variety, sentences are shorter (averaging eleven words per sentence) than the McMurtry example, and the grammar is correct. Sascha has strongly held opinions; she has attitude. She is also passionate, not only about her lover, but also about her reputation.

Even from one paragraph taken from a whole novel, each of these characters comes through with a personality and voice.

VOCABULARY

As you prepare to revise your novel to strengthen the individuality and personality of your characters, expand the vocabulary you used in the first draft. But not just any vocabulary: Make a list of the kinds of professions or activities of your characters but also those that are part of the plot. You can do an Internet search to get words to add to your character dictionary. For instance, you could plug in the search words "art words" or "art terms." All of us unconsciously use words from our interest and work areas—as well as from other spheres of life. Some professions have more "code" than others. Since the genre of crime fiction is so huge, with dozens of subgenres, anyone writing these novels should learn its highly technical and specialized language. And if your sleuth is a detective *and* an artist? Then you'll have those two areas to draw from.

Regrettably, in Danielle Steel's novel *ImPossible*, from which I quoted a paragraph above, the terminology of art is all but absent, even though her protagonist, Sascha, owns a famous art gallery in Paris and another in New York, and even though her lover, Liam, is an artist. The terminology of euphemistic love is in abundance.

Dean Koontz, however, offers a terrific example of a detective who is also an artist. In *Whispers*, Koontz created an officer/artist. Tony's perception of patterns from his artistic eye has led him to becoming a more effective policeman. An excerpt follows of a small portion of over two pages of Koontz's masterful characterization of Tony, as a policeman and artist.

Frank, Tony's partner, is at the wheel, as they drive into Los Angeles:

> He [Tony] stared at the passing scenery with an artist's eye for unexpected detail and previously unnoticed beauty....
>
> Patterns.
>
> As Frank Howard drove east on Wilshire, on the way to the Hollywood singles' bar called The Big Quake, Tony searched for patterns in the city and the night. At first, coming in from Santa Monica, there were the sharp low lines of the sea-facing houses and the shadowy outlines of tall feathery palms—patterns of serenity and civility and more than a little money. As they entered West-wood, the dominant pattern was rectilinear: clusters of office high-rises, oblong patches of light radiating from scattered windows in the mostly dark faces of buildings. These neatly ordered rectangular shapes formed the patterns of modern thought and corporate power, patterns of even greater wealth than had been evident in Santa Monica's seaside homes....

By using the vocabulary from both professions, and developing them as part of Tony's worldview and emotional reality, Koontz builds a unique and memorable character.

METAPHORIC LANGUAGE

A powerful way to develop the personality, voice, and full depth of your characters is to use metaphoric language that directly stems from all of the factors mentioned earlier in this chapter that underlie our attitudes, beliefs, and values. As you build your character dictionary, you can look over the words and create similes and metaphors that directly reflect that character's experience. As Dean Koontz finishes the long description of the neighborhoods of Los Angeles, as Tony sees them, blending his police training with his artistic eye, Koontz shows how Tony extends the idea of literal patterns—rectangles, squares, lines—into metaphors for people, as follows:

> The customers were somewhat more consciously stylish, more aggressively *au courant*, and generally a shade better looking than the crowd in Paradise. But to Tony the patterns appeared to be the same as they were in Santa Monica. Patterns of need, longing, and loneliness. Desperate, carnivorous patterns.

Once you have assembled a vocabulary for your point-of-view characters, I predict you will not have a great deal of trouble crafting similes. Over the course of revising your novel, as you add metaphoric and literal language, based on the individuality of your character's interests and background, you'll build a unity of characterization. Instead of mimicking your own voice, background, and unconscious use of metaphoric language, you'll create characters separate in their own right.

IDIOMS

Every culture has idioms, expressions that often have a meaning different from the literal meaning, and they almost always trip up anyone from another country and culture. Regions within the United States have idioms that may puzzle people who live in other locations. Idioms are another source for giving your characters a unique personality. You can use them in narration or in dialogue. If in dialogue, other characters may respond to the idiom or in some way react, which simply adds to your characterization. Here are examples of idioms from several parts of the United States:

New England: "To lower the boom" on someone, "Three sheets to the wind" (drunk).

New York (Yiddish origins): "Get lost," "What's up," "I should worry."

Appalachia: "It pleasures me," "That was mighty fetchin' of you," "She prettied herself up."

Upland South/Adjacent to Appalachia: "Started full tilt," "As the devil would have it," "Set on him like a wild cat."

Texas: "Cute as a bug's ear," "He's so ugly he has to sneak up on a mirror," "He's ugly as a tow sack shirt."

PHRASES AND SAYINGS

In your point-of-view characters' narration and dialogue, also use phrases and sayings that correspond with their use of language. Earlier I mentioned the Latin/French derivation of many of our words. Common ones that an educated character, or one who has a legal background, might use include:

ad hoc, ad infinitum, alma mater, bona fide, carpe diem, caveat emptor, ego, ego maniac, id, in toto, libido, mea culpa, per capita, persona, persona non grata, postmortem, pro bono, non sequitur, terra firma, terra incognita, vice versa

If your character has a more working-class background or is less educated, you might want to draw from Anglo-Saxon phrases and sayings, which are colorful and always seem to include a literal image used in a metaphoric way:

> on the lam, minding your *p*'s and *q*'s, playing with a full deck, getting your goat, going to pot. It'll cost you an arm and a leg. Mind your own bee's wax. Bring home the bacon.

Now that you have your character's individualized dictionary, you can improve the dialogue you've written.

Dialogue

Listen. Some people speak in long sentences; others rely upon a few words to communicate—and that's it! Some people never complete a sentence and interrupt themselves with another thought. Don't we all use slang, some of it entering the language and sticking and some of it from pop culture, here today and gone tomorrow?

You face a paradox when you go to write and revise dialogue: It needs to sound like natural speech. It should not replicate everyday speech.

In other words, dialogue should fool the reader into thinking it is as believable as talk between your characters, and yet it must meet two primary functions: (1) to characterize the speaker, and (2) to move the story forward.

Here are some guidelines to improve your dialogue.

Dialogue That Works

- Keep it short.
- Make use of incomplete sentences, contractions, interrupted sentences, and trailing off sentences.
- Use occasional non sequiturs—responses to what has been said that have no bearing on what was just said.
- Use sprinkles of dialect; approximate it by sound and syntax rather than using dialect for every word.
- Create movement.
- Imply subtext, reinforced by point-of-view character response between the lines.
- Include conflict or tension.
- Color with the speaker's diction, syntax, vocabulary, idioms, sayings, and so forth.
- Avoid "talking heads," lengthy exchanges of dialogue without any other element of craft such as interior thought, action, description, feeling, or sensation.
- Avoid overuse of direct references—addressing the person by name.
- Avoid using dialogue primarily as a way to dump a truckload of information.
- Omit small talk, introductions of characters, and the "warm-ups" that fill everyday conversation.
- Avoid putting in dialogue what you have just told in narration, or vice versa.

An area that gives some writers grief is the attribution. That means the description of who the speaker is that precedes or follows the dialogue; in other words, the he-saids and she-saids. Above all, you want clarity, yet you don't want clutter. If it is clear who is speaking, don't feel obligated to use any attribution. For example:

"For crying out loud, Davey, will you turn down your blasted stereo?"

"Oh, yeah, sure, I didn't think it was up that loud."

"You can't be serious and if you are, I've got a bigger problem on my hands than I thought."

"Sorry."

The simplest form of attribution is simply to use "he said" or "she said." Generally, the preferred order is subject and then verb, not "said he" or "said she." Of course, you can use the character name in place of the pronoun, but avoid overuse of names as well. Occasionally, use of "he thought" or "she thought" will "sound right," but most of the time, omit this attribution for indirect and direct thought.

In general, don't describe your dialogue. If you've done a good job, the reader should be able to understand the emotion from the dialogue. For instance, in the dialogue I created above, the emotions of each speaker are clear. Yet, sometimes, carefully, you may want to describe the intention or emotion behind the dialogue using words such as "confided, groused, insisted, defended, hinted, explained, or joked." On the other hand, some words for describing dialogue scream novice (except when they "work"), especially if overused: "chortled, snorted, replied, declared, exclaimed, or cried." I personally cringe when I read the word "giggled" used for anyone but children, a personal bias.

A most effective way to improve dialogue is to replace the need for an attribution with a small stage action by the speaker that not only makes it clear who spoke but keeps the reader anchored in the body and setting. Dialogue by itself is cerebral; it exists in a near vacuum—just sound waves. Small actions and reactions can also characterize, demonstrate subtext, and increase tension.

Some novels are dialogue dominant, which may reflect the genre or the fact that dialogue is that author's strength. When dialogue is written well, it vibrates with energy. Because it is an action (after all, the lips do flap), it has the power of movement and the power of immediacy. It has no viewpoint in that it is part of the shared outer environment. If you add narration between spoken lines, then that narration reveals the point of view.

The next example puts all the components of dialogue together: the spoken words, the attribution, the internal response/reaction, and outer action. This excerpt is from a mystery, *Big Numbers* by Jack Getze. I've added bracketed comments to identify the components.

Late that night, Luis's Mexican Grill is empty but for me, Luis, and three sixty-something guys with canvas fishing hats and gray stubble watching baseball highlights on ESPN. [narrated setting] Luis walks into their viewing line, checks his watch, shuts off the TV. [action]

"I must close," he says. [dialogue/attribution]

"Shit," one of the fishing-hat geezers says. [dialogue/attribution]

I push up from my stool, ready to stumble out to my camper, suck up some fresh night air. [action/thought]

"Ten more minutes, Lou," another fishing-hat geezer says. "Till the end of the show." [dialogue/attribution]

Luis catches my eye, flashes me a palm. [action] Telling me to stay. [thought] When I sit back down, Luis approaches the closest fishing-hat geezer. Also the biggest. [action]

Luis saying, "Leave now or I will dismember your body with the sharpened bone of your child's leg." [attribution/dialogue]

Takes eight or nine seconds for the Geezer Fishing Hats to don windbreakers, throw money on the bar, make their way outside. They no longer seem pissed they can't watch the end of *Baseball Tonight*. [narrated action/thought]

In half a page, the reader gets three characterizations—of Luis, the clientele, and the protagonist, Austin, and each of them have a definite attitude. Getze has captured a sense of the ethnicity or dual language background of Luis by his diction and syntax in "I must close." It sounds formal but also gives the sense in context of someone for whom English may be a second language. He hasn't said, "Gotta close up, fellas," which would convey a different character. When Luis makes his threat, I hear it as deadpan and, by the immediate response of the fishing-hat geezers, dead serious. I immediately supplied a picture in my mind of Luis as a bouncer, a big man with a barrel chest and a low voice. Getze has not supplied this description; it is how my imagination was stirred by two lines of dialogue. I was seduced; I gave myself up to the story. That's what you want your readers to do.

Notice, too, how these few lines have conveyed multiple sources of movement and suspense. Getze included outer action, narrated action, anticipation about what Luis will say to their resistance to leave, and suspense about why he wants Austin to stay. Getze also adds the tension of Austin's irritation or disdain toward the men by referring to them, repeatedly, as fishing-hat geezers. Perhaps not taken out of context, but certainly in context, Luis's threat is funny.

Because dialogue is action, it also fulfills the maxim, "Show, don't tell." It is a showcase for characterization and captures personality and character voice like nothing else. Sharpen your dialogue, taking extra pains to delete unnecessary and extra verbiage. Make it lean and expressive at the same time. Although you are most likely to have heard "Show, don't tell" more than any other rule in writing, in the next chapter, the focus will be on "telling well," how to revise your narration to turn it into characterization.

MAKEOVER REVISION CHECKLIST
Character Personality and Voice

☑ Descriptions
- Use a highlighter to mark distinctive (versus general) descriptions or traits of characters.
- Review the list on page 266 for specific ways to create uniqueness in body, emotions/intellect, and attitudes.
- Add "attitude" to each point-of-view character's descriptions of self and others; show opinions, beliefs, values, biases, judgments, prejudices, superstitions, pet peeves, and preferences.
- Endow your protagonist and other characters with passion for their lives and for what they are seeking; use deep listening to "harvest" your own feelings to create authenticity when you revise.

☑ Character Voice
- Create character dictionaries with words specific to each point-of-view character.
- Interview and record a person in your community who matches the demographics of your character—add words, phrases, and diction/syntax to that character's dictionary.
- Read books that have characters that correspond to yours, adding words and phrases to your character dictionary.
- Rent movies for the era, age, gender, and other factors that match your characters and story, adding words and phrases to your character dictionary.
- Go online and use synonyms to find terms and words for your characters.
- Be aware of your own use of language based on your own age, race, ethnicity, income, social class, place of birth and growing up, parental ancestry, and so forth. Make sure you create a character voice and personality that matches the background you have ascribed to that character and not just your unconscious use of language based on yourself.

☑ Diction and Syntax
- Create diction based on selections such as formal, complex, and refined or informal, simple, and colloquial. Craft diction to match

period or era, character age, race, ethnicity, region, education, job, and other attitudinal influences.

- Think about the primary origins of your characters' diction and syntax: Latin/French or Anglo-Saxon/Old English.
- Review chapter two on sentence variety to choose unique syntax for each character.

☑ Vocabulary
- List the profession and activities for each character, then do an Internet search pairing a word with "term" to get lists of words associated with various professions and activities (such as "art terms" or "police terms"). Add these words to your character dictionary.
- Use each character's unique vocabulary in dialogue and narration.

☑ Metaphoric Language
- Use the words from your character dictionary to develop similes and metaphors apropos to your character, taking into consideration all of the demographic factors.

☑ Idioms
- Add and use, in dialogue and narration, idioms—sayings—common to your characters' region of growing up or living.

☑ Phrases and Sayings
- Add and use, in dialogue and narration, phrases and sayings common to your characters' use of language—by education or profession—and often derivative of Latin/French or Anglo-Saxon/Old English origins.

☑ Dialogue
- Review page 279 for guidelines to improve dialogue.

Attributions:
- You can omit attributions for dialogue if it is clear who is speaking.
- Primarily, use the order of subject then verb for attributions: "he said" not "said he."
- Avoid overuse of a name in dialogue or attribution.
- Omit most uses of the attribution "he thought" or "she thought."

- Avoid description of dialogue most of the time: "chortled, replied, declared, exclaimed, cried," and so forth.
- Replace the need for an attribution with small actions or reactions by the speaker.
- With exceptions of carefully chosen passages that are nothing but dialogue, integrate the components of dialogue: spoken words, attribution (as necessary or preferred), the internal response/reaction, outer action.
- Delete unnecessary and extra verbiage.

CHAPTER FOURTEEN

Character-Driven Narration

Options It is essential that you have the skill to "tell," or narrate, as well as the skill to "show." After you turn narration, including description, into characterization, your readers will never think of description as that "boring stuff" they skip. If your problems relate more to style, structure, or even marketing, return to this chapter at a later date.

If you've been writing for even a short while, you have probably heard, if not been told in a critique, to "show, don't tell." Show means to translate what you've written out of a summary and into a scene. Change it from a news bulletin into a dramatized combination of goals, conflicts, actions, reactions, and dialogue. Make readers feel as if the story is unfolding before their eyes. Sometimes writers become overly zealous about portions of writing that are not demonstrated by the characters. Yet, open up most published books and what do you see? Narration.

Narration is the term for anything that is told to the reader. As an umbrella term, it includes the following:

- descriptions of the self and other characters
- named emotions, yearnings, affect
- backstory
- interior thoughts—philosophizing, insights, musings, memories, and strategies for future actions
- descriptions of natural and human-made settings and objects—geography and geology, lay of the land, field and stream, flora and fauna, weather and seasons

As you can see, the types of narration are many. Yet, nearly all instruction and critique fails to advise novelists *how* to narrate. This is not surprising in that beginning writers often narrate when they should demonstrate. And getting a feeling of when narration works is an acquired skill. All forms of telling slow pace compared to showing, which has action at its core. The majority of novels average about seventy percent scenes; they are primarily character-driven action for the purpose of reaching a story goal to resolve an important problem. Yet, showing and telling, like brick and mortar, build a successful story.

All of us have had the experience of reaching a portion of a novel where the pace slows. Like other readers who do not write fiction, we may skip ahead to where the story picks up and becomes interesting once again. Or, we may start a novel but simply can't get through the first twenty pages of narration. Yet in another novel with just as much narration, we can't wait to turn the next page. What's wrong? What is one writer doing that succeeds where other writers clearly aren't?

When any form of narration reveals the unique personality and voice of the viewpoint character, as covered in the last chapter, it becomes characterization. Without the personality, attitude, and passion of a character, this kind of narration often makes the reader aware of the author or a disembodied narrator. Sometimes that narrator seems to be a video camera, objectively panning a scene. Why not skip a few pages? Make sure that narration reflects each viewpoint character's personality and voice.

It doesn't matter how you have written your first draft. Most writers use revision to develop narration and make it character-driven. Most of the time, work movement—action or implied action—into your narrated passages. In her book *Description*, author Monica Wood calls this technique "show-tell." You could also think of it as "tell-show" depending upon which comes first in your sentence or paragraph. The following is an example of well-written narration integrating tell-show/show-tell, as identified in the bracketed comments. The excerpt is from *Polar Star* by Martin Cruz Smith:

During his first months at sea, Arkady had spent a lot of time on deck watching for dolphins, sea lions and whales, just to see them moving. [tell-show] The sea gave the illusion of escape. [tell] But after a time he realized that what all these creatures of the sea had, as they swam this way and that, was a sense of purpose. [tell-show-tell]. It was what he didn't have. [tell]

In this paragraph, the form of narration is thinking and philosophizing about life as triggered by watching the sea mammals and their behavior. The remembered movement within the narration keeps the reader involved in the story setting. The origin of the narration is clearly with the character Arkady, and not from an author-reporter.

In contrast, from this same novel and from the same author is this paragraph of omniscient and objective description that demonstrates the successful breaking of a rule: Limit or avoid omniscient, objective narration; it comes across like a documentary voice, and shows what a camera sees:

The *Polar Star* [name of a Russian ship] had a clinic bigger than most small towns could boast: a doctor's office, an examining room, an infirmary with three beds, a quarantine room and an operating room, [narration] to which Slava led Arkady. [action] Along the walls were white cupboards with glass canisters of instruments in alcohol, a locked red cupboard with cigarettes and drugs, a cart with a green tank of oxygen and a red tank of nitrous oxide, a standing ashtray and a brass spittoon. [narration] There were anatomical charts on the wall, an astringent tang to the air. [narration including telling a smell] A dentist's chair sat in one corner. [narration] In the middle of the room was a steel operating table covered by a sheet. [narration] Soaked through, the cloth clung to the form of a woman underneath. [tell-show] Below the edge of the sheet dangled restraining straps. [show]

What makes this paragraph of objective narration work? After all, it is primarily telling, with a few bits of action, many "to be" or passive verbs, adjectives—which describe [tell]—and nonspecific nouns? For me, Smith's narration keeps me in the fictive world through selective use of specific details, using several techniques, telling the different functions and numbers of the rooms, mentioning colors throughout— white, red, green, red—as adjectives transforming generic objects into specific ones; using the power positions for "brass spittoon," which is a highly specific object and evokes a color and sound, and introducing the body of the woman as the last content of the paragraph. Because Smith includes the told smell, "an astringent tang to the air," as a reader I have a sensation that this telling has been showing. Even though Smith narrates in an objective, omniscient way, I also ascribe the description to the protagonist, Arkady.

Notice, too, that the pace of this paragraph is leisurely. Smith has taken his time to develop details of the setting, and the accumulation of that detail, along with the other techniques mentioned earlier, keep the reader involved, not skipping ahead. Martin Cruz Smith is a superb storyteller, his style understated and subtle. The objective portions of the novel are in keeping, as well, with the style of many thrillers.

As you revise, find places where you have given short shrift to narration or where you have omitted opportunities to fill out the details of your created world by narrating. By riff-writing or by modeling favorite authors, open up your writing. Use the categories covered in the bulleted list earlier in this chapter.

Self-Description

Because characters are all-important as the movers and shakers of your story, I want to single out narrated self-description. One of the most difficult descriptions is the one your protagonist and other point-of-view characters offer of themselves. You'll need to describe them and remind your readers of their appearance, or add details to earlier descriptions. Two mistakes often made by beginners are to stand a character in front of a mirror and to offer a description reminiscent of a list. For example, "Marie gazed at herself in the mirror.

Shoulder-length auburn curls framed an oval face. Her eyes were brown, her lips full but making a downward turn. She was petite, only five-foot-two, but she had a thin and shapely figure." This is a list that could have been given by a reporter.

In the following examples of self-description, notice that some are narrated and some include movements or implied actions within the narration. Especially notice that these self-descriptions are subjective, reflecting the attitude, personality, and voice of the characters. First, from *Black and Blue* by Anna Quindlen, self-description is embedded in narrated backstory. Notice the attitude and emotion Quindlen conveys:

And they [her husband's friends] looked at me and saw a happy wife and mother like so many others, a working woman like so many others. Fran Flynn—you know, the skinny redhead who works in the ER at South Bay. Frannie Benedetto, the cop's wife on Beach Twelfth Street, the one with the little boy with bowlegs. Gone down the drain that morning. Transformed, perhaps forever, by Loving Care No. 27, California Blonde. Hidden behind the glasses. Disguised by the flapping folds of the long dress. California blonde Elizabeth Crenshaw [her new assumed name], with nothing but thin milky skin and faint constellations of freckles on chest and cheeks to connect her to Frances Ann Flynn Benedetto. A bruise on my right cheek, faded to yellow, and a bump on the bridge of my nose.

Entirely different is a straightforward and brief self-description from a genre mystery, *A Rant of Ravens* by Christine Goff. Yet it, too, is colored by attitude, personality, and voice:

Rachel considered herself a combination of the two women. Like her aunt she sported the Wilder auburn hair and trademark freckles. But, unlike Miriam, she'd been blessed with Grandma Wilder's blue eyes and, through some genetic mutation, a long sticklike frame that Roger once deemed "willowy."

Goff used the great technique of comparing the self with another character, which escapes the necessity of a mirror or any other reflective surface.

Description—Other Main Characters

As you revise, look for the first time a character makes an entry into your novel. This is an ideal time for a first description—welcoming a main character into the reader's mind's eye, through the sensibilities of your viewpoint character. In *Prayers for Rain*, Dennis Lehane drops his protagonist's description of Karen Nichols into several spots in the first two pages of the novel, beginning with a narrative hook:

> The first time I met Karen Nichols, she struck me as the kind of woman who ironed her socks.
>
> She was blond and petite and stepped out of a kelly-green 1998 VW Bug…She wore a brown suede jacket that fell to midthigh over a charcoal cable-knit crewneck, crisp blue jeans, and bright white Reeboks. None of her apparel looked as if a wrinkle, stain, or wisp of dust had been within a country mile of it. Her blond hair was cut as short as a small boy's and reminded me of pictures I've seen of women in Berlin in the 1920s. It was sculpted tight against the skull with gel, and even though it wouldn't be moving on its own unless she stepped into the wake of a jet engine, she'd clipped it over her left ear, just below the part, and with a small black barrette that had a June bug painted on it.

Description of Character Affect and Effect

Narration offers you a chance to develop two characters, the point-of-view character and the one being described. You can fill out more dimensions than just physical appearance by using narration to describe one character's affect—demeanor—and his or her effect—influence—on the describer. In *Fahrenheit 451* by Ray Bradbury, notice in this excerpt how his character's thoughts about the girl he met characterize him as much as her:

> Montag shook his head. He looked at a blank wall. The girl's face was there, really quite beautiful in memory: astonishing, in fact. She had a very thin face like the dial of a small clock seen faintly in a dark room in the middle of a night when you waken to see the time and see the clock telling you the hour and the minute and the second, with a white silence and a glowing, all certainty and knowing what it had to tell of the night passing swiftly on toward further darknesses, but moving also toward a new sun....How like a mirror, too, her face. Impossible; for how many people did you know who refracted your own light to you. People were more often—he searched for a simile, found one in his work—torches, blazing away until they whiffed out. How rarely did other people's faces take of you and throw back to you your own expression, your own inmost trembling thought?

Like other masters at writing fiction, Bradbury fully develops the descriptions, *telling*, and mixing movement into telling, to create interior characterization. Find places where you can open up and develop descriptions of another character's charisma or the opposite—repulsiveness, or lesser degrees of each. Remember, let your characters express biases, prejudices, knee-jerk reactions, and "free associations."

The primary problems to spot in your descriptions of the physical and emotional aspects of the hero or another character are (1) their omission, (2) absence of the viewpoint character's attitude, personality, and voice, (3) absence of attitude or opinion, and (4) tight writing—too brief, needing expansion for full impact and dimensionality.

Description—Minor and Bit Characters

Minor characters may have speaking roles and make more than one appearance in a novel. The word "minor" is misleading as no character should be tossed in for the heck of it. Think of the purpose of minor characters as the same as well-written dialogue: to develop characterization and to advance the plot.

Bit characters are part of the ambience. They are the same as furniture; they are necessary for realism of the setting and situation, but they play no role beyond that. They may be pedestrians crossing a street, other guests at a party, the choir at a church.

Minor and bit characters offer another opportunity to characterize whoever has the viewpoint and to add specific details that create that realism and color. In *Truth or Dare* by Jayne Ann Krentz, Harry Stagg is a minor character, a bodyguard, and he appears throughout the novel. In this excerpt, he is described in the point of view of the protagonist's best woman friend, Arcadia:

Physically Harry bore a striking resemblance to a living skeleton. When he smiled he looked like a Halloween decoration. But in the few weeks they had known each other she had come to believe that they were soul mates.

This description is specific, detailed, and unique, but a description of a bit character or characters can be a stereotype. Even so, you can add much to your setting and the ambience. For example, a description of bit characters in *A Dry Spell* by Susie Moloney:

He nodded to the men. All three wore working clothes, outdoor clothes that marked them as farmers. The smell of animals and fresh air cling to them and probably never went away. It was a scene Tom knew well, as well as he knew the smell of dirt after it rained.

Even small descriptions of minor and bit characters add more standout quality and color to your cast of characters while deepening those holding a viewpoint.

Backstory—Exposition

Another aspect of narrated characterization is backstory. Remember that characters become three-dimensional only when you have filled in their pasts to show their deepest motivations. When narrated, information about a character's past is referred to as *exposition*. So often in early drafts of a novel, exposition takes the form of what editors sometimes call "an information dump." You can use the techniques of telling well, or show-tell/tell-show, to transform the "dump" into valuable characterization. Here is a strong example of transformed exposition, using all of these techniques, from *Riding with the Queen* by Jennie Shortridge:

> As a kid, seeing Big Gal Sal made me feel better, not worse. I don't remember a time when she wasn't in my life. In our house she was revered. I knew from birth that she was the Queen of the Delta Blues and that sometimes she was all that kept my mother from sliding into the cavernous sinkhole in her mind. Before I was even school-age, I knew Mom was happy when she'd play Sal's scratchy records on the stereo in the living room. We'd dance, doing sultry hoochie-koochie moves and singing, my baby sister, Jane, bumping along on Mom's hip. "She died the day you were born, Tallulah Jean," Mom liked to tell me in her silky Southern tenor. "She must have given you her voice to take care of for her, because I've never heard a five-year-old who can belt it out like you do."

Thinking—Philosophizing

One of the problems that afflicts rough drafts is characters who never think about anything except the plot or the immediacy of response to other characters. Another use of narration is to develop occasional reflections on themselves or any aspect of life or the world, but make sure these musings are relevant to your story. The following excerpt from *The Joy Luck Club* by Amy Tan goes to the heart of her protagonist's conflict of reconciling two vastly different cultural identities:

> Over the years, I learned to choose from the best opinions. Chinese people had Chinese opinions. American people had American opinions. And in almost every case, the American version was much better.
>
> It was only later that I discovered there was a serious flaw with the American version. There were too many choices, so it was easy to get confused and pick the wrong thing. That's how I felt about my situation with Ted. There was so much to think about, so much to decide. Each decision meant a turn in another direction.

Although I have seen long passages of philosophizing that deepen characterization and add another dimension of enjoyment of a novel, these can backfire. Be careful not to put your character on a soapbox as a mouthpiece for a rant-and-rave of your own. If you turn your character into a politician or priest, you will have turned your story into an author-dominated polemic. Avoid the temptation!

Setting—Natural and Human-made

Your characters act in a world of your construction, and that world includes nature and settings inhabited by or constructed by your sentient beings, whether they are humans, animals, or what earthlings would call extraterrestrials. These settings have a bad rap for being the kinds of descriptions readers most skip. But once they are turned into characterization, they are no longer a still life or backdrop. How much or how little you weave into your novel is dependent on your genre and pacing. Here is an example from a fast-paced, lighthearted mystery, *Briga-doom* by Susan Goodwill:

I set out for the corner and Mama's Deli....A few leaves swirled around my ankles, the casualties of fall. The Arcadia building's eight-foot granite Indians and subdued art deco fixtures stood in solemn contrast to the colorful plaster and riotous Egyptian baroque of the theatre.

I passed the Arcadia's windows, and neon signs for Fast Eddie's Pawn Shop, Lickity-Split Paycheck Advances, and Benny's Bail bonds glowed in the overcast gloom of the day. Our town's seedy underbelly enjoyed one-stop shopping at the Arcadia.

In particular, notice how Goodwill used the fall leaves with a breeze to create movement and to tell us the season. She has but light touches of her viewpoint character's attitude—"the casualties of fall," "overcast gloom," and "seedy underbelly." Her character shows her humor with the sarcastic comment about "one-stop shopping."

A more developed narrated setting, with more implied movement than actual action is demonstrated in this example from *Starlight*, in Warriors: The New Prophecy series by Erin Hunter. For clarity in your reading, the protagonist is Brambleclaw, a cat and part of the Clans:

A cold breeze blew, ridging the surface of the lake and rattling through the reeds that edged the shore. The shining gray water stretched in front of Brambleclaw for almost as far as he could see; above the hills that rose on one side, a glow in the sky showed where the sun would shortly rise. Back the way they had come, the land sloped up more gently to bare moorland. The Twoleg fence stretched across it, and in the growing light, Brambleclaw could just make out a couple of Twoleg nests in the distance. He let out a faint sound of approval; such small nests couldn't hold many Twolegs, and being so far away they were unlikely to interfere with the Clans.

I recommend that you overwrite setting, natural and human-made, rather than underwrite it. Use nature, the seasons, temperature, and the flora and fauna to build a place like none other. Select unique details of offices, bedrooms, kitchens, and so forth, as well as ordinary details. A common mistake is to use too many nonspecific descriptions of setting, which leaves an unfocused image in the reader's mind. Later, after writing what may feel like too much setting, exterior and interior, natural and human-made, you can trim back for other needs: pace, suspense, and flow.

Full development of your characters is one of the most important of all revision tasks, simply because every element of craft—scenes, sequels, subtext, dialogue, exposition, flashback, description, sensory details, setting, and theme—is filtered through the fine fabric of your characters.

When you finish with your many revisions to create character-driven structure, character-colored style and voice, and character-created theme, you are ready to revise your marketing devices and present your novel to the world.

MAKEOVER REVISION CHECKLIST
Character-Driven Narration

☑ Definition of Narration
Anything told including:
- descriptions of self and other characters
- named emotions, yearnings, and affect
- backstory
- interior thoughts—philosophizing, information, insights
- descriptions of natural and human-made settings and objects

☑ How to Narrate
- Turn into characterization by using "show/tell," "tell/show," and "tell well."
- Incorporate action words and a sense of movement.
- Develop highly specific details.
- Accumulate details, colored by the character point-of-view.

☑ Self-Description (of point-of-view character)
Don't use:
- The device of a mirror
- Reporter-like lists

Do use:
- Action words and implied movement
- Subjective description reflecting attitude, personality, and voice
- Emotion
- Comparison of self with another character

☑ Other Main Character Description
- Use point-of-view character; describe when main character first appears.
- Use "Do use" list above for how to describe.

☑ Character Affect and Effect
Affect: demeanor of character
Effect: influence on describer
- Open up and develop affect—from charisma to repulsiveness.
- Let POV characters express biases, prejudices, knee-jerk reactions,

and free associations as they describe other characters' affects
and effects.

☑ Problems with Physical and Emotional Descriptions
- Omission of them
- Absence of viewpoint character's attitude, personality, and voice
- Absence of attitude or opinion
- Tight writing—too brief for needed development

☑ Minor and Bit Character Descriptions
- Develop as part of the ambience.
- Describe to reflect on viewpoint character.
- Use details to add to realism and "color."
- Stereotypes okay but add other details, too.

☑ Backstory—Exposition
- Avoid: "information dumps"
- Use: show/tell, tell/show, and tell well
- Use the same prior techniques—implied movement, action words, viewpoint character emotion, attitudes, opinions.

☑ Thinking—Philosophizing
- Avoid: limiting thinking to only plot or response to other characters
- Avoid: pontificating, getting on a soapbox by using your POV character
- Develop occasional reflections on self, life, or world, as relevant to character and story.

☑ Setting—Natural and Human-made
- Incorporate action and implied movement.
- "Color" with viewpoint character's personality.
- Overwrite setting, exterior and interior, rather than underwrite.
- Select unique details of interior settings.
- Use nature, seasons, temperature, flora, fauna, etc.
- Develop exterior and interior settings and objects, natural and human-made.

PART FOUR

Marketing Pays

CHAPTER FIFTEEN

Copyediting

Options When first impressions count and you have five to ten seconds of an agent or editor's attention on your query, perhaps a few minutes on your sample chapters, typos and errors in grammar, spelling, and punctuation spell *R-E-J-E-C-T-I-O-N*. For a patient and generous-minded agent or editor, these mistakes warn them of a probable amateur not yet ready to be published. This last revision for the "mechanics" is as important as the substantive corrections mentioned in the rest of the book.

At last, when you have finished revising for style, structure, and characterization, you can give your creative right brain a nap. Now is the time when your inner editor can have a heyday with what I call the "nit" corrections, after which you can move on to polish your marketing and your pitch. Before you begin proofreading your novel, I believe you should do one more thing, an important thing: Give yourself credit for the creation of a work of art, for completing your novel. It is no small task and few people who do not undertake it understand the magnitude of this work of ours. Thankfully, you will not have to use Wite-Out or ink erasers, and you won't have to start over every time you find or make an error on your Royal or IBM Selectric typewriter. Those days are behind us! Love your delete button, I say. Love your cut-and-paste functions. And love your backup system even more.

Copyediting

For the linguistic purist, I am going to use the terms "copyediting" and "line editing" synonymously, although fine distinctions can be made. For our purposes, this revision process involves correction of mistakes in grammar, spelling, punctuation, and format.

Different types of publications use different guidelines for aspects of copyediting, and most book publishers use *The Chicago Manual of Style*. Using a style guide allows uniformity, even though there is still plenty of room for fine points of disagreement among copyeditors. Language is fluid and popular usage changes grammar, spelling, and punctuation. Every few years, the editors of *Chicago* print an updated edition, and the rules, or preferences, will change—an iota.

Should you buy a copy of this tome, retail price $55? It is a terrific manual and you will find answers to nearly all your questions, and then some, but it is not an easy reference book to get used to. You'll probably never use the two-thirds of it that applies to nonfiction and technical publications and to in-house editors. The fact is that an editor who works for the publisher will change your punctuation to meet the "house style," which is usually according to *Chicago*.

Use a current dictionary and update it every few years. *Chicago* recommends *Webster's Third New International Dictionary* and their latest edition of its desk version, *Merriam-Webster's Collegiate Dictionary*.

THREE MOST COMMON MISTAKES

If you're old enough to get the Denny's discount, you probably *still* put two spaces after punctuation that ends a sentence. This rule changed shortly after personal computers took over the world. Manuscripts aren't typeset anymore; digital computer files are used. Now the rule is this: *One space after all punctuation*. If you have a thumb that is untrainable, and are using a PC, then click on Edit on the tool bar and select Find. In the Find blank, hit the space bar twice. Then click on Replace, entering one space in its blank. Then click on Replace All, repeating this process until the menu box returns with "0" results.

The second mistake for those who select off the "honored citizen" menus is the absence of a comma before "and" and "or" in a series of three or more items. Although *Chicago* comes down on the side of clarity of understanding, which means there are exceptions when you omit the comma, they do indicate that *a comma should precede these conjunctions in a series of three or more items*—most of the time. Thus, you can throw out your old grammar books, notes from high school, admonitions from college English teachers, and any advice to the contrary. Henceforth use the comma.

A third mistake has afflicted writers of all ages. It is a mistake in flux, not universally viewed as a mistake, and the fault falls entirely at Bill Gates's feet. Word processing programs come with a default font setting of Times New Roman. The problem with using Times New Roman is that it was created for use in newspapers so as many characters as possible can be crammed into a column inch. As a result, Times New Roman can cast upwards of 400 words on a page when an average of 250 is standard. Times New Roman is more difficult to read because it is a condensed font. Agents and editors who do not yet require bifocals don't seem to mind receiving manuscripts in Times New Roman.

Courier is the former standard font for typed manuscripts because it was the same as "pica" on typewriters. I recommend that you *use a noncondensed font, which will put no more than an average of 250 words on a page* (using standard, 1", not 1.25" margins—another default setting to change). Noncondensed fonts are easier to read as well. That means fonts like Bookman Old Style, Century Schoolbook, Georgia, and Courier, formerly the preferred font but now falling out of style. The first three fonts allow you to directly italicize, but if you use Courier, you must underline because the italics are thin and hard to read.

CORRECTING GRAMMAR MISTAKES

A computer will catch most spelling errors, but not all computer programs will catch grammatical errors, and they weren't programmed with *The Chicago Manual of Style*. Use the built-in grammar programs, but then use the following guidelines developed by editor Carolyn J. Rose and I to help our editing clients find the most common errors we see.

Comma splices: Use a semicolon to separate two sentences that are related. Some copyeditors allow a comma splice in dialogue, but to be safe and grammatically correct, use two sentences.

Parallelism: This refers to repetition of same forms of grammar, imagery, rhythm, or other elements of craft. The most common form of a parallelism problem involves prepositional phrases. For instance, notice the parallel repetition of the preposition "to" in this sentence: "To make a convincing argument before a colleague or to pick up the pace in a paragraph, replace passive verbs with active verbs." If the preposition is part of a short phrase, then the second verb does not require repetition of the preposition, as in the use of "to" in the following sentence: "Use short, tight sentences to make a point or pick up the pace."

Paragraph flow: Make sure sentences within paragraphs flow in a logical sequence, including following a stimulus with a response and not the reverse.

Passive construction: Rewrite any sentences constructed passively. *To be* verbs create passive sentences. They include: *is, are, was, were, be, being, been,* and *am.* For example, change "coffee was brought to the table" to "a frowning waitress slammed a mug of coffee onto the paper placemat in front of me." Get rid of *begin, began, do, did, has, had, seems,* and *seemed* whenever you can.

Pronoun reference: When sentences become complex, it's easy to lose sight of which noun a pronoun refers back to. Take a close look at the the usual suspects: *he, she, they, we,* but most especially at the pronoun *it.* Trace backwards to the prior noun and make sure the pronoun is the right substitute for it.

Subjective tense: This refers to using "if–were," such as "If I were rich, I would…" This tense has all but dropped out of American usage. Change to "if–was" unless your character uses high diction, your genre is literary, or your story is set in the past.

Subject-verb agreement: If your word processing program shows a red line under words, that line signals a grammatical problem. Plural subjects require plural verbs. Single subjects require singular verb tense.

STRENGTHENING YOUR WRITING

All of the prior chapters have addressed how to do a "manuscript makeover" to strengthen all aspects of your writing. Below are some additional problem areas to look for in your final revisions.

Adjectives: Use sparingly and consciously. Overuse indicates a need to find more precise nouns and to show rather than tell. Overuse can turn your writing into "purple prose" that is melodramatic and "flowery."

Adverbs: Too often, writers use these to beef up weak verbs. Your goal should be to make verbs strong enough to do the work themselves and kill off your adverbs. You won't be able to get rid of all of them, but circle each one in your draft and use a thesaurus to find strong verbs that characterize and carry emotion as well as convey action.

Awkward phrasing: Reading pages aloud can help you hear what sounds rough and what sounds smooth. If your sentence includes four or more prepositions, it probably needs simplifying and that may smooth out the rough spots.

Clichés: Take a look at your similes, idioms, and expressions, and toss out any that are trite. Trite is okay when a character is speaking, because most of us fall back on clichés dozens of times every day and you can use clichés to further characterize, but readers hope for more from the author in the narrative between stretches of dialogue. Here's a chance to create original imagery.

Dead language and repeated information: Eliminate "dead" words, ones that are extra or repeated, except for reasons of style. Shorten sentences to create clarity. You can get rid of many uses of "could, up, down, unlikely, looked, walked over to," and other words that aren't making contributions. Find places where you tell the reader the same information, either in the same words or in similar words. Some writers develop a habit of telling then offering the same information in dialogue, or the reverse.

Direct thought: Limit use of direct internal thought for moments of strong emotion, realization, or resolve. Avoid use of direct thought for musing, puzzling, or thinking about matters of low emotion.

Negatives: Convert negative construction into positive. Change "He would not disagree with her" into "He agreed with her."

Nouns: Choose which nouns you want to leave as general nouns such as "car, flower, tree," and choose which nouns should be specific, concrete, and colorful such as "Prius, carnation, sycamore."

Qualifiers: As part of the "dead" words you should delete, include the hesitant qualifiers, words such as "a little, a bit, rather, probably, kind of, pretty, might be." Except in dialogue, also eliminate qualifying adjectives that add superlatives that don't increase the noun's meaning: "very, incredibly, awesome, enormously."

Repeated words: Everyone has "pet" words that are unconsciously repeated. If necessary, ask someone else to read a portion of your novel specifically to determine which words you most often repeat. Then use a thesaurus. The most universally repeated words—I call them wimpy—in novels I edit are various tense forms of *look* and *walk*. The second most-repeated wimpy verbs are *see* and *run*. Limit your use of any simple verb that is likely to be in a child's first reader, unless it fits for purposes of style.

Sentence structure: Vary your sentences. Use short, tight ones to make a point or pick up the pace. Separate run-on sentences or trim words within them so the reader can take a breath—unless you have chosen the extra-long sentence for reasons of style.

Transitions: Check your flow and clarity between sentences, paragraphs, sections, and chapters. Avoid abrupt transitions.

Verb usage: Open your thesaurus and dig out stronger verbs. They not only carry the action, they characterize and describe. Use strong verbs that convey emotion and conflict.

CORRECTING PUNCTUATION

Editors disagree with editors over punctuation, and in many cases, *Chicago* offers alternate usages. Punctuation seems to be moving toward "open," which uses less punctuation if the meaning is clear without it. For now, here are the mistakes that I see and correct in the manuscripts I edit.

Abbreviations/Use of initials: When initials are used for agencies, organizations and countries, no periods are necessary. Write them US, FBI, CIA, and so on. If you are concerned about misunderstanding with a particular abbreviation, use periods.

Apostrophes: The apostrophe takes the place of a letter or indicates the possessive. Review the rules on its use. The most common mistake is using an apostrophe for *its*, which means possessive (see the use of "its" in the former sentence). The word *it's* means "it is." The other common mistake is using an apostrophe before an *s* when the *s* is meant to show a plural noun. Incorrect usage of the apostrophe shows up often with the plural of decades such as "1960s." In olden times, the apostrophe was used and that is probably why people still make the mistake.

Bold Type: Do not use bold type for emphasis or to set off a word. Use italics for emphasis.

Breaks: See *Scene breaks.*

Capitalization: Do not capitalize every letter in a word to create emphasis. Capitalize the main words in titles of books, plays, television programs, movies, works of art, constellations, and specific names of ships, trains, and the like. Capitalize titles when they are specific and used before a name, as in Mayor Sam Stone, or when used in place of the name in direct address as in "Don't sign that, Mayor." Don't capitalize a title used like this, "I'm going to call the mayor and give him a piece of my mind."

Capitalize signs and notices, if short. Treat longer notices as quotations. Treat mottoes like signs and notices, except for mottoes in foreign languages; then italicize the entire motto and capitalize only the first word. Capitalize proper nouns and proper names, including brand names and titles of huge natural phenomena, like hurricanes, plagues, and fires.

Ellipsis Points: To show the omission of a few words in the middle of a sentence, use three dots with spaces between dots and words. If there's a legitimate end to a sentence that trails off, use four dots. The first dot indicates the period at the end of the sentence and comes up against the last word. Add spaces between the others. Use ellipsis points sparingly for impact. Avoid use of ellipsis points where you take a breath. It is meant to show a trailing off of thought but not to represent every pause in the dialogue or narrative. So...

Foreign words and phrases: Italicize the first time they appear, if readers are likely to understand them. Do not italicize foreign words that are well known or have been adopted into standard English. "Hasta la vista, baby." After that, the words and phrases are in the same font and type as any other word. Do not italicize foreign proper nouns (such as names of streets and monuments). Follow phrases or sayings (italicized) with translations in parentheses or make clear from context.

Hyphens and dashes: Hyphens hold words together: mother-of-pearl. These hyphenated words are called "compound nouns." Hyphenated compound words are in constant flux. Dictionaries will differ on these nouns and other words that use hyphens. Is it "e-mail" or "email"? For now, the hyphen holds (and lowercase *e*), but that may not be the case in the future. Also use hyphens for an adjective that modifies another adjective that in turn modifies a noun. One exception is the omission of a hyphen after any compound formed by an adverb ending with the two letters *-ly* plus an adjective or participle ("a closely held secret"). Dashes (two hyphens snugged up to each other and the words on either side) indicate an abrupt change such as interrupted dialogue or set off explanatory words and phrases: Golf is a relaxing sport—if you forget about that pesky ball. Using the Word program, the two hyphens are instantly changed into the "em dash" that they are supposed to represent. For instance, in the above sentence, if I retyped it and hit the space after "if" in "sport—if," it would automatically change the two hyphens, as it has here. Dashes are like spices: use too many and you forfeit a subtle flavor.

Indenting: Five spaces is the standard indent for a paragraph (use your "tab"), but you need not indent at the beginning of chapters and following a scene break. This change will be made by the publisher as a matter of design choice, but many writers now omit this indentation.

Italics: Reserve these for words that are emphasized, titles of books, movies, and television programs. (Titles of songs or stories are set off in quotation marks. Titles of constellations are not italicized.) Dramatic, direct internal dialogue (which should be in short bursts only) should be italicized (except in Courier font where it's too thin and difficult to read, and then it should be underlined).

Dream sequences or visions set in "now time," like direct thought, may be italicized. If these are told in indirect thought, do not italicize them.

Quotation marks: Most of your uses of quotation marks will be to enclose dialogue. Punctuation at the end of a line of dialogue, including the dash and ellipsis, belong inside the end quotation mark: "Hey, Bob, want to go fishing?" he asked. If you are setting off a word in quotation marks, perhaps to create an ironic meaning, and a semicolon, colon, or question mark will follow, these punctuation marks follow the quotation marks. Use quotation marks for titles of chapters, articles, poems, and songs.

Scene breaks: This is the break between sections in your story. If the point of view remains the same and not much time has passed, the break is indicated by a double-double line space. If the point of view changes and/or there is a larger shift of time or space, double line space then use one or three asterisks or pound signs, centered on the line. Use another line space before you begin your next line of text after the break. You do not need to indent the first paragraph after the break; indentation style will be determined when the manuscript is typeset.

Song lyrics: Lyrics identifiable to a particular song not in the public domain may be used with permission only. A song title can be used without permission.

Spacing between sentences and after all punctuation: One space only.

Time of day: This is indicated as a.m. or p.m. or through the use of small caps without periods.

Titles: Titles of books should be italicized. Names of ships should be italicized. Titles of songs and short stories should appear in quotation marks. The Bible (and other holy books), however, is not italicized. Books of the Bible are not italicized and the word "book" appears in lowercase, while Gospel and Epistle are capitalized when they appear. Sections of the Bible, such as the Old Testament, are usually capitalized, but not italicized.

Trademarked names or terms: You can use trademarks, but you must spell them correctly, and you must not alter the words in any way: no hyphens, abbreviations, or switches from singular to plural. Trademarked words and terms, like Porsche, Post-it, and Realtor, must be capitalized. However, omit the trademark symbol.

Verb tenses: If your story is told in the past tense, when a character talks or thinks about events in the more distant past, you'll need to use "had" or a form of it to "take us back." In flashbacks, drop "had" once the past is established. Indirect thought in a story that uses past tense remains in past tense. Direct thought always uses present tense.

MANUSCRIPT FORMAT

The most important thing in formatting your manuscript is consistency and professionalism. Appearances count. At a glance, an editor or agent will know if you are using standard formatting.

Chapters: Begin each chapter on its own new page and one third down. Leave no more than four line spaces between a chapter heading and a first line of text.

Chapter titles: The Chicago Manual of Style advises that chapter titles (or the word "chapter" and a numeral) should be written in upper and lowercase and left justified. Often, I see chapter titles and numbers centered, and I don't know any agents who object.

Font: Use any noncondensed font such as Bookman Old Style, Georgia, Century Schoolbook, or Courier. Once the preferred font, Courier is dropping out of style. Change your default font in your word-processing program from Times New Roman (condensed) to your choice of one of the noncondensed fonts.

Headers: Type your italicized book title, or part of the title. Remove italics and add a slash, and then your last name, leaving no spaces between these items and putting all of the data flush left. While there is no requirement for where page numbers go, when there is a header, most of the time page numbers are inserted on the upper right. Enter two hard returns at the end of your header so that the header and first line of text are well separated.

Indenting: Five spaces is standard. Indenting the first line of a chapter or the first line after a break is optional. Indent the first line of dialogue. When the speaker changes, start a new paragraph and indent. Use two indents prior to writing a newspaper article, poem, letter or note or e-mail, or story within the story.

Justify: Justify the left margin only.

Line spacing: Double space vertically, between lines of text. Do not double-double space between paragraphs, except for scene breaks.

Margins: Use one-inch margins on all four sides. Change the default setting of your word-processing program from 1.25" to 1".

Page numbering: There is no rule for where your page numbers should appear. However, the most common location with the use of headers is in the upper right of the page.

Title page: There should be no header and no page number on your title page. Drop down about one third of a page and center and type your title on one line. Double space, and center and type your name (or pseudonym). It is fine if you wish to use a larger font size—14 or 16—for your title and name, and it is okay to use bold. Your contact information (including e-mail address) should be single-spaced and justified right in the right-hand bottom corner of the title page, beginning with your name, then address, phone, e-mail, and website (optional). Remove the hyperlink (use a right click) so that e-mail and web addresses don't print blue with an underline.

Underlining: Underlining means italicize. Italicize directly. Use underline to represent italics only if you use Courier font.

Word spacing: Leave a single character space after all punctuation.

Any reference book on grammar, spelling, and punctuation will give you "the rest" of the rules on use of our language. After you make all of these copyediting corrections on your manuscript, make sure to apply them to your last draft of your marketing manuscripts—the query letter and synopsis, covered in the next chapter.

MAKEOVER REVISION CHECKLIST
Copyediting

☑ Three Most Common Mistakes
- Use one, not two, spaces after all punctuation.
- Use a comma before conjunctions in a series of three or more, most of the time.
- Use a noncondensed font (avoid Times New Roman—condensed) such as Century Schoolbook, Bookman Old Style, Georgia, or Courier.

☑ Correcting Grammar Mistakes
- Comma splices—use semicolon or make two sentences.
- Parallelism—check grammar, imagery, rhythm, or other elements of craft. Check parallelism of prepositions in particular.
- Paragraph flow—check logical sequence, stimulus then response.
- Pronoun reference—check which noun a pronoun refers back to. Especially check for problems with "it."
- Subject-verb agreement—check singular or plural subjects and that the verbs match.

☑ Strengthening Your Writing
- Adjectives—use sparingly and consciously.
- Adverbs—use sparingly and consciously. Use a thesaurus to find strong verbs that characterize and carry emotion as well as action.
- Awkward phrasing—read pages aloud to catch. Scrutinize any sentences that include four or more prepositions; simplify.
- Clichés—check similes, idioms, and expressions and toss out any that are trite (except in dialogue to characterize).
- Dead language and repeated information—eliminate extra or repeated words, except for style; eliminate or replace blah words such as *looked*, *up*, *down*, *unlikely*, or *walked*. Reword verbs of potentiality: *could* or *would*. Avoid telling information and then showing it in action or dialogue, or vice versa.
- Direct thought—limit use to moments of strong emotion, realization, or resolve. Avoid using for musing, puzzling, or thinking about matters of low emotion.
- Negatives—convert into positive construction.

- Nouns—select which general nouns to change into specific and colorful nouns.

- Qualifiers—delete hesitant qualifying words such as *little*, *a bit*, *rather*, *probably*, *kind of*, *pretty*, and *might be.* Except to characterize in dialogue, delete adjectives that add superlatives such as *very*, *incredibly*, *awesome*, and *enormously.*

- Repeated words—find and replace "pet" words, your unconsciously repeated favorites. Use a thesaurus to replace the most used verbs, *looked* and *walked*, with stronger verbs.

- Sentence structure—vary types (simple, compound, complex, compound-complex, complicated), beginnings of sentences (any part of speech). Use short and tight to make a point or pick up pace. Separate run-on sentences. Let style be your guide.

- Transitions—check flow and clarity between sentences, paragraphs, sections, and chapters.

- Verb usage—other than for reasons of style, replace wimpy verbs— *see*, *run*—and limit use of simple verbs likely to be in children's readers. Use strong verbs that convey emotion and conflict.

☑ Correcting Punctuation

- Use *The Chicago Manual of Style* for reference.

- Abbreviations/Use of initials—omit periods after letters in most abbreviations of organizations or earned degrees.

- Apostrophes—use in place of omitted letters such as in contractions and include to show possessive. Especially check mistakes in usage of *its* and *it's* and in use of plural, possessive, or a contraction for the *s* at the end of a word,

- Bold type—use italics, not bold, for emphasis.

- Capitalization—use italics, not all caps, for emphasis of a word or phrase. In particular, avoid capitals for job roles, unless they are used as a part of a proper name. Review rules of capitalization.

- Ellipsis points—use to show omission of words in the middle of a sentence or for the trail off of an incomplete thought or sentence or phrase in dialogue. Use sparingly and with correct punctuation, spaces before and after the periods.

- Foreign words and phrases—italicize first appearance only, if used often. Repeat italics if used infrequently. Do not italicize if adopted into Standard English or familiar to readers. Do not italicize proper names. Do italicize phrases and follow with translation in parentheses or make clear by context.

- Hyphens and dashes—use hyphens to connect separate words that create compound nouns. Also use a hyphen between an adjective that modifies an adjective that in turn modifies a noun. Exception: Never use a hyphen after an adverb that ends with the letters *ly*. Use dashes to indicate abrupt change, interrupted dialogue, or to set off explanatory words and phrases. Use an "em dash," which has no space before or after it.
- Indenting—tabs are five spaces; set your default. You need not (optional) indent the first line of each chapter and after a hiatus.
- Italics—use sparingly for emphasis. Use for titles of books, movies, and television programs. Use for direct internal dialogue—and use that sparingly. Use underlining, not italics, in Courier font. Use italics for short dream sequences or visions.
- Quotation marks—use to surround dialogue, placing the end-of-sentence punctuation inside the last quotation mark. Use quotation marks to surround chapter titles, poems, and songs.
- Scene breaks—use a double-double line space, a soft break, when viewpoint remains the same and not much time has passed. For a hard break, use one or three asterisks or pound signs, centered on a line with a double line space above and below.
- Song lyrics—seek permission to use lyrics not in the public domain. Song titles may be used without permission.
- Spacing before and after all punctuation—one space.
- Time of day—indicate as a.m. or p.m. or use small caps without periods.
- Titles—italicize titles of books and names of ships. Avoid italics for the Bible (and names of other holy books), but capitalize the names of the books and sections of the Bible.
- Trademarked names or terms—spell correctly, exactly as they were created, without any alteration. Most trademarked names are capitalized. Omit the trademark symbol.
- Verb tenses—use "had" when your character talks or thinks about events in the story past. In flashbacks, drop "had" once the past is established. Keep indirect thought in stories that use past tense in the past tense. Use present tense for indirect thought whether the story is told in present or past tense.

☑ Manuscript Format

- Chapters—begin one-third down the first page. Start new chapters on new pages.
- Chapter titles—use upper and lowercase, unless you have style reasons not to. Left justify or center.
- Font—change your default computer setting from Times New Roman to a noncondensed font such as Bookman Old Style, Century Schoolbook, or Georgia. Courier is acceptable but is falling out of style.
- Headers—beginning flush left, italicize the book title, or a fragment of it, click off italics and type a slash, then follow by your surname, leaving no space between any of the units. Enter two hard returns to make sure you have a line space before your first line of text. Omit headers on title pages (which means creating a separate file for the title page).
- Indenting—five spaces is standard for paragraphs, usually set as default for the tab. Indent for each new speaker in dialogue. Use two indents for including an excerpted letter, news article, poem, e-mail, or note, within the story.
- Justify—the left margin only.
- Line spacing—double space between lines of text. Avoid quadruple line spaces between paragraphs.
- Margins—use one-inch margins on all four sides. Change the default from 1.25" to 1".
- Pagination—omit page numbers on the title page (which means creating a separate file for the title page). Insert page numbers on upper right of page.
- Title page—drop down one third of page. Center and type title on one line, double space, and center and type the word *by* and your name or pseudonym.
- Underlining—only if using Courier. For any other font, use italics.
- Word spacing—unless two words require hyphenation, leave one space after all words and punctuation.

CHAPTER SIXTEEN

Query Letters and Synopses: Polishing for Marketing

Options Don't make the mistake of sending out query letters prematurely. You have to resolve a paradox: To gain a request to read and evaluate your fiction writing, you have to write the nonfiction query and synopsis well enough to win agent or editor attention. If you are presently not interested in marketing, then skip to the section in this chapter on the synopsis, which is an invaluable tool during both the writing and revision process, not only just for selling your novel.

The beautiful thing about our art of writing is that we can live anywhere. We can be young or old, handsome and stunning or homely and plain, thin or fat, rich or poor, and still sell our works and even become bestselling authors. Our words get judged, not us.

Query Letter

Unless you meet an agent or editor at a writers' conference or other event, you are most likely to send your sales representative to pitch your novel. Who's your sales representative? The query letter. This is a letter of inquiry to ask if the recipient would like to read a portion of your novel. That sounds easy enough, but when you are in competition with hundreds of thousands of other novelists, the bar rises. Most established agents receive anywhere from fifty to one hundred queries *per week*. Of course, that number includes inquiries about nonfiction books. Even so, your query must show your very best and error-free writing, express your passion for your story, clearly summarize characterization, plot, and theme, and outline your author qualifications. Preferably, in five paragraphs and on one page. The contents of each paragraph are as follows:

1. the hook
2. transition and first paragraph of the synopsis
3. second paragraph of the synopsis
4. author qualifications
5. finishing formalities

THE HOOK

Like any lead you write, the first paragraph in the query letter should draw the reader into what you say and make them eager to read on. That's a hook! The query is a sales letter, not just a description of your novel. Because your letter may get little consideration beyond the hook, put your most important sales pitch first. You may have won or placed in contests, had short stories or another novel published, or you may be writing on recommendation of a colleague of the recipient or a well-known author.

If none of these first-placement items are part of your repertoire for a hook, then choose a business lead or a creative lead. The business lead is straightforward: "I have recently finished my 85,000-word novel, *Great Title*. This psycho-thriller opens in..." This is but one example of a business lead, but notice that I have not used the unnecessary and obvious phrase, "I am seeking representation for." After all, why else would you be writing a query letter to an agent?

The creative lead requires more finesse and carries more risk because it relies upon imagination and skill. You might establish the setting or milieu in a striking way. You could introduce the dramatic conflict and what is at stake, or present the theme in an evocative manner. Least successful in a query letter, I think, is to lead with a dialogue excerpt. It is too out of context to successfully hook your reader, who is not looking for entertainment. She or he is looking for the needle in the haystack, one query out of the twenty that have come in that day, with promise. Or, if a week's worth have accumulated (or more), then one in a hundred.

Here is one example of a first-paragraph hook that establishes the milieu and setting as a creative lead for an historical epic, *Not Between Brothers* by David Marion Wilkinson. Although this novel was not the first one he wrote, it was the first published, by a small press, Boaz Publishing in hard cover, and then in paperback by Signet, an imprint of Penguin USA. It was optioned for an NBC movie, although it was not produced, and it was a finalist for a Spur Award from Western Writers of America.

> *Not Between Brothers* is a novel of the clash of cultures at the time of the Anglo colonization of the American Southwest, and the bloody wars that soon followed. Larry McMurtry's remarkable *Lonesome Dove* chronicled the end of this era; *Not Between Brothers* portrays how it began. Set in early Texas, it's not a "Texas" historical novel, but a solidly researched gut-level examination into the events that shaped the desperate, brutalized cultures that competed hand-to-hand for western North America. It just happened that they confronted one another here, in Texas. At the core of the conflict, as always, was the land.

In this hook, notice how Wilkinson successfully incorporated conflict, stakes, and the cruel side of human relationships. Throughout this hook is passion: "clash of cultures," "bloody wars," gut-level," "desperate, brutalized," and "hand-to-hand." Wilkinson handily deals with the inevitable comparison to the Pulitzer-winning *Lonesome Dove*. And notice the use of the power position, the last word in the hook, which defines this book: land.

TRANSITION AND FIRST PARAGRAPH OF THE SYNOPSIS

If you begin with a business lead, then begin your second paragraph with a synopsis, a summary, of your entire novel, emphasizing the protagonist in this paragraph. In contrast to a business lead, the creative lead may give no information about the genre, word count, or any other important bit of information such as contest wins, publications, or direct experience related to the book's subject, theme, or setting. As soon as you have completed a creative lead, introduce this information. Wilkinson has already made it clear that his novel is an historical epic.

Once you begin the synopsis of your book, use past tense for events in the story's backstory and present tense to describe the story in your novel—even if you have written it in past tense. Present tense is the convention for any synopsis, and it lends more excitement to the writing. Within the first few lines of your synopsis, clearly establish the setting and time period, and the central story problem. Then relate the primary events of your five-stage dramatic arc. You'll have to leave out minor characters or refer to them by role, not name, and you'll have an easier time if you summarize the big scenes of the novel. By all means, avoid the blow-by-blow march of the plot... "and then this happened, and then this happened, followed by this happening."

SECOND PARAGRAPH OF THE SYNOPSIS

Most writers require a second paragraph to finish the summary of their stories. Make sure that you indicate how your story ends, even telling whodunit. Make sure to reveal how the protagonist changed, what he or she learned, and how that transformation relates to a theme. If you find yourself unable to condense your story into two paragraphs, then force yourself to write a one-paragraph synopsis. I'm not kidding. You'll have to strip the story down to its bones. By so doing, you'll have an easier time adding to it, to reach two paragraphs—only if you need it—than if you continue to try to boil down four paragraphs.

Make sure that your synopsis conveys enough characterization to convince the reader that your novel's protagonist is three-dimensional, that your story and plot are unique, and that your hero is desperate to fill a need and passionate about reaching the story goal.

AUTHOR QUALIFICATIONS

If you haven't previously described your accomplishments related to writing, this paragraph is the place to do so. If you are like most novelists aspiring to break in, this paragraph makes you feel nervous and insecure. What if you haven't won contests or published short stories? What if you have "only" spent the last six or ten or twenty years writing fiction for your own pleasure?

With absolutely no credits, or direct experience related to the novel you have written, you can add—and I recommend—a line or two about being an avid reader of the type of novel you've written. Be specific about your favorite authors and write a "positioning statement." This means to specify how your style, or setting, or any other factor is, in your opinion, similar to…and then cite a published novel or two, or an author or two. Keep this short and don't write it in such a way as to claim to be better than a famous novelist. Some agents recommend mention of a current novel or author and a "classic" novel or author. Besides giving an agent an indication that you read in your field, you are also offering a mental picture that an agent can present to an editor about where your book fits, among all time travel novels or police procedurals or historical novels for nine- to twelve-year-olds.

FINISHING FORMALITIES

Whatever information has not been provided in prior paragraphs can be included in this one. Perhaps the author has not yet indicated the word count of the novel, or decides to put the positioning statement here because the author qualifications fill the prior paragraph. If the query letter is sent via mail, then authors may indicate enclosure of SASEs—self-addressed stamped envelopes, for the return of a response letter. I've had agents beg me to mention their need for including SASEs, because they are so often left out. If you forget, then you are unlikely to hear from the agents because they can't possibly afford to pay for postage. Acquisition of new clients is an important but lower-priority job. First, agents must sell works in order to pay the bills. Second, they must respond to their existing clients' needs. Third, they must keep acquiring new manuscripts. And, there are always exceptions. I have read a few queries that run two or three pages and yet secured interest, and later, publication.

Other finishing formalities may be a referral name and mention of how you came to select this agent. Finish with recognition of the agent or editor's consideration such as "I appreciate your time and look forward to a response at your earliest convenience."

There are exceptions to the five-paragraph preference: sometimes a writer will add a paragraph explaining how she was recommended to the agency or provide some other background that is vital to impart. Sometimes, the summary—a synopsis—takes three paragraphs. Shorter is better, nearly always, when it comes to the query letter. I've watched two agents read their incoming mail; they gave no more than ten seconds to most query letters. That means agents make flash decisions to reject as soon as something doesn't match their criteria or meet their standards.

I hope I have convinced you not to dash off this letter, but to spend time refining it, revising it, and revising it. I know one novelist who told me she spent a total of forty hours revising her query letter, setting it aside for days and then picking it up to see it with new eyes. Her effort paid off in the form of a one-third request rate. That means that three out of ten agents who read her letter requested some portion of her novel.

Author Barbara Corrado Pope finished revisions of her first novel, an historical mystery, and wrote her first query letter, revising it many times and getting outside critique before revising it some more. It received a fifty percent request rate, and her novel, *Cézanne's Quarry*, was represented and sold to Pegasus Publishing.

Here is her query letter (with Xs in place of the killer's name in case you decide to read this mystery); a discussion follows:

Dear Ms. Agent:

Cézanne fell madly in love in the spring of 1885. Biographers have never identified the woman in question. The historical mystery *Cézanne's Quarry* reveals that she is Solange Vernet, a Parisian hatmaker, newly arrived in the south of France with her lover, the English geologist Charles Westerbury. In August, when the novel opens, she lies murdered at the bottom of a quarry near Aix-en-Provence.

Because most of the courthouse is on holiday, Bernard Martin, a novice examining magistrate, takes charge of the investigation. His veteran inspector, Albert Franc, tells him that the Vernet case can make his career, but Martin, who came to Aix to escape an arranged marriage, is seeking something else: justice. He does not realize until it is almost too late that Xxxxxxx is a vicious killer who is manipulating him.

As he deals with the sentimental Westerbury, the volatile Cézanne, and the tough unrelenting Franc, Martin confronts the issue of how to be a man in his conflict-ridden society. He thinks of himself as unimaginative, a man of reason devoted to the ideals of the Republic, yet midway through the novel he follows his heart by helping his oldest friend, an anarchist, to escape the army. This lapse, which Xxxxxxx secretly observes, raises the ante. It threatens Martin's life as well as his career.

In less than a fortnight Martin uncovers the tragic past of Solange Vernet and how it became the source of Cézanne's infatuation with her as well as the inspiration for some of his most violent and erotic paintings. Martin also begins to fall in love with the independent Clarie Falchetti. These experiences help him to learn to temper reason with feelings and, finally, to see clearly who the killer is and why.

The novel captures the true character of its historical figures (including Paul Cézanne; his mistress, Hortense Ficquet; and Emile Zola) and embeds them and their fictional counterparts in the controversies of the day: religion vs. science, the changing role of women, socialism, and the development of modern art. Thus *Cézanne's Quarry* promises to be especially satisfying to readers who enjoy learning about the past as they wend their way through a good story.

This is my first novel. It is approximately 110,000 words. I am an historian and women's studies professor and have participated in writing groups for about a decade.

Enclosed are two SASEs for your response. Before August 22, please use the Eugene address. After that time please contact me in Denmark. My email address is xxxxxx. I was referred to you by Elizabeth Lyon. Thanks for your time and attention.

Sincerely,

[*signature*]

Barbara Corrado Pope

As you can readily see, Pope's query letter is seven paragraphs long. Here is the breakdown of what content she has included and analysis of each paragraph:

Paragraph 1: She offers the historical backdrop for her novel and indicates its time period, genre, and setting: 1885, historical mystery, Aix-en-Provence. Notice that Pope has taken advantage of the power position of the first word in the paragraph and the query: Cézanne. She also provides the title of her mystery, which uses his name and, with "quarry," supplies an apt double-meaning. Both words show smart marketing, in the query and for the novel, since most people will recognize Cézanne as one of the masters of modern art.

Pope makes a smooth transition from the historical events and people to the identification of the mystery's victim and two possible suspects: Cézanne and Westerbury, a possible love triangle. She has begun the synopsis.

Paragraph 2: Here Pope continues her synopsis and introduces her protagonist, Bernard Martin, and offers a character sketch that includes his lack of experience—"a novice," a piece of his backstory, and reason for accepting the job in Aix—"to escape an arranged marriage," and his motivating need—"justice." Pope also introduces a central conflict between the protagonist and his inspector, and identifies the killer. In these four lines, and the prior two in paragraph 1, Pope has supplied all of the basics about the crime, the setting and time period, the victim and several suspects, the protagonist, a central power struggle between him and his inspector, and the theme of the novel.

Paragraph 3: This third paragraph takes the reader deeper into her protagonist's psychology and shows how his inner conflicts also relate directly to issues of the times. An agent reading this paragraph will be relieved that the novel promises depth of characterization. She also continues with one of the plot turning points—that her protagonist's loyalty to a friend, following his heart, and his ideals almost cost him his life.

Paragraph 4: This paragraph concludes the synopsis of the story. Pope indicates the "time container" of the novel—a "fortnight," and provides more historical tie-in about Cézanne's paintings. Pope also reveals her protagonist's growth, "to temper reason with feelings," and the dual reward: identifying the killer and falling in love.

Paragraph 5: Pope returns to instructing the reader of the query about history and the larger story reflected in her novel. Thus she is promising that her book has relevancy greater than the mystery story. An agent and publisher may recognize that some of the controversies of late nineteenth-century France are still controversies today: religion vs. science, the changing role of women, and socialism.

Paragraph 6: This paragraph provides author qualifications for the historical accuracy. Regarding qualifications as a novelist, Pope is forthright in stating that *Cézanne's Quarry* is her first novel, but she adds that she has been writing fiction for a decade and participates in writing groups. The reader also learns the word count, 110,000, which is near the upper word count for a first novel, even one that is historical and literary. This information is important to agents and editors who consider the book.

Paragraph 7: In this short final paragraph, she deals with business. Normally, you do not need to indicate that you will enclose an SASE; it is presumed and will be obvious when the envelope is opened. However, Pope has reason to identify the two SASEs because the agent may respond when she is traveling in Europe. Because she was also a student and then a member of one of my critique groups when she started her novel, I supplied her with a short list of agents who know me and I thought might be interested in her novel. She therefore indicates that I recommended the agent.

This is a complex query about a novel made more complex by its tie-in with history. It requires close attention by the reader, which works against the fast reading customarily given by an agent, editor, or a hired query reader. For anyone unfamiliar with French names and language, the number of character names, historical figures, and the location in "Aix-en-Provence" may prove too many.

The purpose of a query letter is to get a positive response requesting to see the whole novel, a portion of it, or more of it if a sample chapter has accompanied the query. The letter you write can always be improved upon. If you do receive a rejection, before sending out another batch—which I recommend doing, about six at a time—revise your query. For instance, I believe that Pope's letter would be better if it had been five paragraphs. I think the second paragraph could have been deleted, the protagonist's name and role worked into the third paragraph, and the last two paragraphs combined into one. However, as the old saying goes, the proof is in the pudding; a fifty percent request rate speaks for itself.

More and more agents are accepting, if not requiring, e-mail queries. As you know, this is a communication venue that is meant for short correspondence. Some agents have websites where they post their guidelines and may even supply a place for you to paste your e-mail for their downloading. If you send e-mail queries, never add attachments. The annual *Guide to Literary Agents* includes contact information, a short profile, and preferences of about 800 agencies. Here you will find web and e-mail contact information as well.

Some agents also request the inclusion of a synopsis separate from your query letter. You will need a synopsis for an agent to use when pitching your novel, in writing or on the phone, to editors. This document, like the query, has specific form, specifications, and artistic challenges in writing it. Once again, you should plan to revise it multiple times before you release it to the world.

Synopsis

Similar to the several-paragraph synopsis in your query letter, a separate synopsis summarizes your entire story and shows the character arc, too. If you're fortunate, you will have written and revised a synopsis, of any length, as you wrote your novel. They are a great tool for writers to talk to themselves and step back and look at how they are fitting the pieces together. Then, at this stage of marketing, your need is only to revise the synopsis rather than to write a first one.

When an agent or editor asks for a synopsis and has not specified the length, you should aim for no more than five pages and preferably fewer, and the pages are double-spaced, with one-inch page margins. If an agent, in a one-on-one meeting or in a directory or website listing, has not asked for a synopsis, you may send one unless the guidelines say "query only." In the case of no mention of a synopsis, I recommend sending a one-page, single-spaced synopsis, leaving a double line space between paragraphs.

To an experienced reader, the synopsis is like an MRI for a novel's structure. In the negative, it reveals problems with logic and organization, the likelihood of inadequate character development, episodic versus dramatic structure, contrived or clichéd plots, and other "symptoms" of a novel not yet ready for market. In the positive, a synopsis will show an original story, developed characters, and increase the reader's excitement to read the actual novel.

If you are constructing a first synopsis for your novel from scratch, or need a review of how to write one, a synopsis requires the following content and style:

- Cover the beginning, middle, and end of your novel. The agent or editor needs to know the end of your story to evaluate whether you know how to complete your story. They are not reading for entertainment, in other words.
- Include backstory as needed, using past tense verbs.
- Indicate the setting and time period.
- The synopsis does not have to follow the chronology of your story. Sometimes the most coherent summary of events does not parallel the viewpoint changes or time and place shifts.
- Because this is a summary, it is not fiction and does not involve writing from a viewpoint. It is like a book report.
- By convention, the summary refers to characters in the third person and in present tense, except for using past tense when relating backstory events.
- Offer clear characterization of the protagonist, revealing his or her reasons for involvement in the story problem, the goals and stakes, and the character wound, need, primary strength, and weakness.
- Describe the central conflict and identify the antagonist or opposing forces.

- Name only characters that are important and necessary to name; use role labels for other characters.
- Make every effort to write lean, and revise leaner, to make every word count.
- Use active verbs, as much as possible, concrete and specific nouns, and convey the emotional and dramatic changes of the protagonist.
- Because of limited space, omit minor characters and subplots as necessary, or refer to them in brief ways such as: "A romantic subplot involves A and B, who has a critical role in x and y."
- Highlight some of the big scenes, the turning points, including the climax.
- Tell in what ways the protagonist changed, what need was fulfilled, and what goal was met.
- Infuse your synopsis with vitality and make sure it leaves a strong emotional as well as intellectual impression.

WHAT CAN GO WRONG WITH YOUR SYNOPSIS

The primary problem with a synopsis is that because it is longer than a query synopsis, it can give erroneous conclusions or raise questions by what it omits. You know your story so thoroughly, you know all the answers. Sometimes the questions raised or criticisms made will reveal problems of logic and structure. But this might not be true. Instead, you may have left gaps in what you should have written. That is why you need to read your synopsis carefully, as if you didn't know all the answers, and look for places where someone else might say, "Why?" "Why now?" "Why there?" and other similar questions.

Think of your synopsis as if it is a letter you have received from a friend you've been out of touch with. What questions might you have as you read the letter? Often, in a synopsis, the raised questions are similar, based on real life. For example: Why would your protagonist leave a good job and benefits to take on the story problem? Why didn't he or she call the police and let them do the work?

What resources did he or she have to live on while doing thus and so? Were there no objections from his family? What is most important to most of us are family, jobs, enough money, health, friends, vacations, days off, recreation, and helping others. Other things go on the list, depending upon the person, or character, but you need to make sure the reader of your synopsis can satisfy questions about why your protagonist will abandon normal routines and requirements to pursue the story.

When you have your revised query, synopsis, and manuscript, with all of the documents copyedited and corrected, you're ready for the secret, unadvertised Marketing Adventureland. Most writers dislike marketing; they are creators and artists and not salespeople. Yet, our career requires marketing skills, just as success after publication requires promotion skills. We can wish that it were otherwise, but the arts in general are not supported well by our government or our culture. With that nod, I do believe that as you grow in competency with your marketing skills, you'll be able to tolerate, and perhaps even enjoy, it.

I have met thousands of writers. I am always delighted when sometime later, I get an e-mail, phone call, or bump into someone and they share their success. They kept improving their skills at writing, revising, and marketing. They believed in their stories and in themselves. I have been struck by two qualities I've noted in these authors: realism and commitment. No one was pie-eyed and thought breaking in would be easy. The statistics about rejection are well known. Yet, these writers remained committed to becoming published, no matter how long it took or how many novels they had to write or how many rejections they received.

There is but one secret to marketing, and that is to persist.

MAKEOVER REVISION CHECKLIST
Query Letters and Synopses— Polishing for Marketing

☑ Query Letter
Sales and purpose: to convince the reader to request the whole novel or some portion of it
Parts of the five-paragraph query letter:
- The hook
- Transition and first paragraph of the synopsis
- Second paragraph of the synopsis
- Author qualifications
- Finishing formalities

☑ The Hook
- Business lead—straightforward
- Creative lead—imaginative

☑ Transition and First Paragraph of Synopsis
- Offer transition from a creative lead to establish genre and perhaps word count, title, or beginning of synopsis.
- Emphasize protagonist.
- Summarize backstory in past tense; present story in present tense—even if your actual novel is written in past tense.
- Establish setting, time period, and central story problem.
- Relate primary events in five-stage dramatic arc.
- Leave out minor characters or refer to by role, if necessary.
- Summarize big events, leaving out minor events.
- Avoid blow-by-blow itemization of the plot events.

☑ Second Paragraph of the Synopsis
- Continue and finish, if possible, the summary of your story.
- Make sure to tell how story ends.
- Reveal how protagonist has changed.
- Reveal change relative to theme.

☑ Author Qualifications
- Summarize accomplishments related to writing.
- Add a positioning statement specifying how your style, setting, or other aspect of your novel is similar to one or several published titles and/or authors.

☑ Finishing Formalities
- Add whatever information has not already been provided such as word count, positioning statement, or author qualifications.
- Can indicate enclosure of the SASE—self-addressed stamped envelope.
- May indicate a referral name or how you came to select the agent.
- Finish with a closing statement such as "I appreciate your time and look forward to a response at your earliest convenience."
- Note: Effective queries may be shorter or longer; exceptions exist.

☑ Marketing Queries
- Mail, with SASE.
- E-mail if indicated by agent, from the agent website or as indicated in directories such as *Guide to Literary Agents*.
- Do not add attachments.

☑ Synopsis
Definition: a summary of an entire story, including the character arc
Length: one page to five pages for marketing
Guidelines to content and style of synopsis:
- Cover beginning, middle, and ending of the novel.
- Include backstory as needed.
- Indicate setting and time period.
- No need to follow chronology of the story in interest of writing a coherent summary of the events.
- Refer to characters in the third-person present tense, except for using past tense for relating backstory events.
- Offer clear characterization of the protagonist, including motivations, goals, stakes, wound, need, strength, and weakness.
- Describe central conflict and identify antagonist or opposing forces.
- Name only characters that are important; use role labels for other characters.
- Write lean, using concrete and specific nouns.

- Use active verbs, as much as possible. Convey emotional and dramatic changes of protagonist.
- Omit minor characters and subplots as space limitations demand. Use one-line summaries as needed: "A romantic subplot involves *A* and *B*..."
- Highlight some of the big scenes, the turning points, including the climax.
- Tell in what ways the protagonist has changed, what need was fulfilled, what goal was reached.
- End on a strong emotional note.

☑ What Can Go Wrong with Your Synopsis
- Omissions can give erroneous conclusions or raise questions.
- Can reveal problems of logic and structure that may or may not reflect actual novel.
- Look for where a reader could ask questions and answer or satisfy them.

Acknowledgments

The best tool for revision and the best source of inspiration is another experienced writer—or better yet, more than one. My good fortune is the support and invaluable critique from six sage writers: Barbara Pope, Geraldine Moreno-Black, Mabel Armstrong, Carolyn Kortge, Carolyn Rose, and Bruce Dodson. Talented writers all, I am privileged to know you, and whatever grace and clarity this book shows is much to your credit.

Special thanks to my friend Carolyn Rose. I stumble for words because of the support you've offered throughout this book project and in the twists and travails of life. And, to my friend Barbara Pope, your concern, caring, and confidence in me have kept me looking forward. You and Carolyn help bring out my best. Bill Johnson, I treasure our long hours of discussion about the deeper aspects of craft, and your generosity as a colleague and friend.

Jerry James, your forest retreat offered everything any writer could want or need right up to the midnight hour of this book's creation. Your friendship means the world to me. Louis Lyon, ever helpful and forever family, I'm grateful to your help with everything and everyone. You and Jerry have sustained me through this project and the immense surrounding challenges of life.

Every writer with a book deadline could use a good psychiatrist, and I'm ever grateful that I've had mine—longtime friend Tom

Kappeler, thank you for the many decades of friendship and doctoring. You, too, are a part of this book's success. Shawn Arbor, DC, your healing touch and fine adjustments have kept this body functioning through days of typing; your compassion, good humor, and friendship have buoyed my spirits. Thank you, Marvin Finger, incomparable masseur, for relief and inspiration.

In the time of this book's creation, I have been privileged to have the encouragement of friends near and far, in the United States and in other countries, including friends I treasure and e-mail friends I hope one day to meet. Please know I appreciate you.

I thank my publisher, Perigee; my editor, Meg Leder; and my friend and agent, Meredith Bernstein. You have been the midwives to help this book reach fruition and publication. Your patience and support have gone beyond the extra mile.

Index

About the Author

An independent book editor for two decades, **Elizabeth Lyon** enjoys the challenge and discovery that are a part of editing works, each one an original creation. Equally she is enthused about speaking and teaching at writers' conferences and events, as well as privately presenting her "I'll Come to You" custom-made workshops for groups of writers. She is the author of half a dozen books for writers of fiction and nonfiction. They include *The Sell Your Novel Tool Kit*, *A Writer's Guide to Fiction*, *A Writer's Guide to Nonfiction*, *National Directory of Editors & Writers*, *Nonfiction Book Proposals Anybody Can Write*, and this book, *Manuscript Makeover*, soon to be joined by a similar book on nonfiction revision techniques.

Elizabeth Lyon lives in Springfield, Oregon, with her beloved Border collie, Riley, and her spoiled black and gray tabby cat, Hunter. You are welcome to reach her through e-mail at elyon123@comcast .net, or visit her websites at www.elizabethlyon.com or www.4-edit .com. Her freelance editing company is Editing International.

A WEALTH OF EXPERT ADVICE AT YOUR FINGERTIPS FROM ELIZABETH LYON

• ***Manuscript Makeover***
Revision Techniques No Fiction Writer Can Afford to Ignore

• ***Nonfiction Book Proposals Anybody Can Write***
How to Get a Contract and Advance *Before* Writing Your Book

• ***The Sell Your Novel Tool Kit***
Everything You Need to Know About Queries, Synopses, Marketing, and Breaking In

• ***A Writer's Guide to Fiction***

• ***A Writer's Guide to Nonfiction***

"Whether you're learning the craft, revising your manuscript, or looking to position it for the best chance of getting published, read Elizabeth Lyon."

—Robert Dugoni, *New York Times* bestselling author of *The Jury Master*

Perigee Books penguin.com